I0059449

1080 NORTH AVALON

1080 NORTH AVALON

An Affectionate Look at US Immigration

A Novel by
GEORGE A. CHALAGONIAN

Copyright © 2015 George A. Chalagonian
All rights reserved.

ISBN: 0692501606
ISBN 13: 9780692501603

FOREWORD

No genuine American likes the United States Immigration and Naturalization Service, whether his persuasion is left, right, or center. But those who like it the least are the souls whose misfortune it is to work there. They are Customs, Inspections, Border Security, and even the officials who work the benefits jobs such as Naturalization - making new citizens, Adjustment of status-making new residents, and finally Asylum. These latter officials are not so well known, but often despised. They're seen as the ones hell-bent to give away the store by welcoming to our golden shores neither new residents, nor citizens, but trenchant liars disguised as refugees.

It might be better to become a pimp; the salary scale would be higher, the career satisfaction greater, and the stress level lower, but to get there from here would require a level of chutzpah and cunning seldom seen among federal employees. So, the story that follows is a glimpse into the lives of the officials who work this little known and sometimes misunderstood subculture of the Immigration and Naturalization Service. Since the recent reorganization, the current and legal name of this organization has changed to Citizenship and Immigration Service. But I shall continue to call it the INS or Immigration, as that is how it is best, or notoriously, known.

One more thing-the following story is not for intellectual snobs. If you're into Dadaism, or Mamaism, or if your Dadists have had sex change surgery to morph into Mamaists, or perhaps you fancy yourself in the camp of surrealism, supra-realism, socialist realism, or whatever realism-read no further. This book is not for you. It is about life and death, hope and despair, depravity and redemption. This book is also work of fiction. The persons, places, scenes, situations, events, and scents of this story are creations of the author's virile imagination and are not to be construed as real. Any resemblance to actual persons, living or dead is purely coincidental except for historical figures. Could these things have happened? Reader, you decide.

DEDICATION PAGE

This story is dedicated to those who have told "the system" to take this job and shove it, to those who expect to soon do so, and yes, to those few good people who labor conscientiously in the immigration vineyard without obsession of power or position. The remainder do not matter.

"Better to die on your feet than to live on your knees."

Emiliano Zapata, Mexican Patriot

This story contains adult dialogue, situations, and themes.

TABLE OF CONTENTS

Chapter 1

A WELL-FUNDED FARCE

Rewrite!

That dreaded word among veteran newspapermen. And Publisher/ Editor Robert Wilcox Robyn, who recently purchased *The Riverside Times and Review,* had once again chained his new Deputy Editor, Steve Melkonian to the weekend rewrite desk to rework the dismal copy of the junior reporters before sending it to Monday's printing press-another "lost weekend."

Rewrites will kill any veteran reporter's career. They turn you into a roosting duck while the aggressive newbie flying ducks grab the by-lines. But someone has to do it and it always falls to those who can write well and fast-hence, a seasoned vet. Not that Steve resents the rewrite desk as much as he lets on. An aging hack reporter whose better days and scandal ridden past are now behind him, you might call Steve the Willy Loman of West Coast journalism, not a loser but not one of life's big winners either. Yet, Steve genuinely loves writing and gives more to the job than he takes. At fifty-seven he is still faster and better at grabbing a story and getting it to the copy desk than any of the snooty Ivy League university cubs. And he's certainly more adept at parsing standard English than the radical reporters newly minted and hired from the lower bowels of progressive journalism at California State University at San Ysidro. Actually, there is a bit of *schadenfreude* (if you prefer pseudo-sophisticated Eurospeak) mixed in with a little bit of smugness at work here.

Steve is happy when the cubs can't cut it and the boss has to call in the cavalry captain to do it. For *The Riverside Times and Review* was once the late unlamented, underground, radical *Riverside Roach*. It was a counterpoint, a pesky tick, a substandard foil to the mainstream *Orange County Register* or the OC version of the *Los Angeles Times* dumbed down to appease local tastes and intellects. Who knows? Maybe big Otis Chandler, perched on his favorite Saint Peter-donated Harley and tooling around on his favorite heavenly puff, is having a booming laugh about it all now. If in fact that is what he's doing and that is where he went! And to Steve's booze-swilling, burlap-suited, floppy fedora, press pass-in-hat wearing Publisher and Editor Robert "Rob" W. Robyn, Steve's loyalty is a quality rare and most welcome, but he would never let on about it.

For time is about to pass them by and both men know it. *The Times* will be their last hurrah, so they had better make the best of it. And that's why the counterculture *Riverside Roach* (as in roach clip), is about to morph into semi-respectability as *The Riverside Times and Review,* and thus end the sordid props that go with counterculture turf: ads for old headshop paraphernalia, tie-dyed fake Woodstock '69 t-shirts, sleazy massage parlors, and naked lap dance joints. Publishing a newspaper in this one-time blue-collar county, thirty miles east of LA, and changing the format should be a great risk. The demographics of this 1.2 million-person spread are in state of constant flux. Ah! The joys of Riverside County!

Cowboy until the end of World War II, then low-end Anglo in the 1950s, the original *Riverside Clarion* started out as a conservative "workingman's newspaper." The University of California at Riverside of the sixties however, brought in student liberals and radicals who formed the nucleus of the early *Roach* readership once the Clarion changed hands.

As the hippie longhairs displaced the blue-collar Ford pickup Anglo, so has the recent influx of Latin American immigrants eclipsed the happy pothead UCR Anglo who once actively supported the beloved *Roach*. Now, neo-establishment Robyn and Melkonian would take the Riverside fount in yet another direction-a modestly sophisticated county daily, a gamble indeed!

Culturally and politically the new executives are very different. Robert W. Robyn, a South Boston blue-collar dockworker's son, is stereotypically "old school." He had the grades for Harvard but chose Boston College instead. Big for his age the sixteen-year-old Rob lied to his draft board to enlist in the army and join the tail end of the Korean War in 1952. He was honorably discharged with Silver Star and Captain's rank after just three year's service. He used his GI Bill benefits and worked his way through Boston College, beginning his newspaper career as a cub reporter for The Boston Globe after graduation in 1959. Moving on to the Chicago Tribune in 1963, Robyn began to cover political events, including both national conventions the following year. At six-foot-two and quite the stud in his day, he boned every "Goldwater Girl" at the Frisco GOP convention and still had enough mojo left to pork what few lefties merited his efforts at the LBJ Demofest in Atlantic City. To compensate for his youth, Rob affected a stereotypical old-time reporter countenance. He stole the rain and sweat-drenched fedora from ace reporter Spuds Turkee, with the Tribune press pass still attached to the hatband.

Today Boss Robyn still pounds out his editorials wearing the same fedora with a loosened brown-toned, well-worn necktie, and manages one hundred twenty words a minute with two-finger touch on a 1930 vintage Royal portable typewriter. He works his craft and does his admin chores from an old rolltop desk where he pigeon-holes rewrites on purpose; i.e. they could be useful to frame a judge or politician he doesn't like. As Winston Churchill never drank a brandy younger than himself, Boss Robyn never used a typewriter younger than he was. He was working intently on an obituary as Steve handed him a rewrite about the Riverside city election and some new ordinances.

Steve Melkonian is thoroughly California. Tall, handsome, and athletic, the dark-haired, olive-toned all-stater in basketball, and weight man in track, led a charmed life during his school days at Fresno's William Saroyan High School and later at Cal State U. at Fresno. He moved through his early life with ease and grace, and a sense of personal style that assured his success in basketball as a forward during the season his team took the Central Valley Championship with a perfect 26-0 record.

Steve is a second-generation native son. His grandfather Aram Melkonian left Turkey in 1915 shortly after the massacres of Armenians had begun, and then left for the West Coast only one week after landing at Ellis Island. Right or wrong he believed the stories of West Coast gold fields and thought everyone who went there struck it rich. With just enough money left to secure third class train passage, Aram headed to the gold fields, only to find that they had be sold and subdivided, if they had existed at all. He worked as a grocery store clerk until he could save enough money to start his own wholesale grocery business which he named the Hye Van Wholesale Emporium, and opened his first warehouse within two years of his arrival in California. During his lifetime, Aram Melkonian presided over twenty-two outlets and had three more in planning when he passed on in 1968. He left the major part of the business to Steve's dad, Kevork, who completed three new emporia in Ventura, Thousand Oaks, and Oxnard.

Steve did not want to be a wholesaler. He witnessed the big events in his senior year at William Soroyan High; the escalation of the Vietnam War, assassinations of Robert Kennedy and Martin Luther King, Lyndon Johnson hanging it all up, the mega-chaos at the Democratic convention in Chicago. At Soroyan High, as editor-in-chief of the student newspaper, The Ararat, he had access to the AP/UPI wires and saw these stories come hot off the presses. He wanted a piece of the action, not the grocery business! Kevork Melkonian planned an upscale "farmers market" scheduled for the outskirts of Malibu for 1972, but by then, son Steve was about to graduate FSU Summa Cum Laude and Sigma Delta Chi, a journalism fraternity. At six-foot-three, and a solid 210 pounds, he found time to letter in track and play forward on the Fresno State Team that made it to the NCAA western regionals. That team got bombed by the UCLA Bruins 105-78. No matter, every other team did too and this was the only dark spot on an otherwise stellar senior season. Ever the family rebel, Steve let his younger brother Arthur, and sister Grace, enter the grocery business while he went to intern at the Monterey Bay Gazette.

After college Steve did the unthinkable-he crossed the color line and religion barrier to marry Elena Maria Calderon, a liberal Democrat but not quite radical Roman Catholic Latina activist from the University of San Francisco. They met over coffee as Steve was writing a series of articles about Bay Area ethnic student activism, just as he was completing his internship at the Monterey Bay Gazette. After dating two weeks they moved into a downtown apartment so Steve could commute from San Fran to his office. They married three months later. Steve's family was Armenian Apostolic Church and staunch Republican.

They would not attend the wedding of their son, and his lithe and elegant bride. Elena's family hosted the wedding of five hundred guests, and everyone drank and danced and laughed and pinched until four the next morning. Steve had his four best friends from his college fraternity, and his best man stand beside him. Only a few of his high school chums showed even though many other friends and relatives had been invited.

After the Gazette, Steve did his time in trenches at the three bugs: The *Sacramento Bee, Fresno Fly*, and the *Gurneyville Gnat*. He worked the three bugs until he found his niche at the statehouse. How ironic he should close out at the former *Riverside Roach*! By 1990 he had worked his way up to a choice assignment-the statehouse beat for the *Rio Linda Republican*, a different sort of bug. The paper was appropriately named. If you are not a Republican the city fathers won't let you live there! It was here that he also wrecked his once happy marriage. A wrecked marriage, yes - adultery.

The statehouse beat did not require it but he let it happen anyway. Twenty years of marriage, two children, two homes, condo in Cancun, a slice of his sibling's grocery interests, and deputy editor of the *Rio Linda Republican*, he blew it all big time with a series of affairs that included a bimbo lobbyist representing the oil industry in Sacramento. Now doing the dirty with offshore dirty oil money is one thing. Doing it with the lady speaker of the Assembly is going way beyond the Northern California pale ale. Steve did both!

A Bay Area liberal Republican, unpopular with the conservatives from the South, Sandra (Sandi) G. Lusepuzi, daughter of a former governor, held on as party leader with the wealth and influence of her family's prosperous newspaper chain: Morro Bay Idealist, Mendecino Metropolitan, Fort Bragg Redwood, and also major stock in the Braggart Lumber Company. When her party unexpectedly won control of the Assembly in 1992 by a one-seat majority, Lusepuzi faced a revolt from within the Republican Assembly Caucus to oust her as majority leader and thus deny her the speakership.

Not to worry! She simply cut a deal with outgoing Democratic speaker Franklin Roosevelt Sutter; he threw his party's support to her on the floor and she won by forming a majority coalition. In addition to covering the oil lobby, Steve did a four-part series on the life and times of Sandra G. Lusepuzi, an in depth bio-portrait of her family's rise to power from pioneer times until the 1990s. It was a span that covered most of California's 150 year colorful state history as well. Steve begins to spend more time on Cal-Hill, less in Rio Linda, and even less with his family. During the first session, dinner and drinks lead to cloakroom hijinx midway through the first session.

Late evening encounters were consummated and unfortunately conceived in the cozy cocktail and hors d' oeuvre bar nicely concealed between the speaker's office and the Assembly cloakroom. Members know about the "O-shaped room," but few have access. It is, or was, an "off-budget" privilege reserved for the Assembly speaker and selected guests. There, Steve and Madam Speaker conceived the fourth of her children - each by different men, and this one was born two years after her first grandchild. Later, the merry miscreants were sharing Lusepuzi's four-thousand-square foot penthouse condominium in an exclusive gated grotto about three miles from the statehouse.

The story broke just before the off-year election in 1994 and was exactly the kind of scoop that his boss did not want in the paper. Republican Publisher and Editor, Hector Horatio Lambug, solid citizen and scion of one of California's most prominent families, Rio Linda rotating mayor and councilman, first cousin of conservative radio cult icon Hush Lambug, and humanitarian and benefactor of many worthy causes, (especially Native Sons of the Golden West) was in extremely foul humor.

He called in his reprobate deputy, read him the riot act about "professional ethics, sub-moral behavior, mockery of community standards, and sleeping with a GOP turncoat," and fired him on the spot. What raised this rage was not so much Steve's trysting with Madam Speaker of the Assembly; after all, about one-fourth her colleagues on both sides of the aisle had done that. No, Publisher Lambug just would not tolerate any further mockery of the *Rio Linda Republican*, the finest conservative newspaper in all of Northern California. Actually, the only conservative paper left in all of Northern California, proudly upholding the patriotic traditions of the Great Golden Bear Republic-rah, rah!

Big Deal! Like, who cares already? The Bay Area dailies buried the details in the B and C sections as everyone of any consequence already knew about Sandi Lusepuzi's prolific love life. But Lambug just knew that the editors of the Three Bugs would front page it, just to embarrass him.

That year, the Assembly also reverted to the Democrats, Speaker Sutter got his old job and old office back, minus the O-room, as it had already been declared an historical landmark. Sandi G. Lusepuzi, no longer needed by either party was unceremoniously dumped by both. Adding insult to injury, a 1995 successful recall effort won by Molesto, California Mayor Harley Halfwood removed her from her Assembly seat and, with intemperate Nixonian sour grapes, she denounced her opponents as shallow men with short penises.

So much for sleeping with the enemy! Sandi Lusepuzi continued to live a colorful life post-Assembly politics. She was elected to many terms as Mayor of Algoba Roja, her hometown, a pleasant little San Francisco bedroom community tucked into the foothills. She purchased the town's nearly defunct newspaper La Yerba Loca, and somehow made it a paying enterprise. It was no doubt supported in part by her other enterprises; a chain of progressive massage parlors, and new age encounter seminars. Eat your heart out Mayflower Madam! She lived a rich full life until she passed away of Alzheimer's disease and herpes in 2007. Over 50,000 people attended her funeral. What many knew and few would say, was that many of the male mourners were loyal customers.

Disgraced in west coast journalism, Steve did a midlife career change and enrolled in University of Pacific College of Law following his divorce settlement. His personal investments, family business, and borrowing from his siblings allowed him a luxury such as few others could enjoy. He could pay off his ex and use personal and family connections to start over. He had the intellect but lacked the passion and temperament to become even a good second-rate lawyer. Seven years into his new career, Steve Melkonian hung it up again, and returned to writing, doing freelance and piece work until his byline saw daylight again. He read an ad for a deputy editor of the resurgent *Riverside Roach* that seemed to be to his liking-a paper emerging from subculture, but not too staid or proper. After two weeks as "monster man," Robyn trusted him enough to promote him to the editorial room and do rewrites.

While rewrites might kill off the remnant of Steve's career, he took that chance. In-depth feature articles were his natural beat and as the rewrites took their toll on his content, he was not a happy camper. It was four o'clock on a Saturday afternoon, early in June 2007. Having worked all day on rewriting an article on the on the city council's new undocumented alien safe-haven ordinance, Steve pushed open the boss' door and slapped the copy down on his desk. Rob Robyn's Saturday morning quart of Jack Daniels was half-drunk and so was he, so he was ready for Steve's weekly tirade.

"Jeez, at 70 grand a year starting salary, we can't get good help? I wrote better copy in high school. I know why we call this inferior California." (Meaning Southern California as opposed to the oh-so-cultured Northern California.)

Robyn swung a 180 in his chair to confront his immediate subordinate. Regardless of staff incompetence, the remark smacked of snobbery and he would have none of it.

"And what was your record in Northern California? Did you ever write for the Examiner or Chronicle. What about the Tribune when it was still a real paper-before Big Bill Knowland shot his brains out? Ever write for any of those or did you just work the scrubs? Did you keep your job at the scrubs or did you wash out because you couldn't keep it in your pants?"

Surprised that his new boss knew about his past and having no quick retort, Steve, in a rare loss for words, said nothing. He glanced at Robyn's obit about a fellow publisher, the illustrious Hannibal Hamlin Hardy of the Arizona Advocate and other media endeavors.

PUBLISHER HANNIBAL H. HARDY DIES IN JAMAICA
Funeral Arrangements Pending

"I thought that crusty old curmudgeon died years ago!"

"We all did, but it appears that when he turned ninety he retired and dropped out of sight to pursue other interests. He turned the daily chores over to his eldest son, Hammy with chief counsel Irwin McTorter as deputy editor, as he was constantly involved in lawsuits. For the past fifteen years he has been publisher emeritus, writing an occasional in-flammatory editorial but otherwise dividing his time chasing pussy on Maui and Montego Bay."

"Judas Priest! He must have been…"

Robyn smiled thinly, knowing what was coming next.

"He celebrated his one hundred seventh birthday January first. Last week he died on his honeymoon with the new Mrs. Hahdy-the fifth. Mrs. Hahdy, a stunning six-foot-tall mulatto island girl of eighteen. Too much for him I guess. But a man ought to know better than to marry a woman young enough to be his great-great granddaughter, heh, heh, heh! Trouble is, he outlived the four other Mrs. Hahdys. Two of them that we know of died from nervous exhaustion. And get this-he left his bride of less than one month half his estate! There's going to be a civil war at the Advocate over assets to be parceled out over six generations. Can't wait to get that scoop!"

"You're going to the funeral then?"

"Wouldn't miss it. It'll be the biggest sendoff in the state's history-a legend in his own mind if there ever was one, and man of the century as he liked to refer to himself! Bigger than when Cactus Harry kicked the bucket a few years back."

"Senator Silvervane, the presidential candidate? My Dad was active in politics and contributed to his campaign."

"One and the same, and both cut from the same cloth - grumpy old men."

Steve might have said something but thought the better of it. The three of them were cut from the same cloth. And what his boss said next was a total, and most welcome, surprise.

"I expect to be gone two weeks, and after the funeral I'll finally get a chance for some golf at the Biltmore Course with the new set of clubs I just bought," he declared proudly, pointing to his $ 5,000 titanium set, with the revelation that he could play on this very private course. Steve thought the better of asking the hows and whys of it and just assumed that his Hardy family contacts were sufficient. "Until I get back you're editor-in-chief and at that time we'll talk about your moving up to features. I have a blockbuster in mind."

Steve knew at that point that he had earned his spurs, or rather re-earned them, and was pleased that he need only manage the rewrite troops one more week. So Robyn returned to his paper chipper in good humor, churlish manner in best form. But as all curmudgeons go, they are at their best in this strange kind of mood. He had completed a short feature about the Hardy funeral and the eminent newspaperman's contributions to American journalism. He turned to his subordinate with a semi-concealed grin.

"Feature articles - the lifeblood of the newspaper business - just the thing to bring back the city edition from the curse of the internet, and we have a sure winner for you, if you're willing to take it on."

"Yes, of course. But just what is it?"

By now, Steven was as much irritated as he was anxious. He sensed that time had passed his boss by, and that *The Riverside Times and Review* would soon tank as another curse of the internet victim.

The craggy leather-faced publisher/editor looked up from the Hardy article that he had been blue-penciling on his beloved rolltop. Fedora askew, and the remaining contents of the Jack Daniels perched perilously close to the left edge of the newsclipping-stuffed mahogany heirloom, Rob Robyn sardonically glared up at his new found protégé. "Steve, do you remember the old story about what the hard-boiled city editor said to his ace cub reporter?"

"Yeah, sure! The one that goes liiike… 'There's a sex maniac loose in this town. Do you know what a good sex maniac does? HE SELLS NEWSPAPERS! Now go get that scoop before we see it in the Daily Planet first! Yeah everyone in the media knows it, sure!'"

"Well Steve, this time the sex maniac is for real and he's loose in an agency of the Immigration and Naturalization Service. A place where you would never expect that kind of thing going on. However, a little bird flew by my window (he pointed to the small picture window), and told me the Feds are hot on the trail of one of their own. That is, a wayward political Asylum officer's been approving applications in exchange for money and sexual favors."

Little birds were always flying by his window. The metaphor is a bit dated but he made his point. Robert W. Robyn had a ready network of moles, spies, deep-throats, and just plain old blackmailers who he could summon at his beck and call to source any expository article or hatchet job he needed at the time.

"I think you lost me. What agency is this and what does it do?"

"Officially, the agency is US Asylum and its officers, usually high mid-level bureaucrats, interview political and religious dissidents and the like to see if they qualify for refuge in the United States. If they are here already, the officers determine if the story of persecution these people tell is on the up and up, and if they should be allowed to stay here."

"Do very many get sent back?"

"This is where it gets dicey. To stay here they need to show that they have experienced persecution in the past or have a fear of persecution in the future that is well-founded. That means that the process of admission to asylum status should go to those who have a legitimate dread of return; like they might be tossed in the clink, sent to the rack, or stood up against a wall. And this is where you come in.

"How is that?"

"The whole process is horseshit; that's how! This branch of the hated INS is a big sham played out through a series of crooked lawyers, form preparers, fact checkers, interpreters, notaries, and even syndicates in the asylum seekers' former countries. Most of the applicants have never experienced any prosecution; they use the process as a back door to immigration. After one year they can apply for full adjustment of status as permanent residents and they never have to go home, but many do, as they never had experienced any persecution or have a genuine well-founded fear. Most come and go like any other immigrant."

"Well, it seems the well-founded fear for the most part is a well funded farce?"

"Exactly, so the Director of the Los Angeles Asylum Office, John B. Ouine has graciously agreed to let you work undercover as an Asylum officer to do a series of articles on the US asylum process. We'll have a meeting with him tomorrow night at the El Malecon Restaurant where the director will assist you in setting up your assignment and introduce you to a few of your new colleagues at Asylum."

"Is that the restaurant that fronts for Party Dolls? Did I hear you correctly? Also, I'm a bit confused. Would it not be counterintuitive for him to help us with this series? After all, you just hinted that a bit of this corruption might be traceable to his own office?" Steve although nonplussed by what he has just heard attempts nonchalance, wondering if his divorced boss has an occasional taste for the raunch. Robyn smiled sardonically, his weathered face braking into a near grin.

Party Dolls is a gentlemen's club located just behind an upscale Cuban restaurant and patronized by immigration attorneys, federal judges, civic officials, and other solid citizens. Members only and you need a key.

"The owner, a Leilo Torquemada is an old college buddy. A Southie like me. We worked the docks together during summer vacation from Boston College. His family emigrated from Cuba during the latter Batista era. Good people, anti-communist; saw what was coming and left. After law school he sets up practice serving the Hispanic communities in Miami and LA. But you're not supposed to know very much about him, got it? He's a personal friend and confidant of John B. Ouine to whom he provides blocks of Lakers tickets for entertaining out-of-town visitors from Asylum headquarters, and some UN human rights officials. Officially we will be meeting at his restaurant, El Malecon. Hope you like Cuban. After we loosen up with dinner and drinks, we'll get down to serious business in the club. It's the Cuban way." He winked. Steve was still a bit baffled by all this, but curious. This might be a challenging assignment after all.

Chapter 2

THREE YARDS AND A
CLOUD OF LUST

Boss Robyn arrived earlier than the rest on a relatively warm June evening. His old dock worker buddy, Luis Leilo Torquemada, the gracious and effusive owner of the Restaurante El Malecon, and associated enterprises, sauntered across the Batista Dining Room to greet his favorite guest as soon as he walked in. A striking, enormous six-foot-six man, he was resplendent in a double-breasted cream silk dinner jacket, formal shirt, black tie, dark trousers, and black patent-leather shoes. He always greeted guests at the vestibule of the cavern-ous dining room. Winter saw a change to a full black tuxedo. It was like a uniform, but with the old-school Cuban émigré, it was style not affectation. He wore it well and complemented the ensemble with im-ported Ashton Monarch cigars, one of which he always discreetly kept in the breast pocket of his jacket. His still coal-black hair was combed back and lightly oiled. A pencil-thin moustache completed the impos-ing countenance. And above it all, the huge man wore a constant sar-donic smile that evoked nostalgia of a Latin American matinee idol, time-warped in the 1930s.

El Malecon was very much his fortress and his 300-plus pound presence seemed to fill the main castle to the rafters of the thirty foot high ceiling. More than his machismo good looks and imposing size, Leilo spoke with the charm of a Caesar Romero or Antonio Bendares - a truly lovable rogue. A slight scar running down the side of his left temple was only indication that he was once something other than a Latin gentleman. A remnant of his dockworking days, when a pack of Southie toughs made the mistake of hassling him about his heritage, he sustained a minor switchblade cut before dispatching the five badass micks into Boston Harbor.

It was this incident that steeled Leilo's friendship with Robyn, as much as their army days during the Korean War, and college years that followed. Robyn was working a neighboring dock when he saw his friend was in trouble and ran to help. A knife-wielding little Southie, the eerie image of a lost Kennedy brother, lunged at Leilo and cut the left side of his face. Surprisingly agile for such a large man, Leilo ducked and parried. Grabbing one of the burlier toughs, he shoved him toward the scrawny knife-wielder. They collided, sending the smaller man reeling into a pylon. Choking and nearly puking, the little bastard managed to hold on to the switchblade and lunge again at Leilo.

By now Robyn had entered the fray and helped his good friend make quick work of the pack. He cold-cocked the Irish lug and tossed him into the drink. Grabbing the knife-wielder's wrist, Robyn bent it back and broke it. The little mick shrieked 'gaahddaahm' and the two Boston College seniors grabbed the Southie by the seat of his tweed britches and flipped him ass over head into the "hahbah." Those were the days! But both young rogues had broken the crude unwritten rule of dockworker bigots: micks do not help spics beat-up other micks. A couple hours later, the union chief steward heard about the rumble, approached the loading area, told them the boss had already drawn up their pay, and they better leave and not show their faces anywhere else on the waterfront. When the chief steward dimwit mouthed out the rule, Leilo and Rob grabbed his legs wishbone style and also dumped him into the hahbah.

"Aha, my good old friend Rob Robyn, I've been expecting you. I am especially pleasantly surprised that Mr. Ouine of the US Asylum Office will be joining us this evening. Have an imported Ashton, my favorite you know!"

Robyn had to laugh in spite of his cool cynicism. "Still the same Leilo. Always ready with a bone crusher, cigar, and quip. How the hell have you been?"

"Ah, my friend, I have never been better, but business has been very slow, and so it was chivalrous and fortuitous of you to invite your friends from the Los Angeles Asylum Office to join us tonight. For you and our esteemed guests, nothing but the best."

"Cut the bullshit, Leilo! We share the same accountant, so I happen to know that your business is booming, thanks in no small part to the free ads you get in my paper. I also know what goes on in the 'club sections' and why we are here tonight. Mr. Ouine owes you some big-time favors for those blocks of Lakers tickets, use of your condo complex in Cancun and Cabo for his personal get-aways, and those of visiting dignitaries. You need him to grant status by hook or crook to your off-the-books service personnel. Do you think I was born yesterday?"

"Ah, my friend, Citizen Robyn, ever the syndicate cynic, what would we do without the incorruptible press lords, aheh, heh, heh? Tonight the finest batch of my Torqemada Plantation Jamaican dark rum, garbanzos con chorizo y albondigas, falda de ternera con vinagreta de almendras y alcaparras, esparragos con citricos y pistachos, patatas con chorizo ala riojana, with a fine dry sherry. Bueno?"

"Leilo, you know me. I'm a meat and potatoes man, so corned beef and cabbage for me, and a few Budweisers to wash it down. But I'm sure the Asylum group will appreciate your going all out for them."

"Ah, yes, of course corned beef and cabbage."

Leilo may wonder about his friend's culinary tastes, but he and Rob were lifelong buddies so he always maintained a resident cook who specialized in making the best of this Irish favorite.

Torquemada thundered a Mephistophelean laugh that shook the plaster off the walls as he regarded with pride this most picturesque of his enterprises. It was a sprawling Latin American dinner and dance emporium, a renaissance posada carved impregnably within the south rim of the San Gabriel Mountains, just outside Pomona off Interstate 10. At one time it was exactly that. Constructed as a fortress built into the mountainside, the rear part once served as an occasional stockade for miscreant Mexican army troops before it went over to the Americans following the Treaty of Guadalupe-Hidalgo.

Engulfed in a parade of one hundred foot-high palms, sensually gyrating with each Santa Ana breeze, El Malecon offered guests elegant dining and dancing plus clubroom facilities at Party Dolls for members only. The restaurant décor was a bit eclectic; a collage of 1940's copacabana, overlain with New Orleans bordello, with just a touch of colonial Spain - very Creole indeed. The ambience was a unity of subtleties. The Party Dolls room was a remnant of the original stockade. Within its cavern's, a fifty-occupancy backroom offered discreet privacy to those holding club cards.

The floor consisted of the usual two poles descending from a twenty-foot ceiling. But the subdued lighting and mellow music assured a pleasing ambience. No punk rock here! Five guestrooms located discreetly off the bar area offered romantic encounters for members sufficiently shrewd to negotiate an interlude with an exotic dancer. Or they might bring their own guest. Each suite was a well-appointed den of iniquity; replete with fully-stocked wet-bar, twelve-foot-diametric circular massage beds (hey, there orgy girl!), soft-pink walls, and push button mirrors discreetly placed at the choice of guests and company. To complete the delectation, El Senor Torquemada offered mellow Latin American and English music selections. Ethan Allen Tuscan chairs, sofa, and oaken conference table appointed an adjoining conference room to assure executive privilege for privileged executives.

About fifteen minutes later, Steve arrived, just shortly before the INS group. He huddled with his new mentor at the discreet table selected by Da Torque; one just close enough to the Party Dolls area without making it seemingly obvious that some members of the group might find their way there. The circumstances of the delicate relationship among the three parties, i.e. the press, the proprietor, and the public official, Steve had not yet fully grasped.

"Boss, I can't understand why would you chose this gin joint cum nudie bar to do business with these INS people?"

"This is the business of a good friend who has owned this restaurant since 1970, and two more like in it Boston and Miami. As for his other activity, I don't pass judgment and you shouldn't either. Leilo has been a model citizen and credit to his community since his family emigrated here in the 1950s. He has always been anti-Communist (always a plus for the boss), and has helped many other good immigrants settle here. Also, he's been on the Pomona city council, and has won many awards for his civic contributions. In any case, we may see an example of INS efficiency. A little bird told me one in our party is to be set up, and an arrest might be made this evening... right under our eyes."

Chastened, Steve backed off on this one. He wanted the assignment badly and understood that his boss did not trust him enough to clue him in on all the intricacies that might eventually play out. The others arrived and Da Torque gave them a Cuban hale-fellow-well-met welcome. Introductions were made and battle lines drawn, or so it appeared. Da Torque selected a discreet table for the party near the back, but close enough to the oaken doors that separated the restaurant from its other activity.

First to arrive were the top dogs; John B. Ouine, Director and Sean Faggerty, former immigration attorney and now his recently appointed new deputy director. Director Ouine sought out the boss straightaway.. They shook hands and sat down to join the others. Two of the three others expected soon follow: Karl Kirel Keibalski, an AFGE government employee union representative and brawny ex-football player, nearly as big as Torquemada, and Harriet McCornnell, a bit moody and withdrawn but not without cause. Once the odds-on favorite to become the next deputy director, she disagreed with Ouine over issues of local policy and was abruptly bumped aside in favor of the more genial Faggerty. Conspicuously absent was Theodore T. Penrod, resident sex maniac and arrestee apparent.

Da Torque ordered drinks and dinner for the group and surprisingly put it 'on the house;' or perhaps, not so surprisingly. He had just hired three new dancers, one from Afghanistan and two from Egypt. Ouine introduced Steve, as his new Asylum officer, but it was not at all clear which of his subordinates was tipped off about Steve's assignment, if any. Might they not think it odd that a new mid-level employee be treated to dinner at the director's favorite watering hole? A voluptuous six-foot-tall waitress named Berlin, dressed in El Malecon miniskirt and blouse arrived to serve dinner and drinks.

A Heidi Klum wannabe, both Karl Keibalski and Harriet McCornnell lasciviously eyeballed her but it was the ex-football jock who turned on the effective charm. With an ill-concealed leer, Karl nodded toward the oaken doors, asked Berlin to go 'East and West' this evening, and handed her a business club card with a fifty-dollar 'reservation tip,' the usual custom at Da Torques for those seeking action later in the evening.

Director Ouine feared the worst - that his distrustful assistants might form a cabal and whistle-blow to OSI about such shenanigans. Moreover, this was scarcely the time or place to introduce a new mid-level employee to the kind of power dinner a director usually reserves for the out of town execs. Add to this an already sullen Harriet, peeved by the non-direction her career had been taking, and Ouine might not only lose his job, but do serious time in the San Pedro Club Fed too! He hoped Faggerty, McCornnell, and possibly Keibalski were out of the pipeline on this one, and figured he must keep them isolated until he could arrange his own dream transfer.

Not to worry! Faggerty, a company man but not a party man, excused himself after the elegant dinner and one drink, and went home. Karl Keibalski gave Steve a pep talk about joining the union.

"I just gotta tell ya. Ya gotta join AFGE. The union makes us strong, ya know?" He announced that he, of all persons, would be his Asylum mentor for the next two months. Did Keibalski know? Was he clued in on the ruse? The last thing that Ouine needed was a union loudmouth aware of an underground reporter in the midst. Or was he part of the action?

It was understood that after the Penrod issue was settled, the articles would be generally favorable to the Asylum office and its personnel. No byline would appear in *The Riverside Times* until the project was finished. Steve would resign his position as an Asylum officer six months before any articles would appear in the paper. Should Lazarus Longstreet, the national director, get wind of the project and complain, the byline would temporarily go to the most promising of the new people and Steve's name would disappear from the masthead until he was promoted to deputy editor - all in the name of plausible deniability. Apparently, Keibalski did not know this or was preoccupied with other matters. He glanced toward the door and took the beckoning index finger of Berlin as the signal that it was time for them to retire to the club for the evening. Ouine did not approve it, but couldn't prevent it.

Harriet McCornnell, stared downcast into her Cutty Sark and soda while Ouine began to outline Steve's responsibilities as an Asylum officer. At five-feet-nine, with medium-brown hair cut in a duck's ass flat top, cinderblock head, short thick neck, broad shoulders, two modest mounds that might be construed as breasts, a rounded abdomen, and narrow hips, she resembled a 1950's era Big Bopper, only without the letter sweater. Harriet instead was wearing a Harris tweed sportcoat, shirt and tie, dark tan skirt, and flat lace-up brown badly-polished shoes... always. She changed to a silk-tweed as the only concession to the warmer months. Hers was an ice-queen countenance that could do Hillary Clinton proud!

Now, Ouine began to wax proudly about the Asylum mission; i.e. the UN Charter and Convention on Refugees, Overseas refugee pre-screening and processing, and that his efficient management style maintained the credibility and integrity of the application process. Sensing that she was about to be sidelined by higher management, Harriet continued to sulk. She occasionally interrupted to mumble an anecdote or two about her experience in private immigration law practices, her academic credentials (BA, Valedictorian and Summa Cum Laude, University of Oregon, University of Washington College of Law, top of class), or her success in establishing the quality assurance and diversity training' classes for the office. All truthful, but a bit pathetic. She finished her drink, shook hands with all present, made her way to the front, and strode off in an attempted power gait. The boss noticed and then remarked about, "hands too large and powerful for a woman," almost like a longshoreman's. Somewhere down the line she had done some hard physical labor.

Around ten in the evening, Steve and the boss returned to *The Riverside Times* office to have one for the road, discuss his assignment, and the people he will work with. He made a mental note that it might have been better to discuss the assignments with Ouine in his office and without the others present, but he knows better than to raise the issue. Bosses have their quirks.

"Remember; cover, cover, cover. Do not blow your cover! If you do, *The Times* is screwed, blewed, and tattoooed, and so is you job here!"

"Unless," he sneered, "you *want* to return to you old job as an underpaid tort lawyer!"

Much like Captain Quint of *Jaws* fame, the boss could lay on the Boston soul and exaggerate it, sometimes with comic effect.

"Well, since you put it that way, mum's the word!"

"Yeah well, one more thing; don't write clichés like that in your copy."

With a quick wink that said no hard feelings, the boss continued to disclose his game plan.

"My inside source was the one that sang, but he got it wrong. No bust tonight for whatever reason. Not the time or season, I suppose. Find out why, only don't act like a snoop. You're not supposed to know about the Asylum house fiend, got it? Over and above this little schmuck, there is more monkey business going on in this unit per employee than any other government agency that it has been my misfortune to cover, and we haven't even hit the motherlode yet. Tomorrow you'll report to Sean Faggerty at Los Angeles Asylum who will introduce you to your supervisor. After an incoming briefing, you'll be working closely with Karl Keibalski as your unofficial mentor. Why they're letting you work with the union rep is something of a mystery." He hesitated a moment then completed his thought, "Possibly Ouine suspects we will not be objective and they've clued him into this already."

"Where exactly is the asylum office?"

"1080 North Avalon Road. You turn north at the corner of Kuchel Street and Kugel Way, just above the 91 at Hahbah Boulevahd it's the cross street two blocks north of Disneyland. You know, the happiest place on earth? Except that this place isn't, heh, heh, heh!"

The thirty-mile drive from his eight room penthouse condo with a breath-giving view of revolting downtown Riverside was leisurely enough for Steve to engage in some idle speculation as he coasted through moderate rush hour traffic. He had left at six thirty, more than enough time to grab his usual yogurt and bagel breakfast at his favorite Carrows, and make the nine o'clock briefing. While taking a final leisurely sip of coffee, Steve pondered the next few months of his strange return to the newspaper business. The name Karl Keibalski sounded familiar, but he couldn't recall precisely where he had heard it before or when. Vaguely, it had something to do with sports. Oh well, he could always ask once he got there.

Steve easily located the brownstone and oak-trimmed three-story building at the north edge of Anaheim just below Old Town Fullerton. It was tucked away unassumingly, about fifty feet behind a row of date palm trees and desert foliage that masked the outer wall. Eucalyptus and palo verdes tree, and poinsettias also enhanced the style of a building. Although certainly not classical, it was at least an attractively landscaped government structure on a dead end, a block from historic Kuchel Street. How appropriate! Indeed. it had become a dead end to more than a few lost federal souls.

Steve eased his subdued gray-toned Porsche into a small space in the employee's underground lot. To get his bearings through all the vegetation, he passed the elevator and took the walkway to the façade facing the main thoroughfare. A timeworn 1940's vintage address plate gave the only clue to its location: 1080 North Avalon Road. A name perhaps, not just an address.

There had always been rumors about it. The original building, put up in 1880s was at one time a saloon with a second story hotel and brothel. Later, the German American Club owned it as a hofbrau restaurant and patriotic meeting hall to evoke fond memories of the fatherland, until memories of the fatherland became decidedly unpatriotic, i.e. during World War I when the krauts got the boot. Five years after the US Marshals seized the hofbrauhall, the building was turned over to real Americans, i.e. the French. Pepe Le Peckre, an immigrant from Rouen bought it from the government, turned into a Eurobistro, and his family operated it until greener pastures beckoned them to the Malibu Canyon area in the early 1980s. The building remained closed until it was bought by the city of Anaheim in 1990 and leased to the Asylum office at this agency's inception.

Steve reported to Deputy Director Faggerty for a brief orientation and introductions to his new colleagues. Introductions were always made at the Tuesday morning 'all-hands' meetings held in the mini auditorium on the first floor. It accommodates about 100 people, usually the officers and supervisors who worked the applications files. Director Ouine did not relish this type interplay and rarely took part in them. Faggerty, a nondescript ex-immigration lawyer left private practice in the Bay Area to secure a steadier government paycheck. Once he was athletic and good at sports, a former AID official in the 1980s who organized and coached village basketball teams in the Republic of Nkookoo, or some country like that. Now a gangly, balding, middle-aged, slightly flabby, androgynous male with a girlishly nervous laugh, he liked to refer to himself as 'the new deputy in town.' It was a subtle slap at the recently-ousted 'old deputy in town,' an old mama-type bureaucrat who moved to the Riverside office before she was scheduled to forcibly retire for incompetence, malfeasance, misfeasance, and cronyism. He took the podium while his subordinates listened in studied boredom.

"It is my extreme pleasure (of course his pleasure is extreme when it comes to initiating a fellow lawyer to the Asylum office), to welcome our most recent selection to the asylum corps, former attorney Steven Melkonian, who comes to us from private practice in the greater Fresno area. Steven, we welcome you to Los Angeles asylum, and assure you that we in management, and the members of your assigned team, will cooperate to the utmost to help you succeed in your career."

Steve stood for the introduction, amid polite applause among the twenty rows of officials. Only the applause in the back was affected and mockingly boisterous, if only because Karl Keibalski jumped up from his chair to lead the jeers, "Let's hear it for private practice - rah, rah, rah! Just what LA Asylum needs - another failed lawyer...hoot, hoot, hoot!"

The back-row majority as they are called, are the six or so officials who always take the back row seats during all hands meetings and always harass the quality assurance people or junketing dignitaries from HQ with their snide whispers and occasional cat calls. The back-rowers were in general a few DODs, disgruntled old deadwoods, those who had been officers for ten or more years, had failed to make supervisor, promote themselves to a better career, or those who were marking time until retirement. Most hung on because they needed the money.

"Mr. Keibalski," retorted Faggerty, "try not to embarrass yourself or discourage a new officer who is about to begin a promising Asylum career, as opposed to the one you have had!"

Keibalski sat down and sulked as the deputy continued with the introduction of two more new hires. The meeting and the usual half-hour training briefing ended at ten with Faggerty motioning to Steve that they would return to his office for a confidential follow-up briefing. Faggerty's office was spare, even by the standards of a mid to high-level federal bureaucrat, and contained the usual family photos, fake Norman Rockwells, and an eight by ten glossy of himself shaking hands with National Director Longstreet. He sat down behind his oak-wood desk and offered Steve a chair.

"Steve," he intoned, "this can be the beginning of the most rewarding career the INS has to offer. You, as an Asylum officer, will save persons of conscience from the perils of persecution in foreign lands. As I drive to work every day, I think of the good that we have all done in advancing the cause of universal human rights. Like Doctors Without Borders, we the US Asylum Office do our wonderful little part. If you share our vision, you may one day take your place at headquarters, or possibly the UN High Commission on Refugees." As he said this, the deputy gazed wistfully out his corner office window, to a better time and a future place.

"However, I must tell you in all confidence, that you will be under close scrutiny during your probationary first year. You shall have no choice of your first-line supervisor or mentor." He shook his head slightly as he mentioned it.

"I wish it were not so. For your own good though, be careful about whom you choose in this office as close friends and associates. Some here, hold beliefs that run counter to the goals of this organization. You will know who these people are after a short time. Avoid them! That is all I shall say about this, and this conversation never took place. It's ten-fifteen. Your supervisor, Isaac Chaiklin, will briefly discuss your duties and then you will be working with a mentor for in-house training. The director has waived the requirement that you attend the law enforcement training center as is usually the case. You may find Chaiklin a bit eccentric, but he's very conscientious, so I'm sure you will learn a lot from him. As for the mentor, it will be Karl Keibalski. Why he selected him I don't know. I just do not know."

"Isn't he the union rep?"

"Yes, but I don't think it had anything to do with his selection."

Faggerty reached for a well-worn stencil on his desk, a map of the offices of each employee. "This will orient you but please return it. The information is secure, and shows the name and office of each official. You'll find Chaiklin and Keibalski on the third floors, in offices 325 and 330. You will be assigned to 305. Good luck."

They shook hands once more and Steve went for his supervisory briefing. The deputy was right. He did not know anything about the Keibalski selection. Chaiklin did not say much, preferring instead to send his new team member directly to the mentor and then report back for his assignment. A nerdy looking little man in a starched white shirt, dark green tie, khaki trousers, and tortoise shell glasses, he mumbled about this whole process 'not being ethical' and then motioned for Steve to leave. Irritated at working with an employee who had slighted him for no apparent reason, Steve was nevertheless determined to make the best of the arrangement as he had no choice. Still he was curious. Why the attitude of the new supervisor? And why would management trust an aging adolescent to mentor a new officer?

He went to Keibalski's office. Karl stood up and, with his eighty-inch plus reach, extended his hand from behind his desk and greeted Steve with his usual Ohio State University bone crusher. At six-foot-four his now 240 pounds was about fifteen more than his playing weight had been. But most of it was still solid. An imposing figure on the football field as fullback, he loomed even larger among a bureau of girlie-men Asylum officers. The partly balding blond hair combed back, quizzical expression, and wide-set blue eyes of the typical northern Slav, half Pole, one quarter Ukrainian and Russian, he slightly resembled the late Pope John Paul II, but that was where any resemblance ends. They hit it off well. Steve was also tall, athletic, and a bit leaner, but part of the same tribe and there was an instant camaraderie that always existed between has-been jocks. As they shook hands, Steve remarked that he had heard the name Keibalski before and that he thought it once had 'something do with sports' but couldn't recall the details.

"I wouldn't expect you to. Hardly anyone does anymore, and that's just fine with me since it's all behind me now. Anyway, you may be thinking of Ohio State U. 1970-73 seasons."

"The one that had the two Heisman candidates in the same backfield? Hailed as the greatest since the Four Horsemen?"

"Fuckin' A. And I was one of them! In addition to me, I bet you remember Harvey Grissom. He got the Heisman two years in a row. Canya believe it dude?" He railed and pounded his desk, as he said with a Clevelander steelworker brogue, "One a dem shoulda been mine!"

It was starting to come back to Steve, like déjà vu all over again! (with due apologies to Yogi Berra).

"Oh yeah! And Bill Shcheister was quarterback, and Lex Fern at the other half. The OSU Fullhouse T. Three yards and a cloud of dust. Those were the days."

"Fuckin'A!"

He grabbed an autographed 'game ball' from a desk drawer and tossed it in the air, giving Steve a big high five for his astute memory. "I played fullback on the national champion team. Or, at least I did until I had a little mishap that involved the head coach's daughter."

"You mean…"

Anticipating the name recognition straight away, Keibalski went into flashback mode, a nostalgia trip to his long past heyday.

"Yep, Stoney Oates, Ohio State football coach for thirty years; five Rose Bowl trips, one Cotton Bowl, and three Orange Bowls. A real legend, especially in his own mind. I remember it all like it was yesterday. Last week of November 1973. Just before the big game with Michigan. You *know,* every OSU-Michigan is the big game."

Keibalski tilted his head back and his eyes went into in a semi-trance, evoking remembrances of long ago…far away. "It was like this….sort of…" Keibalski rambled on in typical aging jock jargon.

"During my senior year I started dating The Stoneman's youngest daughter Esmeralda. She was like seventeen. The pretty one… that means, the one that looked like her mom not her ugly dad. Only he didn't know about it, see? And, like, she was real hot to trot…" He turned his eyes back toward Steve now. "Know what I'm sayin?"

Of course Steve knew, it *is* a guy thing, after all!

"Well, like, we were ranked number one in the final AP/UPI polls. Just above USC who we ended up losing to by a field goal in the Rose Bowl after edging Michigan in the final conference game. Only, I didn't get to play in either game. Man if I did - National Championship trophy! Weeda creamed Michigan by forty points and pounded USC by three touchdowns. Fuckin' A!"

Another high five. This was getting a bit redundant!

"Anyway we had a real bad, I mean, a baaahd final practice early Thursday afternoon before the game, yah see. Cause, like, the tackles couldn't block, the ends dropped passes, and the backs fumbled, except me, of course. But, like, Grissom dropped the ball four times in practice. Like four fuckin' times man! So like, Coach Oates was one pissed-off dude! Now, my big fumble came a couple hours *after* practice. Right smack bang, I mean literally, a bang on the 50-yard line."

Save for the peculiar overuse of 'like' as a general modifier, and common misuse of the gerund that denotes a kind of fornication, ex-college jocks do make great storytellers, and Keibalski was no exception. "So Coach had us go to the film room after practice and starts to reem our asses. He kinda had this growl, like a rottweiler ready to bite off your leg."

"All right you guys stink and here's why... no blocking, no ball-handling, and you pussy receivers, my seventeen-year- old daughter could snag a pass better than you candyasses."

"Anyway, me and the other backs, we're sitting in the back row, and I'm like, right behind our tackle Ed 'King Kong' Lodazhit the monster that devoured Columbus. Or, at least Luigi's Pizza joint just off campus. One night he bet the owner that he could eat up every pizza he could make and he did! Ten large ones in all! Like, can you *believe* it? Poor little Luigi went broke and closed his joint the next month because of Ed. Maybe you remember Lodazhit? He went on to play for the Browns and had a couple good seasons, made All-Pro even. But after seven years, he starts dating this flakey New Age chick and hangs up his cleats right after the Pro Bowl. Like, I couldn't believe it man! He had it fuckin' made!"

"So what happened to him?"

"Last I heard he moved out here with his New Age chick. They facilitate at this nude therapy encounter center in Ojai and sell desert flowers from a stall at the Ventura County Farmer's Market. Like, can you *believe* it, dude?"

"Well, uh, no."

"So like, Ed is six-foot-eight and 380 pounds, and he's hunched over and reading the December issue of Playboy, the one that has all the pin-ups of the whole year, instead of watching the game film and Coach's diagrams on the board. So, I don't think Coach can see me behind Ed. So I nudge him in the back and said. "yeah she can snag a pass all right." Ed was my roommate at Opra Phelta Thi Fraternity, and my close bud. The only one who knew I was going to bone Coach Oates' daughter. For real. So me, Grissom, and Ed can't stop laughing and Coach hears us."

"So he says, 'Did I say something funny? What is it with you shit-heads, anyway?'"

"Hardass disciplinarian that he was, The Stoneman threw down his chalk and stormed to the back of the room to confront his recalcitrant gridders, beginning with King Kong Lodazhit. With a primeval growl, he grabbed the mag from his mammoth right tackle, tore it to shreds in front of all 60 of his players, and while the benchwarmers snickered, Coach Oates stomped on the torn pages. "

"You creeps are supposed to be the cream of Ohio manhood - not cream all over this disgusting pornography."

"He continued to stomp while Lodazhit, Grisom, and Keibalski looked on in rapt amazement. Afterward, there was little more to the December issue but angry footprints. Oates stomped to the font of the room, threw his clipboard at the ashcan and rocked on."

"I've spent thirty years at this fine institution of higher learning, and none of you losers belongs here. After I pull your scholarship, I'm going to write your parents that they raised an ungrateful degenerate and that you should be locked up in the pervert section of the State Funny Farm at Sandusky."

Actually, the State of Ohio has no state mental health facility at Sandusky but it's the thought that counts.

"He really did none of these things, but what he did next was the stuff of which OSU legends were made, much like the time a few years earlier when he got pissed at the ref for calling a holding foul and stomped the sideline, tearing up all the ten-yard line markers. He told us all to bring our watches to the front of the film room and go sit down. Fortunately I never wore one, but like, some of the guys had expensive ones their parents gave them at high school graduation, or like, they even belonged to granddad, too. Well, he stomped on every player's watch and broke about fifty-five of them in all. So Lodazhit yells out, 'But Coach, that was an old family heirloom!'

"I'll put your cock hairs in a loom if you miss even one damn block on Michigan's outside linebacker, got it bud?"

"Like, Lodazhit was first team All-America, but he had one minor fault and that was that he had trouble blocking the other teams' outside linebackers - a real thorny bee in the Stoneman's bonnet."

"I've got a $500 bet with Coach Bum Schumbunkler that we win by three touchdowns, got it bud? Now you pansies get outta here and take a trip around the field, on the jog - five laps. Keibalski you lead, you're the team captain, and I use the word loosely."

"So, like we had to jog the laps around the practice field in street clothes and shoes just because of Ed's magazine."

By now Steve was getting a little bored, and he knew that Chaiklin wanted a few words with him before he left for the day.

"So how is it that you missed the final two games?"

Replying with as ill-concealed a smirk that in general summed up his attitude to his job and everyone around him, Karl countered "I'm getting to that."

"So after the intense practice session and the jog, a lot of us seniors were going off campus for beers. But guess who was waiting for me outside the Opra house just outside the main stadium? Esmeralda! And I mean that night she was really hot. Like we got into a little 'hand sex' in my red and gray Volks stationwagon - the Buckeye Bomb. But like, she gave me the look like it was going to be cherry-pickin' time tonight!"

Karl grew misty for a moment as he recalled his first car, the one that wore as many buckeyes on its hood as he had on his helmet - one for each score.

"I really miss that little piece of shit. Uh, I mean the Volks, not Esmeralda. So, the Phelta Bros had an idea of what was coming, they said a mocking hello to Esmeralda, and pretended to go off downtown. You see, we had a little custom. Like I lived in the student dorm under the stadium until the middle of my junior year, but I used to hang out with the Phelta Bros. They'd been hasslin' me to join, but my family wasn't that rich, so I didn't want to spend the money on dues. Anyway, after I saved enough bread, I joined late in the second semester of my junior year so I had to wait until the next fall for my 'final rites.' Anyway, we had this custom. Any bro who has a steady, and can persuade her to do it on the fifty-yard line, like where the band sousaphone player dots the Ohio-'I' passes his initiation without Hell Week. So there was a lot of incentive right there. Of course it wasn't easy. You needed witnesses, and of course they had to be discreet enough not to reveal themselves. So I take Esmeralda to my car, we drive around the stadium, park and mess around a little bit more until her panties are soaked. She's already wild, and ready to dot the 'I'. We get out of the car, and hit the turf on the fifty. It's already dark; OSU has no stadium lights, so we were safe, or so we thought. At the far corner of the field I notice Lodazhit and Grissom in the shadow of street lights, giving me the thumbs up and like, go for it! So like, I got her mini up and knickers down as the Brits would say, and I'm like ready at ramming speed with fourteen inches of Polack sausage, when the awful happens. What I didn't notice and should have, was Coach Oates stomping across the field toward his car in his reserved space behind the stadium office. He usually left for home right after practice, but he sometimes worked late before a game. Some said that doing his admin chores was the only way he could relax before the "Big One." Again, the faraway semi-stare.

"So Coach Oates crosses midfield, growling to himself...'What a lousy practice. Creampuffs, all of them. Not one of them worthy of the red jersey. And why the hell can't we get stadium lights put in? Dammit, we're the only Big Ten team that doesn't have them. Gotta take a flashlight with me just to find my car. It's always the same excuse - not enough funds in the budget. That's an *excuse?* The administration is too damn cheap and the president is a bastard! Why, football pays for everything else at Ohio State. Grrrowl! Just fire a couple profs in the too-liberal arts college. Get rid of those damn protesting pinkos and we'd have enough funds for stadium lights! What's more important anyway?'!"

"Right then she goes, 'Oooooh, Karl...it's soooo enormous!'"

"'Whaats this? Who the hell is messin' up my football field? I know all about what you creeps do here and I'll have your ass!' Coach Oates dashes to midfield and flicks on his flashlight just as we were about to go *in flagrante delicto* as they say in court."

"Keibalski, it looks like you and if it is you're through at OSU, and so's that tramp your trying to bone."

As Keibalski and Esmeralda grasp for their clothes and dash in different directions away from the fifty-yard line, Coach Oates finally recognizes his precious little gem.

"'My own daughter...my own daughter' he sobs. 'You ruined my daughter you bum. I'll have you arrested for rape, incest, child molesting, perversion, and assault and battery.'"

Keibalski, ever the broken field runner, tries to zigzag to the nearest clump of bushes. Grissom and Lodazhit figured out what's going down and they're outta there ten minutes ago in a mad dash for the parking lot.

He can't get his pants on, so Coach zigzags toward after him kicking his bare butt all the way to Stoney Oates Drive. Yep! They named the stadium drive after him, too!

"You filthy pervert. When you get done doing time at the Penn State, uh...state pen, forget about turning pro!" Kick, kick, the left foot followed by the right foot. "The NFL won't take a degenerate like you."

Karl Keibalski carried 225 pounds with a thirty-two inch waist. Coach Stoney Oates carried 225 pounds with a forty-two inch waist. No matter. On his best day, Crazy Legs Hirsch could not have outrun Coach Oates kicking Keibalski's bare butt across the field. And Jim Thorpe could not have done so many drop-kicks in one season!

"And don't even think about running north. I know every damn coach in the Canuck League, and I'll tell them never to hire you!" Kick, kick, kick. "You're through at Ohio State. Your scholarship is pulled!"

Grissom reaches out and grabs Keibalski as he reaches the edge of the bushes. Coach Oates stumbles over a rock and falls, smashing his flashlight, so he was never able to make out who had helped Keibalski escape. Ed quickly tosses him into Grissom's car and helps him put on his pants.

Next day, the president of the university, no less, calls Keibalski to his office. He informs him that his football scholarship has been cancelled, that he is to turn in his gear to the athletic office, that he will not play in the Michigan game or the Rose Bowl, and that he is expelled following the fall semester.

"Yeah, now I remember. I majored in journalism and played basketball, and that was a scoop at the time. But none of us student reporters could figure out what happened, except that you left Ohio State for... 'disciplinary reasons' that were vague."

"So now you know, 'the rest of the story' as Paul Harvey would say. And it's pretty much true, except that Oates couldn't keep me out of the Canadian leagues. They doctored my name a bit - called me Bullhead Kazurski, and I played halfback until this knee injury. See this game ball, my buds stood by me God bless 'em. And after the Michigan game, they all autographed the game ball and gave it to me. Here, have a look. You can still make out a few names."

The ink had faded after thirty years but Steve could make out the buds: Lex Fern, Ed Lodazhit, Bill Scheister, and the other OSU immortals.

"It seems that you might have done a little reporting, at least you know who Paul Harvey is."

"I did a little sports analysis in Cleveland after I moved back to the US but then Scheister, who was an attorney by that time tipped me off to a couple opportunities to join the justice department and work in Investigations - mostly fraud stuff and anti-trafficking. Really fascinating work and I can't wait to get back to it."

"So is this just a temporary assignment for you?"

"In a way, yes."

He seemed put off by the question and Steve wondered whether he trod on some agency taboo.

"Not that I'm complaining, it's just that I've had more experience as an investigator. Like, that's what I do best."

Steve wasn't quite certain that he should start prying, but he did need the scoop, and it was becoming apparent that Keibalski could play 'deep throat.' But until he earned his confidence he would have to be circumspect.

"I've heard some strange things about this office."

"Like what?"

Keibalski returned the game ball to his desk drawer and seemed to regard Steve a little suspiciously. Is this newbie just curious about rumors or was he a management mole out to get him? Keibalski was union after all. And no one hates unions more than government executives. Although to the last suit, they would deny this on a stack of Bibles. Likewise, Steve was not at all sure that Keibalski knew about his undercover reporting for *The Times*, or that Ouine played a clandestine part in allowing his hiring. Steve gambled that it was better to chance it and be straight up about what he knew, if not how he knew it.

"Like blackmail and sexual misconduct by some officers toward asylum applicants."

"Whew, you're right on top of things. I'm not saying there's a lot of that shit going on, but there is enough for a minor scandal if and when it breaks. But by that time I hope to be back in Investigations. If you're interested, drop by Friday afternoon. I know where the bodies are lying; living and dead. But you need to keep all this in strict confidence until you and I are outta here.

So, he is tossing the onus of secrecy back to Steve - very clever. A win-win situation only if…

Steve glanced at this watch and excused himself reminding his new mentor that he had to go back to Chaiklin's office to get his assignment. Keibalski nodded with a wink that said it all, i.e. 'everything's cool.' No more doubts about his participation. And Steve was rapidly gaining focus of an assignment that just might reignite his career.

"Until *you* and I are outta here - got it?"

Karl knows.

Chapter 3

NIGHT WITH THE WIFE OF BUREAUCRAT FALABENKO

Earlier, the introduction at the all-hands meeting was a bit of comic farce as they sometimes are, but in general it went well. After Deputy Faggerty finished his spiel, quality assurance trainer, Meg Wynter, spoke briefly. A plump midlife careerist whose wardrobe betrayed a fondness for Carnaby Street minis and stilt shoes that were no longer becoming on a frame that had packed on 60 pounds since her Twiggy days as an exchange student in London. Meg waxed grandiloquently about the pride everyone had as an Asylum officer defending human rights everywhere on this troubled planet. She then proceeded to inspire the bored room with a lecture on female genital mutilation in the glorious Peoples' Republic of Humunga Ramboogie, or some hell-hole like that. But during that first meeting with his new boss, Steve was not about to reveal his true feelings about the all-hands lectures.

It was now five-fifteen; just about closing time. So after meeting and greeting the rest of the ground troops, Steve dashed to Ike Chaiklin's office for his first assignment.

Isaac Chaiklin, measured, insecure, and a bit dour as always, asked Steve how the meeting went and whether he felt he could get along with the "problematic" Karl Keibalski, an officer he obviously did not like. Reaching in his desk drawer for the tranquilizers he discreetly kept in a Bayer aspirin bottle, Chaiklin further inquired about the all-hands meeting, and whether anyone mentioned his name to Steve? Or what might have been said about him? Steve sensed that his new INS boss had deep-seated paranoia issues, and discreetly said that no one mentioned anything.

The resident power couple, Isadore "Izzy" Falabenko and Hortensia Luz Martinez de Falabenko, his athletic over-sexed wife arrived next. Chaiklin introduced Steve to the two mighty players. You could call them the Los Angeles Asylum's answer to Juan and Evita, only without the prerequisite style.

"I think you will like working in Asylum very much," Hortensia purred. "We Asylum officers love humanity and we are very sharing people."

Recalling Voltaire, Steve thought to add, *but it is people you despise.* Best not to reveal such sarcasm though, at least not until he began to work on his articles. In any case, Hortensia did seem very hot to trot.

Before Supervisor Chaiklin and new Officer Melkonian were allowed to discuss his assignments, Hortensia completed the brief introductions. She offered Steve any assistance he might need, and left the bedraggled, slightly scruffy Isadore saying very little, except affirming his wife's point of view in his Eastern European accent, "I dink zo doo." Such are the joys and sorrows of maintaining a young wife!

They left after introductions, but Steve would soon meet up with one of them again, and how! He returned to business at hand and it was clear his boss was very distraught about something.

"I understand you wanted to see me about my first assignment?"

"Yes, but I can't understand why higher management would do this to an untrained officer. They have their reasons, I suppose. In any case, I would not blame you if you turned it down. I can try to arrange it so you can go to Georgia for your introductory officer's training, assuming I have that option. This isn't right, it just isn't right!" he moaned.

"I'm sorry, Isaac, but I don't follow."

"Your first assignment will be a monthlong detail to US Commonwealth of the Northern Marianas. Principally, the islands of Tinian, and possibly Saipan, near the US territory of Guam.

"The islands fought over during World War II?"

A streak of pacifism runs through the Asylum office, especially so in the management ranks. Disliking anything having to do with the military, Chaiklin seemed a bit irked by this innocent name recognition.

"Yes, but that is not of our interest now. Ocean vessels carrying Chinese nationals entered US territorial waters, and were interdicted and detained by the US Coast Guard and Border Patrol there. Some just within US jurisdiction, and others at dockside. Your employee file indicates that you spent six months in coastal Guangdong Province covering trade issues for the Sacramento Bee, and that you have a rudimentary knowledge of the Cantonese dialect from two college courses. Accordingly, management has decided that as your first assignment, you will travel there to interview the detainees for the part of refugee processing known as 'credible fear.' You will determine if the Chinese nationals qualify for a full Asylum interview before an Immigration judge."

"So, how soon do I need to leave?"

"Two days from today, early morning."

"What have you been smokin?"

Career bureaucrat that he is, Isaac Chaiklin hated any kind of originality, confrontation, or satire. Unaware of the circumstances of Steve's employment, he was beginning to resent his new subordinate on all three counts of his cavalier attitude. He tried to dismiss Steve's comment with a withering warning.

"I'm sure you are aware that during your first year as an Asylum officer you are on probation and your employment may be terminated without cause?" he intoned. "Your comments are not appreciated. In the future do not besmirch the character of any person employed here. Is that understood?"

Steve wanted to jerk the petty small-minded geek from behind his chair and slap him silly, but he knew he had to eat this one to assure that he would remain in this assignment, discourage any probable lawsuit against himself or his publisher, and do no additional damage to his journalistic career other than that which he had already done by his indiscreet lifestyle.

"Of course, and my sincerest apologies. I meant no offense. It's just that I don't know whether I can make travel arrangements so quickly."

"The arrangements have already been made by Omega Travel Service. You will be leaving Thursday morning from Los Angeles International on Polynesian Airlines to Honolulu, where you will transfer to Blue Hawaii Airways. You will receive your ticket and boarding pass at the Polynesian terminal. Your travel orders have been processed and you may pick them up at the secretary's station. Your briefing you may obtain in Hortensia's office. You have two days to attend to personal issues. Is there anything else?"

"Just like that?"

"Yes, and this is how it is normally done! Also, while you are there, your team leader will be Hortensia Falabenko. As this is to be her first supervisory detail, I know you will want to give her your utmost loyalty and effort."

A recalcitrant Steve wondered if it was normally a part of the routine for first-line supervisors to suck up to Hortensia just to bond with the office establishment? Once again, he put his foot in his mouth. "I can hardly wait!"

"Don't get snippy," Isaac countered wearily.

Having quickly developed antipathy toward his new boss, Steve left before he could get any more steamed than he already was. He had all of two days to get packed, cut off his mail, notify his credit card companies, gardener, housekeeper, and decide which of his two significant others would stay the night before departure, while he made a viable excuse to the not-so-significant other. Steve had developed a grudging liking for Boss Robyn's cantankerous manner, curmudgeon though he be, but after just one meeting, he began to despise Isaac M. Chaiklin. After all, private enterprise bosses are pricks because they have to be, government bosses are pricks because they want to be, that's the difference! Steve's flight was irksome during the LA-Honolulu leg, surreal on the Honolulu-Guam leg, and paradise during the layover in Saipan, almost.

The irksome part was the come-on from the motormouth leader of the interpreter team, Mamie Chen. Having eyed Steve from the check-in counter where Hortensia introduced everyone, Mamie decided that Steve was her kind of stud and made her move about an hour after the 747 left Los Angeles International. The logistics were a bit awkward but where there is a will, Mamie finds a way. Ms. Chen pranced her way downstairs from the first-class section where she obtained a frequent-flyer ticket to the coach fare section where Steve and Hortensia, seated next to each other, were having a cordial, but not quite intimate, conversation. Not just yet.

"I understand that Steve speaks Cantonese, I would like to give him some practice before he begins his interviews. May we exchange seats? I'm sure you will like my billet in first class, it's certainly more comfortable!"

In the words of *Casablanca*'s Captain Reynaud, Hortensia does, 'a good tactical retreat.' The briefing, or perhaps debriefing of Steve Melkonian could be postponed. And besides, it's not often that an entry-level supervisor gets to fly first class. With a "let's get cozy" introduction, Mamie Chen started to regale Steve about her great life as an Immigration officer and erstwhile interpreter, while she leaned in on his torso to look for any sign of arousal. There were none.

She complimented him on his athletic build, rather good for a man of his age, snuggled close, and continued with her favorite subject - Mamie Chen. At midlife, Mamie was pleasantly attractive; medium-height with a slim build, auburn-shaded hair, slightly naughty smile, a bit brainy, and at least she had ranked high in her graduation class at UCLA. Now the single-mom of a seventeen-year-old daughter, this was not the sort of relationship Steve should take a chance on and he should know it.

"I'm a supervisor in LA Natz (Naturalization). I'll be supervising (she loved that word), the team that will do the interpreting for you and the other officers. I'm Chinese-American (as though he could not figure that out), you know. I speak Cantonese, Mandarin, and some Shanghaiese. I understand you learned some Cantonese from your neighborhood in Fresno. Would you like to practice? It would be beneficial during your interviews."

"That's very kind of you and I certainly need a break from this boring briefing book."

As Steve lays the briefing book down, Mamie makes a subtle move casually touching her palm to his lap - not laptop! They engaged in a couple hours of light conversation in Cantonese, but about 100 miles from Honolulu International, the idiot 747 pilot does the usual, "We are now beginning our descent into Honolulu International." then banks the bird too sharply. So instead of the passengers getting a breathtaking view of Diamond Head they get a breath-choking, gut-wrenching, up-chucking dive during which, Mamie Chen got a heart-stopping 'feel' of Steve's legendary soujouk.

"Oooooh, that was awesome, but I feel safe in your strong arms. I wish you didn't have to change planes. I'll be flying straight through, couldn't you change your plans?"

"No, that's the itinerary and the Travel Management Office won't let me make changes. Sorry."

"Maybe sometime again in Saipan."

"I'd like that, but I think Hortensia has other plans."

"Back in LA maybe?"

"We'll see."

Hortensia's team of three deplaned at Honolulu International where Steve had hoped he might enjoy a rare indulgence - a Cuban cigar he had purchased on a recent trip to Tijuana. And maybe a mojito in the Trader Vic's Lounge during the one hour layover. Fat chance! As soon as he ordered his drink at the bar, Hortensia blindsided him even before the bartender had finished mixing it.

"I hope you've taken the time to read the briefing book. I just made supervisor and I take employee loyalty very seriously. I understand that you are a former litigation attorney, so we have something in common."

Steve had heard the line before. For him it had become the chick lawyer equivalent of, come here often?' But Steve was not amused. For the moment he stared into his drink, searching for the appropriate non-commitment words. "Well yes. I did a little litigation, but I really didn't care for it. Basically I was a gofer filing pleadings, doing an occasional slip-fall, medical malprac, and general immigration issues. After several years practice, I decided I just could not stand it any longer, so I accepted an offer to go into newspapers as a legal affairs writer in the Bay Area. It was okay, but not enough action." He had to watch it there. Steve could mention his reporter career, but must be clear that it was now behind him.

"Through a mutual friend I learned of openings in US Asylum and decided to apply. I think this kind of work covers my full range of experience - from law to journalism. So I'm quite satisfied with it." The bold-faced lie worked and diverted attention from his scandalous past. With a sullen glance into his mojito, Steve muddled over how he might handle this awkward moment.

"We have a twenty-five minute layover; would you like a drink?"

Turning syrupy, Hortensia leaned in. "Yes, I'd love a Bacardi martini, light on the vermouth. But I insist on buying. After all, I am the team leader."

It didn't take much to make her purr. While not a full-blown nympho-maniac, as a naturally horny young professional woman married to an ag-ing cardiac patient, she had her frustrations! Steve had no knowledge of this - yet. Their light conversation and exotic beverage imbibing was soon interrupted by..."Blue Hawaii Airways Flight 69 to Guam, The Marianas, Easter Island, and Tierra del Fuego - now boarding at Gate 00."

The boarding call came at the right time as Steve pondered the un-easiness of Hortensia's attitude, and his possible actions. Was he not al-ready dating two women casually? Should he risk his career last chance with a relationship that would involve a triangle with an INS power couple? Had he not wrecked one career with an indiscreet liaison? Moreover, after a difficult marriage, divorce, and at least one long-term affair, he was no longer attracted to the Amazon woman type, especially one that was sexually loose player.

The last leg, the twelve hours from Honolulu International to Saipan, capital of the Northern Mariana Islands, would be the pleasantly surreal part. The 747 took off over Diamond Head. Actually every in/out Hono-destined plane takes off over Diamond Head as this procedure keeps the gullible haole tourists thrilled, and the lusty locals raking in tour-ist bucks. This one disappeared into the clouds with sensual Hawaiian chants evoking images of half-naked Polynesian hot chicks and catama-raner hunks on screen for the passengers' delight; a sort of a high-end *Baywatch* - hayah, hayah, hayah. Not a bad way to spend twelve hours in the southbound sky.

A pitstop in Guam and a Piper Cherokee hop over verdant Mariana coral reefs, put Steve in more of a holiday mood and so it should. He could have been suffering newbie drudge assignments full of boring paperwork, redundant testimony, and aging interpreter mamas bounc-ing off yet another divorce or unfulfilled relationship. Had he not had enough of his own, after all? Still, this tropical end-of-the-earth special assignment might sweeten the spirit, provided that a colleague didn't sour it. The coral reefs reach out into hundreds of miles of mini islands of serene coco palms. They swayed sensuously above turquoise and copper vistas which yielded their way to the sheer enormity of a tropical moonlight. It would have made James Michener weep if Stephen Spielberg hadn't used it as a walk-on in his *Joe and the Volcano* movie.

Upon arriving, Steve did his usual to unwind after a typical Ripoff Airways cattle-car ride. He checked in to the Saipan Sukiyaki Plaza Hotel and went for a short run - just to get the lay of the land and refresh his spirit before the short hop to Tinian Island the next morning. He did not know it, but would soon find out that Hortensia had checked into the room next door with her own idea of the 'lay of the land.'

She wasted no time. Before Steve got to wash and change, Hortensia rang him up and asked his help in removing the top of her pill bottle. Steve's approach was anticipated, the door opened before he even knocked. She had just bathed, perfumed, and dressed for bed, but not in the manner of one who expected to sleep solo. She was draped in a loosely fitting three-quarter length, royal blue and cream trimmed Dolce & Gabbana silk gown which revealed just enough cleavage and transparency to fall evocatively over toned limbs and tightly ripped abs. It was the kind of rendezvous every healthy straight guy hoped for just once in his lifetime, but a chagrinned Steve instinctively drew back from a shag at which he would once have salaciously plunged. Steve winced.

Reading his mind like the shrewd lawyer she was, Hortensia beckoned. "Come on in, please! It's okay, I'm in my nightgown."

It was not okay for Steve, a man given to way too many indiscretions in the past. One more could wash him out of this final career if he risked it. Especially one with an old supervisor's young wife. And he knew it well enough. Yet, it might it be a frame-up might it not? A frame-up with a cover-up? Yes! It's been known to happen in US Immigration and only the Miami Asylum office is totally immune, as just about everyone there is in bed with everyone else. Like, chick, what is your game anyway? A former three-sport college athlete, basketball forward on the women's NCAA champion team, with gracefully large hands and she can't flip the top from her sleeping pill bottle? Perhaps she had a different top in mind. Steve made a mental note of the worst case scenarios.

Hortensia would play the lure - entice him into a sexual advance, grab the phone, summon hotel security and charge him with sexual assault. His undercover ruse is exposed - end of problem for the establishment. Ouine, and perhaps Faggerty, are fired and her tired old man moves one promotion closer to the Asylum headquarters, the Holy City where they answer only to Pope Lazarus himself, the Holy Father. Risking a sexual assault to take one for the team, Longstreet would owe them both - big time! That presupposes she knows about the ruse, however. Now, what if she is not aware of the ruse and is using sex to form her own cabal of loyal Asylum officers whom she can promote and manipulate if Izzy moves up? Never mind that this might ever so subtly violate the Hatch Act. Where there is a will, HQ will find a way when it comes to promoting their sycophants. Or possibly, Izzy just isn't and Hortensia is simply horny. Reader, you decide!

"So, where is the bottle you need opened?"

"Oh yes, that, of course! Just a sex, uh, sec. I'll bring it from the bathroom."

Retrieving it from her travel pack, Hortensia placed it gently in Steve's hands and then cupped her own around his, as her face animated with a seductive smile. Again, Steve noted that her hands, while feminine, were exceptionally large and powerful. They were nearly as large as his, with athletic fingers that could hold a basketball in one hand. She had been captain of the University of Connecticut women's team that won the 1995 championship, after all. Together they flipped the top - the one on the bottle, that is.

She stepped into the bathroom again, presumably to rev up her engine with her two aphrodisiacs - they were not sleeping pills after all. Steve hesitated, but he should have seen what was coming, excused himself, and left immediately. However, when Hortensia emerged from the black-marbled tile bathroom, she was wearing only her blue and white trimmed basketball jersey, emblazoned with her team logo plus mascot, and matching blue and white trimmed thong panties. Too late now guy, it's gonna happen whether you like it or not.

"You seem nervous. Haven't you seen an All-American before? I bet you have."

Now, she became more menacing than purring. Hortensia drew close, pressed herself against his chest, stroked the nape of his neck with her well-manicured, but powerfully elongated left hand, and in a deft move, locked her right hand against his shoulder and forced her tongue into his mouth in a very aggressive French kiss. This course of events would move downward quickly.

Thrusting her left leg between both of Steve's, she flipped and pinned him to her bed, deftly pulling up his muscle shirt and rolling it to shoulder level to quickly immobilize. Then she jerked off his tropical shorts and briefs. Encircling Steve's neck in the crook of her elbow and bicep, she kept him focused and unable to slide off the bed and escape.

Tossing her thong, Hortensia enveloped his midsection with legs that could press a ton and a half on the Hammer-strength machine, and groin muscles that a few years earlier had popped out a twelve-pound baby without anesthesia - by a previous relationship, of course! She went into a piston squat and humped, him in an erotic full-court press that assured her a most enjoyable slam dunk. Take one for the team, Steve! UCONN Huskies, symbol of might to the foe, rah, rah, rah!

She came a few seconds before he did, so they climaxed in an ecstatic, if not altogether harmonious, sigh. As Hortensia had neglected to draw the curtains of her ocean-view suite, the typically grand Pacific full moon shone through the breeze-caressed palms and glistened on their naked flesh as they lie motionless and silent for nearly fifteen minutes. Then, Steve slid from her side, retrieved his Tony Banana beachwear and tried to leave without saying a word. She calls or rather smirks a parting shot.

"Now that you've been debriefed I hope you'll review your briefing book. I'm sure you'll find it more stimulating now. We'll touch bases again in Tinian."

Steve mumbled a quick 'yeah, right,' and shuffled dejectedly to his room, and rightly so! He knew that he did not have to let it happen. A polite rebuke that suggested inappropriate conduct for a team leader would have given Steve the high ground and ended it there. Certainly, any sort of unwelcome sexual advance by a superior is considered by department standards to be absolute grounds for disciplinary action to include demotion, removal, or criminal sanction, depending on the nature and severity of the incident. Had it gone to an investigation, he would have been cleared and Hortensia's career and joke of a marriage would have terminated. That he let it happen surely left some self-doubt as to whether he was actually penitent. It would chew at him again.

The shorter thirty-minute Piper Cherokee run, from Saipan to Tinian over even more sand, sun, and coral, went smoothly and without compromising incident. As the group of eight Asylum officers and two interpreters boarded, Hortensia gave Steve a salacious wink, but he nodded politely in return. Then he took the seat next to the pilot where he could be safe and also try his hand again at the stick. He had taken flying lessons at the college aero club and passed a visual rule flight test, but had never pursued a full pilot's license. The check-in at the Marianas Paradise Hotel and Casino went quickly and well, and this time he was not placed in a room next to Hortensia. Fortunately, her room was not even on the same floor. As Steve was not scheduled to report to work until early the next day, he took a quick shower, changed into a fresher set of Tony Bananas. As a modestly competent blackjack player, he went down to the first floor to check out the action in the main casino.

Developed and constructed by Singaporean bon vivant, and notorious gangster Wu "Chao" Nih Mah, 'The Para' as it was affectionately known, is an ostentatious display of post-colonial decadence. A crystal chandelier of brobdingnagian proportions suspends from a 350-foot-high ceiling and greets patrons (they are never guests), in an imposing yet beckoning display of a thousand points of light. It was an over-opulent art deco monstrosity if there ever was one. Done in pink outer-tones and black marbled fixtures, it sits in the middle of a former World War II Japanese stronghold which the American GI's overran while the low-level Nip administrators and grunt soldiers jumped off one hundred-foot cliffs in hopes that dying for their emperor would assure their place in heaven - as opposed to a billet in an underwater canyon with enough drink to bury Mt. Everest a mile deep. At least that was what their officers told them, their last image of this life being the salubrious vistas of the Mariana archipelago.

Now, The Para boasted twenty-five floors of luxury hotel suites with Victorian bay windows facing the ocean. Not quite a "green hotel" but one immaculately cultivated with tropical foliage topped by over a hundred perfectly situated undulating coco palms. Good luck picking the nuts off these! The other kind of nuts were to be picked once the sun went down, so the palms were not alone in their swaying as the tropical ambience lent to various styles of undulation. On the outer rim Chinese, Japanese, Korean, and Western restaurants catered to every culinary taste. Straight, gay, and tantric massage parlors catered to every erotic taste. It was all organized in enormous concentric circles, the better to serve drinks efficiently and have patrons ordering more.

At ground zero of this Pentagon of Pleasure, a twenty-thousand-square foot casino housed baccarat, roulette, blackjack and poker parlors. Within its bowels, three cocktail mega-lounges, and four underground pleasure palaces stocked various Western, Asian, and Pacific Island liquors. Of particular pride were Johnny Walker scotches, ranging from the common man's red to the tycoon's blue. The casino tables were presided over by the vivacious, curvy, Sino-Korean-Filipina mix, Yu Bang Mi, who ruled the pleasure palaces like an empress. Also known as the sperm sponge she catered after-hours to those of no particular taste, but appealed to the manly well-hungedness of the U. S Border Patrol and Bureau of Prisons enforcers whose official job was to process in and manage the detainee population, and discourage rioting. Her younger sister, Yu Fook Mi, worked the palaces and solicited orders from desirable gentlemen. "Me love you long time!" After the not so welcome tryst with Hortensia, Steve was rather turned off to the whole gaudy oasis with all its vulgar luxury, garish casino houses, and come-ons from the pretty-pretties.

Slouching toward one of the tables at the middle rim, Steve sought what he thought was a quiet area, ordered his usual mojito, then began to muddle over his fate. He was still dejected over the previous evening's events and it showed. He sat alone for about twenty minutes, brooding over his third drink and pondering his sorry fate at midlife; no viable career, estrangement from his family, and now a possible player in a sex and security sting. All self-directed, of course. But his level of reflection, if not candor, might not allow him a personal catharsis leading to any level of healing. Rather it was taking on the quality of a self-pity binge.

Unscrupulous friends, relatives, and associates are out to screw me, figuratively and literally. Fortunately, Steve's low-level stream of consciousness was about to be interrupted.

At a table nearby, a strange theater-in-the-round was playing itself out. Senior border patrol agent Rachel Chin, an attractive, petite but very athletic Chinese-American woman, was holding court with two male colleagues, Miguel 'Mike' Sanchez and Jose 'Joe' Cordova. All three had returned from the flight line where they had completed their twelve-hour shift guarding the detainees. They each still had their 'heat', i.e. 9mm pistols holstered in their belts. An animated conversation ended with Mike, the larger and more colorful of the two yelling at Rachel, "You think I'm a *puto*? Finish your martini and get outta here! You're drunk and disorderly! And gimme your weapon before you shoot some poor guy's nuts off with it!"

Rachel sulked, spat out something about gender equality and a woman's right to pay for sex too, but did as she was told, as Miguel was her team chief. Steve began to bend his ear and lean in their direction, curious about the comic opera that ended with Rachel angrily stomping off to her room without her weapon. Aroused by her spunky manner, Joe said something like, "What a little bobcat, can you believe it?"

"Yeah, I'd knock her up, if my old lady wouldn't find out about it," roared Mike in reply.

Both men roared with laughter and slapped the table, spilling good primo Polynesian suds from their full beer mugs. They continued their conversation laughing and swapping stories of their boyhood days in barrios of Matamoros, Texas. They played football at rival schools and that meant a lot. Home of *Friday Night Lights*, high school football is a religion in the great Lone Star State, and the best players are deities. Mike and Joe surely qualified as both had made All-State; Mike as a monster man at middle guard for Matamoros Union High, and the lighter, swifter Jose as tight end for Lyndon B. Johnson Mentally Handicapped High. The rivalry was intense as both schools played for their division championship and the right to go to the state 7A finals. Their parents, cheerleaders, student body, and even the faculty joined in mocking the other team from the opposite sides of the stadium:

> Mata more ass
> Mata more ass
> We'll kick your ass
> Mata more ass!

OR

> Dumbdumb High
> Dumbdumb High
> 20 IQ
> At Lyndon Johnson High!

Unlike his school's namesake, arguably our only mentally handicapped president, Joe was 'retarded' like a fox. His IQ was in the neighborhood of 120, quite a bit above average and certainly way above the Stanford-Binet score of 80 that mandated enrollment at LBJ. He deliberately botched his test scores so he could play at the perennial football powerhouse, get straight A's in his classes, and win an easy athletic scholarship to any Texas college of his choice. Joe also played basketball and baseball, was elected class president, aced all his courses as the school 'genius,' and was offered scholarships even in his sophomore year. About this time the ruse was discovered.

Joe's postgame press interviews began to reveal a rather gifted, charismatic, and self-assured young man. As a result, he was retested under strictly controlled conditions, booted out of LBJ Mentally

Handicapped, and forcibly enrolled in the rival Matamoros where he and Mike, once bitter rivals, became fast friends. During their senior year, after Mike's bone-crushing tackle forced LBJ's quarterback to cough up the ball on the twenty-yard line, Joe added insult to injury by scoring the winning touchdown in a hard fought 21-17 victory over his old teammates. This was the first time in fifteen years Matamoros 'went to state' and won the 7A football championship. They reminisced, laughed uproariously, and regaled mightily over the past glories, wild parties, and juicy pussy that was theirs as Texas football gods. Why did it all have to end? But end it always does - college ball if you're good enough; military service, or dad's hardware store if you're not. They were clearly good enough. Mike 'freight train' Sanchez even went on to the pros; as a six-foot-one, 355 pound nose tackle that could stop any running back or combination of blockers up the middle, he began what might have been a promising career with the New York Giants. But in his third year Mike made a most unfortunate disciplinary blunder.

One week before the Giants were to meet the Redskins in the playoffs, Mike and his good buds went up to the El Cabron Grande, the popular bar and grill just off Seventh Street. There, he and ten of his football buddies drained the "Cabron" of all the good and bad bottles of tequila in central Manhattan's only Mexican watering hole. Monday morning he showed up on the practice field two hours late and in no condition to scrimmage. Worst still, it was the last full practice before the divisional playoffs and four of the buds did not show up at all. Line coach Harold Cocksell suspected Mike was the ringleader and immediately got in his face and on his case, railing against the team slackers. This was too much. Mike took his helmet off and beaned the nerdy 130-pound jerkoff, who had never played the game, and then picked him up by the seat of his britches and collar of his oversized Giants windbreaker, and tossed him over the polo grounds chain link fence and into the third row of the bleachers.

The water boy and trainers rushed to Cocksell's assistance, and when he came to, he began raving like a madman about Mike Sanchez being through in football and that even the 'Canucks wouldn't hire him. Now where have we heard that before? Mike was told by the front office to report to NFL Commissioner Peter Rosepetal personally to explain his conduct.

Rosepetal read him the riot act about player deportment on and off the field, dismissed, and permanently banned him from the league, fined him $20,000, plus a forfeiture of a major portion of his pension to compensate Coach Cocksell's expensive physical and psychological rehabilitation. It was a bit harsh for such a minor infraction and the punishment was deemed unfair by a consensus of his teammates, coaches, and owners. Everyone knew Cocksell was a pain in the ass and had it coming. But Commissioner Rosepetal was also known for his strict disciplinary measures and a fair amount of cryptic race prejudice.

Mike went back to his spiritual home, the great and sovereign state of Texas, the most glorious in the union, and the good Lord's home state to boot. For a couple weeks he moped about the A & M campus, wearing his old letterman jacket and looking to his old mentor, head coach Teebone Prickins for a job as an assistant coach or statistician. Nothing doing. His reputation had followed him all the way back to the greatest place in the world, Texas!

"Yankee Boy," he said, (Prickins called all his players Yankee Boy, regardless of geography or ethnicity of the player), "Y'aint got the brains of an Austin Democrat."

Prickins especially hated the city of Austin, the state capital, home of arch rival University of Texas, and habitat of registered Democrats and other social refuse, therefore doubly cursed. In addition to his job as head coach, Prickins has been a consistent lobbyist to move the state capital to College Station. "Y'all bopped the Giants line coach on the haid, so y'aint gittin' no coachin' job heah. Ah, insist on discipline heah! Ya got that Yankee Boy? Now ya'll mosey on down ta Mata-mo-ass and I can getcha a coachin' job at your old high school. Ain't that grand?"

"But Coach Prick," Mike countered, with an obvious Freudian slip, "I bopped the line coach there too, right after the state championship."

"Lahk I sayed, Yankee Boy, y'aint nevuh, haid no lick a sense! Ya can try LBJ Retarded, if they'll take yuh, else wise ya'll shit outta luck!"

Mike did not think it so grand, but he shook hands with his old mentor and thanked him for his kind offer. With his head down, Mike shuffled the distance to the main gate, waving to the new generation of Aggie players, who gave him the Aggie salute with a high five, "Waytago man, I woudda tossed that geek, too!"

Small consolation for a man now married and with two children to support. Things change once you get the diploma and family responsibilities. It's always about tomorrow and not today. Nice gestures were no help, but before he walked off campus, Mike noticed a bulletin on a kiosk that would change his life for the better. The ad offered good pay and benefits with the US Border Patrol to those who qualified; i.e. college degree, under age thirty-seven, and bilingual. Mike met all three criteria, applied, and was selected. And so Mike looked up his old buddy Joe, who was now managing one of his dad's hardware stores, and talked him into joining too. You and me in the Border Patrol. Now, how about that! At the border patrol academy, Mike scored near the top of his class, so he was pretty well set for life – a responsible family man with a viable career.

Where had the last twenty-five years gone, indeed? A few more Primos, football stories, border patrol anecdotes, and Mike and Joe became increasing boisterous as each war story gained a little more color and a little less credibility. Life doesn't get any better than the Texas life, Friday night lights, cold Lone Star Beer, and warm cheerleader nookie after the game - if you win. Why, them sorry-ass politicians in Washuntun oughtta pack up the whole dang US Capitol and move it deep in the heart of Texas, then the guvmint would be run raght. Yeeehaaah!

Perhaps at this moment, Mike recalled his own 'down time' and called out to the dejected Steve. Ever the enormous, jovial Mexican-American border patrolman, Mike yelled out from the nearby table.

"Hey compadre, why so glum? Sunny beaches, nice rooms, beautiful girls, good travel pay. You Asylum dudes got it made here."

Steve picked up his drink and eagerly joined the zanies, anxious to end his doldrums. Also, he was curious, especially since the BoPas were responsible for the safety and security of the Asylum personnel and their interpreters. And who knows? A good sex maniac story always sells newspapers. Miguel Sanchez and Joe Cordoba, the two agents who would become an integral part of Steve's Tinian experience might know a few. Why, it seems one had just occurred, or rather one that could be safely newsworthy. Mike stretched out his ham leg-sized hand and offered one of his Rio Grande crunchers. Even Steve, who had also played sports and met a lot of big dudes, had to be impressed.

"Mike Sanchez, and this is my buddy Joe Cordoba. Senior Border Patrol at your service. Join us for a pitcher. We grew up together and played football in Matamoros, Texas and later at A & M. We were just talkin' about the old days when we joined Border Patrol and went to the academy together. Joe was down on the idea at first, but I knew he was tired of working in his dad's hardware store, so it didn't take much to talk him into it."

"We've had some great times in the service, right Joe?"

"Yeah, and especially here!"

"So I heard," Steve smirked caustically.

"Oh her? That was Rachel Chin. Good agent, smart, speaks five languages, but horny as hell. Says she wants to have a big Mexican baby so she can raise him to play professional football and make a lot of money so she won't have to work hard when she gets old. A real head case. Hell, she even tried to offer Joe and me $250 each to double-team her. Like, can you believe it? The Chinese here call her the Gonggong Chiche. It means 'public bus' and she certainly carries a full load of riders. Ahahahahah. We had to ban her from Camp Purgatory duty after she pistol-whipped one of the big snakeheads that wouldn't put out. What a little bobcat! Ahahahahah!" Mike roared and pounded the table again, loosening its foundation.

Steve was beginning to feel a bit awkward, like it was déjà vu all over again after he tried to put the previous night's attack out of his mind and convince himself that it really didn't happen.

"Uh, it seems there are a fair number of aggressive females in the INS, wouldn't you say?"

"Yeah, well we have a saying, what happens on Tinian stays on Tinian. Everybody gets a little loose down here. You'll have your chance."

Mike gestured toward the roulette room with his tree trunk arm. "Would you like to meet a couple of the nice ladies who work the wheel?"

Steve pensively swirled the liquid in his glass and answered in a coolly haughty James Bondian fashion, "Oh, you mean the sperm sponge?

I've had a little bit of action already. It was pleasant enough, but I can't say that I require more. Actually, I'd like to get in a blackjack game, or even some baccarat. Might you know the best tables?"

Not too knowledgeable about the tables save for the two sponges, Mike changed his tone. He suggested that Steve check it out with agents who regularly played the tables and offered Steve a ride to the camp next morning.

"Well, compadre, good luck at the tables. Say, how would you like to ride with us out to the camp tomorrow morning? If you're out of action and out of the sack by five forty-five, meet us in the lobby and you can ride in our van instead of with those *puchucos* who ride the bus."

"Five forty-five a. m. it is. I think I'll even get up at four and take a dip in the ocean and a quick run through these hills first. The ocean views here are the best anywhere except for Carmel-by-the Sea.

Steve took his dip before sun-up, did a short jog up the mountain-side, and watched "the dawn comes up like thunder outer China crosy the Bay." Too bad Tinian didn't have a Moulmein Pagoda, elephants pilin' teak, or flying fishes at play on the road to Mandalay; all the stuff Steve promised himself that he would see one day. During his dark period, some ten years earlier, Steve started to frequent temples, took up Zen, and thought about converting. That was when he took more Chinese courses and developed a passing interest in things Asian. But the Pacific Basin glitz he saw at The Para was not what he had in mind. These things went through his mind as he headed back to the hotel to change, and meet Mike and Joe in the lobby. They left at 6:05 a. m. a little too late to make the 6:15 shift at the camps, but Mike the Monster Man had his own manner of shaving a normal fifteen-minute drive into five. Mike looked at Joe and winked.

"We're running late, so I'll drive. Now let's give our new buddy, Steve, a real friendly A & M welcome to Tinian. Waddaya say?"

"Jeez Mike, we better not get another complaint. You know how the OIC hates those things."

Joe was referring to the shortcut Mike took when they were running late or anxious to get back to The Para for some action. He drove his van through the gardens of a small Shinto shrine instead of slowing down and passing around the circle that enclosed it. The shrine honored those souls fortunate enough to have died for the emperor during the American landing on Saipan and Tinian islands. *Sakura shiawase wa tenno heika banzai!* The Japanese embassy protested, of course, especially since no part of the war was ever their fault. The governor of the Northern Marianas forwarded the complaint to the state department Nervous Nellies, who chewed out Officer-in-Charge, Melvin Wimpfrumple, who then confronted Mike about causing an international incident.

"Oh, stop worrying about that little *maracon!* Will ya trust me? I got it all under control!" That, of course was the best reason not to do so! So today, no banzais for the emperor, only *"Yeehah, arriba la raza,"* as Mike tore through the Meiji Gardens South. Laughing and enjoying himself on his way to Camp Purgatory, he managed to take out two prayer tablets, three stone markers, and a bonsai palm tree.

What Mike meant by what he said about the little *maracon* involved the confrontation he had with Wimpfrumple two weeks earlier when he held blackmail stuff over the OIC's head. "I hope you realize that you just caused an international incident and ruined my career. I want you to know that. What do you have to say for yourself, hmm?" he exclaimed, with his usual nervous tic and flick of the wrist as he reached in his desk for a well-stocked supply of tranquilizers.

"What do I have to say for myself? Well, let's start with…does the INS Director know you've been leaving your luxury quarters at The Para after midnight and driving out to Camp Hell, sneaking into the detainee's tents and molesting underage Chinese boys? Do you think he might like to find out about that, bub? I've got five border patrol agents as witnesses who can testify against you, and photos to back it all up unless you cut this bullshit about my driving. And who won that war anyhow? Last time I heard it wasn't the Nips, so screw 'em!"

"Who told you this? It isn't fair. I can't stand it! I can't stand it. You're a horrible person. Get out of here, you brute!"

The Gods were not amused. Neither the ones the Nips worshipped, or the ones at the state department that the OIC must pretend to worship. But this time, he knew better than to call Mike on the carpet. Wimpfrumple fell ill, suffered a nervous breakdown, and was replaced. Within the next month, he would be replaced twice; first by his deputy, Regina Skankfield, a double-hatted Asylum and refugee supervisor, and later by a former FBI section chief, Neil 'The Wheel' Von Rothweiler.

No one knew how sick Wimpfrumple was until he showed up at Camp Purgatory wearing his favorite pair of white hot pants, Dolce & Gabbana tennies, bottle-green fishnet stockings, and his favorite purple pullover silk t-shirt. Joe Cordoba was happily munching his favorite, a bag of sunflower seeds, and spitting shells on the tarmac when Wimpy approached the tent area.

"A lot of seeds. You *know* how I feel about seeds. Why do you exhibit such disgusting behavior?"

Joe only regarded him with mild contempt and between bites and spits uttered, "Why not? You're pretty seedy, yourself! And we all know what goes on in those tents at Camp Hell, so that's why you're busted and outta here!"

"Agheegh! You're a horrible person and I hope you catch some horrible disease from one of your girlfriends. I, personally will have you dismissed from Border Patrol. I have friends at high headquarters, you know!"

"You mean the Department of Homo Security? Yeah, right! More than likely those friends are at your tailquarters. And I hope you get AIDS and herpes from Regina Skankfield on your way outta here. There's a rumor she's hermaphro-just your type. You might even give it to each other. Put that in your lace panties and rub it!"

Screeching like a banshee, Wimpfrumple put his hands to his ears and ran from the command tent shrieking, howling, and bawling, "Those barbarians. So insensitive!" Shriek, shriek! "I'll fix them. the Asylum Director will hear about this!"

Yes, the director did hear about it, and after examining all the facts, and against the strenuous protests of Wimpfrumple's friends at high headquarters to the contrary, Director Longstreet reluctantly removed the miscreant from his cushy GS-15 job for conduct unbecoming an Officer-In-Charge.

Regina Skankfield would prove no better. Arrogant, belligerent, and demanding, yet characteristically neither very industrious, nor very bright, she divided her time between driving her rental car up and down the flight lines and snorkeling off the coral reefs. Thus she did no more than a couple hours real work in a day at best. And the 'at best' amounted to no more than riding the backs of the first-line supervisors and demeaning the refugee officers. At midlife she was already falling apart and it showed. Haggard looking, her once semi-attractive face and tight body were now turning to droopiness and flab after countless affairs and two abortions - the most recent having come as the result of leaving her birth control pills in her condo while she globetrotted at taxpayers' expense. So Regina took a chance with a husky pineapple-headed refu-gee officer in Kuala Lumpur but the chamber was still loaded.

The refugee part of the Asylum corps tends to attract the sex-ually promiscuous. Those without family ties or connections, who like living out of suitcases and in hotels, who love multiple partners. Please apply, we've been expecting you. Regina was typical of that lot. A feminist ice-queen rumored to be bi-sexual from her Mills College days. Intellectually lacking but not extremely so, Regina played her minority card into easy admission at UCB, Frisco Bay, Hastings College of Law.

Having been born in Alabama of racially-mixed parentage dur-ing the post-war Jim Crow south, Skankfield learned how to make her way in the world, playing this card; i.e. white when it was convenient, black when it was even more convenient. Through family connec-tions, like those who have a friend who has a friend, and regular Baptist church attendance, she gained admission to Mills College. It was there that her survival instincts took over. Sympathetic profes-sors and other bed partners assured her smooth sailing from L-1 to L-3, so she was never at any time scared to death, worked to death, or bored to death, the common lot of American law students. Upon graduation, and with the earnest recommendation of many of her professors, Skankfield was immediately hired by the Gavin Bully mega law firm and clerked for the Duke of Contracts himself, who took her under his wing, and other parts, and it was here that she lost both her AC/DC cherries.

Only one year after graduation Skankfield was immediately fired by Bully himself for having the temerity to "share the wealth" with his man-aging partner, and worse still, two junior associates. Not cool! From that time, her career went downhill, and like many failed lawyers, she went to the government. Forty-hour workweeks, GS-12 salary, and monthlong vacations sure beat grinding for success in a smaller litigation firm, or worse yet, doing immigration lawyering for a hole-in-the-wall immigration consulting firm.

Mike, Joe, and Steve arrived at Camp Purgatory in time to make the shift change and begin their twelve-hour rotation. Boring work really, but they were needed in order to keep the coolies cool, from overrunning the island, and making the Marianas a part of the New Celestial Empire. As Mike and Joe set up their gear and strapped on their heat, Steve reported to Hortensia who behaved as though not a damn thing had happened between them.

"Good morning, Steven. An absolutely lovely tropical morning to begin our detail, don't you think?" Not expecting a reply she gushed on, "I will be your team leader, of course. And Regina Skankfield is the Officer in Charge as of yesterday. You will report directly to me, but Regina can answer any questions you may have concerning the overall operation. Do you have any?"

He might have asked how one goes about filing a sexual assault complaint but thought the better of it. And after a short briefing (the debriefing occurred the night before), Hortensia walked him over to her majesty's tent to meet Regina Skankfield. "Regina will take you to your work area after a short drive around the camps where the detainees are housed, and introduce you to your team of interpreters who will translate for you. Then you may begin your casework. I'm sure you will find your detail here a most enriching experience. I know I have."

Without rising from her makeshift bamboo throne, Regina Skankfield extended her right hand, palm tilted over slightly as thought she expected a kiss. Not quite Steve's style though, so a handshake would have to do.

"How nice you will be working for me," she gushed. "I'm sure we'll get along well. Everyone does."

Not quite true as the next week's events would play out. Steve began his work interviewing refugees real and imagined, while Ms. Skankfield sunbathed, snorkeled, and lounged throughout the next two weeks. Foul enough, but mouthing off to a three-star admiral is quite another matter.

Vice Admiral Amos P. Mothbauls, retired, led a Department of Justice fact-finding team of five former military brass to ascertain the budget requirements and cost overruns that usually fund such operations. The Marianas Paradise Hotel was among the redlined items. More ominous, his team was also sent to survey the situation and assess any potential military or espionage threat. Admiral Mothbauls, always on a tight schedule even in retirement, was not a happy camper even at this luxury camp. Especially not at this luxury camp. Blaming his forced retirement on a lack of a good war to fight, he was all military and no nonsense, especially civilian nonsense.

Moreover, his stock portfolio, the one he used to buck up his military retirement pension had been performing poorly. After a four-hour search, (five hours too long for him), Mothbauls finally located Skankfield on her reserved deck lounge sunning herself beside the super Olympic size pool, rolls of fat hanging over her bikini bottom, wearing no top to better reveal boobs that had long since lost their estrogen, and holding a reflector sun panel under her jowly face. She would not even stand or render any proper greeting or courtesy, but only announce herself as, "Regina Skankfield and I' m in charge here. You'll be working for me." Before she could say any more the 'good old salt' showed her the error of her ways.

"Like hell I will, aarragh!" Mothbauls retorted with his classic Blackbeard the Pirate snarl.

"You a muthufukuh! I'm in charge here, so yo'all stay outta mah camps, ya heah?"

"Aarragh! I've deep-sixed the meanest, saltiest, sons of bastards under the seven seas, so I'm damned if I'll take orders from a quadroon like you, I'll run you through with my cutlass, I will, aarragh!"

Horrified by the buccaneer's shiny cutlass and pistol the grand admiral wore even with his Hawaiian shirt, Bermuda shorts, Panama hat and sandals, and with a sonar boom deep from the bowels of Davy Jones' locker, Regina Skankfield quickly leapt from her chaise longue in full retreat, and high-hurdled tree and shrub to the safety of her penthouse suite at The Para. What a sight that was - gross!

It turns out that 'Old Mothy' was a friend of the Bush family going way back to the era of Hitler's tire salesman buddy, Senator Prescott Bush. So all he had to do is say the word about the OIC's expense paid vacation which he did as soon as he got back to Washington, and George Dubya told the Department of Homeland Security to humor the slightly demented old family friend. Skankfield was removed from the detail, sent back on the next plane, and an official reprimand was placed in her employee file by Longstreet, himself. No chance to go to HQ now! Skankfield would end her Asylum career as a first-level supervisor like it or not. Sometimes, there is just no justice.

With the Skanks given the boot, Steve was getting good copy to his boss after only a week on the job. The part about Horny Hortensia - better leave it out. With her sister-in-crime recalled, Hortensia, not so hi-tone now, left Steve alone, except for an occasional salacious wink. The new OIC, the third on this operation, was Neal 'The Wheel' Von Rothweiler, a short roly-poly FBI section chief, and quick with a scowl, growl, or howl if need be.

The Wheel did not want to leave his cushy job at the DOJ, but orders are orders. He took his job seriously and expected others to do the same. No excessive partying or lounging. So Steve could now switch his efforts from dodging the amorous aims of lusty bimbo supervisors, to doing the work for which both bosses would pay him - namely refugee casework that would morph into feature articles.

The work effort broke down thusly: About twenty Asylum officers did the casework of processing six boatloads of refugees that sailed from the Fujian Coast to the Northern Marianas Islands just north of the equator in the Eastern Hemisphere. Coast Guard vessels interdicted three of them as they entered US territorial waters and convoyed them to the Tinian Harbor. Crew leaders and snakeheads testified that two more boats had sailed with their party, but one had disappeared from sight days earlier. Another was taking in serious water, so the Bureau of Prisons and Border Patrol had to remove the refugees to the Coast Guard vessels while still in international waters.

Another boat had made it to shore and landed on an inconspicuous beach, but after a few days, the local Chamorro population was quick to spot the band of about one hundred ragged-looking Chinese aliens foraging about or looking for work at The Para or any of those sweatshops and restaurants in Saipan not covered by US labor laws.

The warning of the local people to the Justice Department authorities in Washington was clear: Get down here and take care of the situation or we will take care of it ourselves in our own way. The our own way happened once before. After the US war effort in Vietnam failed, a boatload of Vietnamese squatters made it to the Marianas, only to disappear. Both US and local officials questioned a few of the local big shots who might have seen them, but to a man they claimed no sightings or knowledge of any boat people. Thus began the official part of Steve's assignment for *The Riverside Times.* The nucleus of series had already formed. All he had to do was write about it.

Steve did his refugee interviews under a cabana, as did all officers, and retreated to the US Public Health Officer's tent to complete write-ups into a short recommendation or denial for Hortensia and exaggerate the effort up into journalistic copy for the boss. The USPHS tent afforded him a measure of privacy as it was secluded from the cabanas. Hortensia never ventured into the area reserved for the 'health people.' Whether she blended same gender hostility with an attitude of superiority, only she knew the reasons. USPHS was only 'uniformed services' as opposed to the lofty humanitarian endeavor that US Asylum surely was.

So Steve wrote:

The one word that best describes this rescue operation is *surreal.* You might call it a little bit *M*A*S*H* blended with a lot of *Bridge on the River Kwai.* The Officer-In-Charge, Neal Von Rothweiler, nicknamed 'Neal The Wheel' because of his rotund appearance, oversees the entire circus like a feudal lord. Discreet about his hanky-panky, his pick of the ladies excludes those who run the casinos, but he does an occasional hook-up with a public health nurse or 'hot doc" with whom Neal The Wheel can cop a feel.

Neal The Wheel is more "hands on" than Directors Skankfield and Wimpfrumple before him. He's present at the camps every day and maintains constant cell phone communication with the DOJ for subtle changes in refugee policies or procedures. No lounging about the pools or sex scandals for him!

The new deputy OIC is one Vincenzo del Piano who gave his boss 'The Wheel' nickname. Del Piano is a veteran Border Patrol supervisor with more than 30 years service. Add his travel pay and he caps out at somewhere around $130,000 a year. By law, a federal employee cannot earn more than a member of the US Congress, so as Del Piano's salary has reached this level, he was paid no more money for this detail. Okay, no pay, no work! Therefore, as soon as he reaches the required six hours, he leaves the refugee camps and hits the gambling tables. Vinnie the 'godfather' was popular with his troops. "Nothin's too good for my boys," he loved to say in his Hoboken accent, so he assures that 'his boys' and sometimes 'his girls' get the best lodgings at The Para, laundry facilities, 'extended use' of government vehicles and 'odder tings!'

The 'Pubic Health Babes' as they are affectionately known, are rather attractive, even in combat boots and fatigues. The effort is called, not without a fair amount of irony, Operation Saipan Security. It is not certain who should be made secure and from what.

Most of the Chinese coastal peasants paid their snakeheads anywhere from US$30,000 to $80,000 to bring them to the US Commonwealth of the Northern Marianas Islands, but they surely did not expect to stay in the Marianas. Many had visions of opening restaurants in New York, becoming movie stars in LA, or even entrepreneurs in Honolulu. All believed they could make it happen with little effort or talent. "And all the stars that never were…do hot massage or cut the grass." The lot of the few who sneaked in under the radar and joined the local underground economy of Saipan, would remain part of the unregulated, unprotected, and underground labor force. The US Department of Justice authorities in Washington really do not give a damn what the local indigenous authorities in Saipan do, so long as the commonwealth capital makes a discreet livelihood taking administrative stipends from Washington, and so assure they are not about to make any Mariana waves.

Most, if not all of those interviewed, experienced no religious persecution in China, but this ruse makes for a credible claim. Although the Chinese government officials in general discourage extreme religious expression, mainline and evangelical churches operate above ground. The refugee applicants get around this by memorizing and rehearsing false testimony and submitting equally false documents in order to gain secure passage into the United States where they pursue their own American dream. The first-line supervisors lean hard on their officers to grant these people "credible fear." If a refugee is granted "credible fear," this person appears before an Immigration judge in Saipan for a more extensive Asylum interview, or the courts temporarily resettles the persons in the US, depending on the number of cases on the federal judicial dockets. Some do not show up in court; they go on the lam and join the underground economy as sweatshop laborers, exotic masseuses, or low-paid restaurant workers. The snakehead takes their wages to repay the "loan" back in China. If any protest there is no recourse, as they are in the country illegally having not shown for their Immigration court hearing.

On Tinian Island, the refugees are housed fifty to a tent in processing centers called Camp Purgatory and Camp Hell. These are located on the old World War II runways, the very same ones used by the planes that dropped the atomic bombs on Hiroshima and Nagasaki. US Border Patrol segregates males from females to assure that they create no new US citizens while they await interviews. Border Patrol also disarms any snakeheads making the trip as they are usually the boat captain's enforcers and often carry pistols.

All this has an air of comic farce, however. Petty gangsters known as snakeheads work the US Immigration systems through its many flaws and inconsistencies. Beginning at the source in coastal Fujian Province, the snakeheads recruit uneducated, gullible peasants to sign charter contracts for boat fare, lodgings, false documents, and fabricated testimony which guarantee them passage and settlement in the mainland United States.

After the peasants arrive at the ports of entry, or through the underbrush of the territories, the syndicates offer the services of immigration lawyers, translators, interpreters, and document preparers to usher them through the labyrinth that is the US Immigration system. Thus, they safely enter the underground economy. By and large the process is safe for the criminals and parasites who game the system. Once the peasants are in the hands of the consulting services, the owners of such enterprises often demand as much as $2,000 to $3,000 for continuing the process, especially if the "refugee" is found not to be credible and is referred to the Immigration court.

At this juncture, an Immigration judge usually makes the final decision whether to send the person home or grant asylum. A few cases may win on an appeal to the federal judicial circuit if the Immigration judge makes an unfavorable decision and the refugee is exceptionally wealthy. A referral costs money and most persons exhaust their funds paying off their snakeheads and lawyers.

Some of the snakeheads make the trip with their clients and file their own claims to assure the syndicate process works smoothly on both sides of the Pacific and the asylees continue to pay their tribute money after they have been granted. Border patrol identified and removed twenty-five snakeheads from one of the boats. They were all armed and heavily tattooed, instant giveaways. The irony here is that the snakeheads often offer up the best testimony. They are shrewd, well coached, and well connected through their respective networks.

This reporter interviewed one who claimed to be a "home church Christian." He alleged that the public security police in his town, Pingtan in Fujian Province, arrested him and six other worshippers during a Sunday home church service. The police grabbed their Bibles and songbooks, duck-walked them to a police van, and removed them to seventy-two hour detention for questioning. A fat cop and a skinny cop questioned him. The skinny cop accused the snakehead of "disturbing the social order, practicing an evil cult, and supporting reactionary politics." It was always the same boilerplate affidavit. When this reporter asked the snakehead how he acquired his gang tattoos, he stated that he had them done before he was converted. When asked about the brass knuckles, nunchakus, and sawed-off .38 that Border Patrol took from him, he simply replied that the ship's captain put him in charge of maintaining order - a likely story!

What is curious about this whole comedy of crime was the business card that this "refugee" submitted at the interview. It was the card of suspended Los Angeles attorney O. D. Barfield, Esq. The applicant also stated that Mr. Barfield would represent the him upon arrival in the continental US. Further investigation has revealed that "O-don, Da Barf, or Old Barfey" as he is sometimes called, is a former employee of Los Angeles Asylum and classmate of Sean Faggerty and Malcolm Muddleston at La Jolla University's Mahatma Gandhi College of Law and Meditation. It is believed that these two officials were responsible for his hiring, but after a few months he was fired under mysterious circumstances, allegedly due to a conflict of interest between his private law practice and his duties as an Asylum officer. Confronted by Asylum Supervisor Oswald H. Hinkel for working on his cases after authorized hours, and with an unauthorized visitor, Hinkel fired him on the spot. The visitor, his Chinese girlfriend, had been making phone calls to solicit business for his firm, a serious conflict of interest! Barfield continued to practice immigration law after his dismissal two years prior and often escorted clients to the Anaheim office wearing expensive-looking suits. When asked about the specific details of Barfield's employment, Director John B. Ouine and Deputy Director Sean Faggerty declined comment. Veteran Asylum Officer Karl Keibalski, not quite so reticent, declared that the whole incident "stinks" and that Ouine had "a lot of egg on his face because of it." Barfield is currently under investigation by the California Bar Counsel and State Attorney General Feather Lockliar for ethics violations.

Chapter 4

ZOO LA-LA

"**W**hat's shakin' big guy? How's your golf game?" With this acquired-Keibalskiism, Steve bounded into Robyn's office, very much the swashbuckling sailor of fortune back from the far-flung seven seas. With booty for the sovereign, he was confident that his big scoop would not just impress his boss, but that his thoughtful expose on INS corruption might even earn him the next Pulitzer Prize, or least his own name on the masthead as co-publisher. This was not how it was going to play out. Slumped over his rolltop and reviewing copy, Robyn did not regard his delinquent deputy editor until he heard him storm back from the bounding main at which point he did his usual angry 180.

"Is that all you have to say after smoking out my moles, wrecking the marriage of the LA Asylum's highly respected (hah!) power couple, and contributing to an international incident?"

"Whaa?"

"A little bird flew by my window and told me you raised three different kinds of hell on Saipan!"

He took an embossed envelope from one of the many pigeonholes of his rolltop and slapped it down. "This is a formal complaint lodged by the Consul General of Japan under the seal of the Emperor. You and your Border Patrol hoodlums defiled a Shinto shrine dedicated to the poor souls who died for their Emperor during the war."

"And all this time I thought *we* won that war."

"I bet you think this is all very comical; well I don't. Ouine was going to terminate your job, so I had to go to Leilo to chill him off. For a price, of course, always for a price. You think I have enough ad-funds to cover freebies on his restaurants, chains of massage parlors, and all his other dens of iniquity? I want you to know, it's coming out of your salary. Now, John B. will likely reign in Keibalski and one other mole whom I won't mention by name. So I've got to persuade him that you're not going to do any more off-the-wall antics like at Tinian. Otherwise, he cancels our deal and your job goes with it - here, there, anywhere. Capiche?"

He gave Steve no chance to accept or say, "Take this job and shove it!"

"Oh, one more thing before you say, 'Take this job and shove it.' Izzy Falabenko was rushed to the hospital two nights ago after a mild heart seizure and tests reveal that he needs another bypass surgery. Can you imagine what might have brought this on? No? Well, I will tell you what it was. Hortensia was so juiced after her detail the night after her return that when she was jump straddling her old man, guess whose name she was hollering?"

Now, the boss was pouring double rations of Jack Daniels and slamming his tumbler down on the rolltop with ice cubes flying in all directions, the least he expected a was a contrite answer.

"Uh."

"You know whose it was! It was 'Oh, Steve,' So don't try to lie your way out of it! After an awkward confrontation, he keeled over, and Hortensia Hot Twat grabs a see-through nightie, calls the medics, and they wheel him into emergency cardiac at Loma Linda wearing only his birthday suit. Can you think about what a sight that was? Can you? You can thank your lucky stars he didn't die of embarrassment or they didn't lose him in intensive care. And another thing... the next day I get a very irate call from J. B. Ouine. He was set to fire you and cancel all cooperation on future feature articles. Or, maybe you think *The Riverside Times* and Los Angeles Asylum are joint chahptahs of Club Med just for your leisure?"

"Well, I, uh, in a matter of speaking, the incident with Hortensia was not exactly consensual. She is a very forceful lady."

"Are you trying to suggest that you were a victim of sexual assault?"

"In a matter of speaking, as the law might define it, you could say…"

"I can't stand double talk - you know that! And another thing, everyone knows she's the office nympho," he rambled, gesturing with his half-full tumbler. "And Izzy was nuts to marry a woman half his age, and a Division One college athlete to boot, especially with his history of heart trouble. But that's neither here nor there. What I do know is that you might have averted the entire slimy mess, but you did not."

Robyn said this with a slight smirk as he tilted his glass, letting the remaining ice cubes cool the amber liquid and his temper with it. His chastisement had left subordinate visibly shaken, but he also knew that Steve was as fireproof as an Otis safe deposit box.

"A leopard can't change his spots… can it?"

"Well, uh…"

"I'm transferring you to a different beat. It seems US Immigration in downtown Los Angeles is a real zoo parade of illicit sex, and a little bird told me there's some friggin' in the riggin' going on at The Federal Building. It's more than the usual stuff between the old geezer federal judges boning their hot babe district counsels," he mused. "No, this time it is big time. The 13 floor where nobody goes except 'the somebodys' is a virtual Playboy Club that pays no royalties to Hugh Hefner. All this began to surface after Hernando Da Silva retired as District Director two years ago. No wonder those in the know and the blow still call it Hernando's Hideaway." The allusion to the 1950's pop tune was totally lost on Steve who was now non-plussed yet piqued at the prospect of a federal building beat.

"Wasn't he director before…?"

"Yes, yes," replied the boss impatiently. "Before Laura Schmelbalz left Asylum to take over the District. Wherever she goes, she always reaches her level of incompetence. It's taken Sean Faggerty two years to locate the backlog of two thousand case files the deadwood officers had hidden around the offices of sympathetic supervisors, and fire a few of them, as she had continued the proud tradition of Sloppy Joe Michelson. But that's neither here nor there. For reasons I cannot fathom, she always manages a promotion or a transfer out before all the shit hits the fan. You could say she always comes out of all her desperate straits smelling like a rose. Your job is to make it all surface and expose it. This should win kudos with John B. who hates her, and in addition, keep you out of Hortensia's orbit while Izzy recovers. You start as soon as you turn in your Tinian casework to Ike. One more thing… Chaiklin knows about the Hortensia incident and he is not a happy camper, so you consider yourself warned and walking on eggs."

Steve was about to roll his eyes at such clichés, but though the better of it.

When Steve arrived at 1080 North Avalon, Ike Chaiklin was pacing the floor of his office. He was wearing bandages where he had bitten his fingernails hard enough to draw blood, and doing one of his many free-association binges.

"This is not ethical, this is not ethical," Ike moaned, to no one listening. Actually, no one was ever listening but he hadn't figured that out just yet - more valium. Steven Melkonian should not have been allowed to go on a detail without completion of the Asylum Officers Training Class. It clearly states this in the Asylum Official Policy Manual on page 69, paragraph B, Roman numeral Iaiii.

"This is an outrage! I am so distraught. No one understands me and the Universe has forsaken me. What shall I do?" Ike moaned between sobs, and acting like some Hollywood finochio.

Lear raging on the moors could not have been more pathetic, but the good king did his jeremiad with so much more style. Steve, of course, heard all this bleating through the closed door and hesitated to knock. Once Steve developed a visceral dislike of anyone, he would not, could not, change his mind, and so it was with Isaac Milhouse Chaiklin III. There were two previous? Lord, help us! Moreover, it was enough to suffer the ramblings of a competent boss, but he had little patience for those of a fake boss, and a genuine head case at that!

So, Steve headed to Keibalski's office first, just to raise his own morale, even though his boss had declared him persona non grata and his domain off-limits. Da Keibals would be good for gossip, scandal, and a few new war stories - always good for news copy despite Robyn's not so convincing no-fly-zone warning.

"Hey, Steve, welcome back! Howthehellzit hangin? From what I hear long and loose and fulla juice!"

Steve rolled his eyes Al Gore-style but understood he would not get in a word edgewise until he let the Keibals' gas off.

"Speak of the Devil. You'll never guess who I saw last week up the coast? Like, my old lady's outta town on one of her three-week Euro spending sprees - good thing her dad is wealthy! So, I hop into my 1950 vintage Ford station wagon and cruise the 101 Freeway listening to my Fleetwood Mac disc like *You Can Go Your Own Way.* I mean can you dig it? No old lady around for three weeks, and like, who should I run into while I'm checkin' out vapid babes at Ventura Beach, but my old football buddy Ed 'King Kong' Lodazhit and his New Age mama Bacchanalia, with their five grandkids having a day at the beach. Like, can you believe it dude? Where the hell did the time go? Like, I didn't recognize him at first because Bacchanalia has him on this macrobiotic diet and like, he's real skinny - only weighs 300 now! Like can you believe it, dude? And like, he's got this three-foot-long beard and white hair, and looks like King Neptune crawled outta the sea. Fuckin' A, I ain't lyin', dude! So like, I spend the afternoon with them and they try to hook me up with one of Bacchanalia's friends, but like, this chick's total vegan, and like, I'm total carnivore, and total married, so we didn't hit it off. But I got her cell phone number if you want it. I mean like, if Hortensia is totally out of bounds now!"

Steve noticed with some amusement that Karl crossed his fingers when he got to the "total married" part, because his marital infidelities were well known by the office, but he fidgeted at the Hortensia part as he did not share Karl's braggadocio about his own indiscreet behavior and moral shortcomings. Now, it was exit time.

"I need to turn my Tinian work into Isaac and I hear he's really pissed!"

"Aw, don't worry about the whiney little nerd! He just thinks he has more power than he really does. No one likes him here, not even management - especially not management! He only keeps his job here because his fellow bum-buggers at headquarters won't let Ouine fire him."

By this time, Steve had worn out his brand of bourgeois liberalism. He hated Chaiklin and felt that what Karl just said was on point, but he would not let his conflicted feelings show. He had straight and gay friends after all, but none like this misanthrope.

"Well, I'd just as soon get this over with, so wish me luck."

"I don't know why you think you'd need it, or why you should even be afraid of this turkey," Karl replied, with a semi-disgusted glance. "You're not permanent… here." A careless slip of the tongue, and before he caught himself, Karl just revealed that he knew about Steve's delicate situation at Asylum.

With the fifteen-minute motivational speech from Karl full-of-himself Keibalski thankfully over, Steve trudged upstairs to the office of Mr. Woebegone, Karl's temperamental opposite. Steve knocked, entered, and found Ike pacing the floor, checking his Rolex watch (a gift from the previous deputy director) and biting his nails. His trusty bottle of valium in full view.

In his best bureaucratese, he turned to Steve and shrieked, "Did Mr. Weizenheimer enjoy his US Government expense paid vacation? Where is your completed work product?"

Steve sneered a bit, and then answered, "Got it right here, 175 interviews on CD-ROM, twenty-five over my quota. Got a problem with that?"

Unable to belittle Steve on productivity, Chaiklin went into yet another pathetic free-association binge. "That's not the point. What you
did was unethical. And you will stay away from Ms. Falabenko while you
are here. Hortensia Falabenko is one of our most competent supervisors, a respected lady, and a beautiful person. You defiled her person-
hood and right before she runs the Yorba Linda Marathon. Moreover,
you caused her beloved domestic partner to suffer a coronary seizure.
Your conduct has been dreadful since you arrived here, just dreadful."
He sighed then reached for his valium. Now, Steve had all he could take
of Asylum p.c. blame-speak and said so.

"Well, I am getting damn tired of all these bogus accusations from
federal management parasites like you - especially given the facts of the
case. Just the opposite happened. HORtensia," he stressed the first sylla-
ble for effect, "resident office nymphomaniac, will hump anything that
has a dick and even force the issue, except on you of course, but that's
because you are an ugly, hatchet-faced, haggard old prig and everyone
knows *your* persuasion. And why not? Her old man has one foot in the
grave and the other on a banana peel, and your pathetic liberal-speak
psychobabble is just so much cover-her-ass spin doctoring. It would be
better if he did croak and they removed him from the federal payroll."

"Screech! You can't say that to me. I have a PhD in abnormal psychology from California State University at Pebble Beach and I am very
important here."

"Well, if that's true, you have done a piss poor job of curing your
own case!"

"Screech, get out of my room, now!"

"In case you're still interested in my work product," he sneered
with a good deal of contempt, "here it is." Steve swaggered over to Ike's

pill-laden desk slapped the CD-ROM down on it, and turned and left without waiting for more admonitions from his temp boss. His mojo restored, Steve left for his new "first day on assignment," and the one that he would know the best - the courthouse.

Steve took two hours to detox from his meeting with Chaiklin and enjoyed a luxury rare for himself, a nice lunch of vichyssoise and white burgundy at Schnellings, the new seafood restaurant a few blocks east of his office. He deserved as much.

It had been a trying month, after all. Shenanigans in the Marianas, a disgruntled publisher, and an effete government supervisor left their emotional mark. Had he done the right thing by leaving the relative comfort of his litigation firm? Might he have made partner with a few more clients on his billing record? It was the like poet Robert Frost's "Road Not Taken" and would always be so. Yet, mightn't this new beat offer the professional challenge he sought?

And this one would be a genuine challenge. It was an intricate web of corruption characterized by lies, deception, and extortion on the part of immigration attorneys, federal judges, and district directors. A byzantine world that infused the cosmic energy of the Los Angeles Federal Building - stuff of which exposes are made and careers ended - or in Steve's case, resurrected.

It would not take long. As soon as Steve arrived at the fed, parked his car, and approached the magnificent edifice in the heart of El Pueblo de la Ciudad de Nuestra Senora, la Reina de los Angeles (that's LA downtown, off Olvera Street; like, the original burg to all you monolinguals), what appeared to be a civil disturbance or probable riot awaited him. Yes, an incongruous and fearful sight beckoned him to the side entrance of The Federal Building. Great reporter that he was, Steve surveyed the scene, analyzed the facts, whipped out his iPod and wrote:

The vicious, notorious, ruthless, and depraved 19 Street badass Guatemalan gang, the feared Mamacita Putas, replete with demon and skeleton tattoos and full dress uniform; bandanas, bare chest, ball-buster jeans, shit kicker stiletto boots with Cuban heels, is now leading a crowd of "innocent bystanders" in the cheer: "Gringos and pueblomos, we can't hear you! Jump, jump, jump, jump! You *pachucos* gotta do better than that, now let's hear you! Yeah, you, up there, yeah, on floor thirteen. Be a man! Jump, jump, jump, jump!"

Thirteen floors above the original site of the elegant, cultured, historical Spanish city of Our Lady, Queen of the Angels, a dweeby little man stands trembling on the east ledge of the fed. Wrapped in the US Department of Justice flag, ready to bid good-bye to this cruel world that has never understood him. His plaintive cry inaudible to those gawking below, poor, misunderstood INS Asylum Supervisor, Ike Chaiklin, appears about ready to make his mark (we hope) on the world - and a messy mark it might well be!

"No one else is ethical in this department. I am the one. I, Isaac Milhous Chaiklin III, am the only one."

Now, before he could, jump and splot the glorious pavement of El Pueblo, his spiritual advisor appeared on the scene to coax him off the ledge. Pabu Punjah Punjahbih Pootahngheehr, licensed Kumbayah practitioner, US Customs agent, part owner of the Anaheim Lime Street Poontahngheehr Hotel, and fulltime Hindu mystic appeared in saffron robes. He set down a recording of Ike's favorite music to soothe his soul - Ravi Shankar's "Greatest Hits" followed by Magdalena's "Multicultural Girl." From the sitting lotus position, he was chanting and burning incense when a team of federal marshals broke down the double pane 13 floor teakwood doors. And what an incongruous sight it was, indeed!

Led by former US Army Green Beret, former Texas Ranger, now US Marshall Billy Bob Rednick, in full battle regalia of LBJ-style white Stetson hat, $10,000 handmade crocodile cowboy boots, and desert camouflage fatigues with general's star on the collar, the team stormed the thirteen floor to rescue the tormented soul of Isaac Milhouse Chaiklin III.

"Whew!" yelled team chief Rednick. "What stinks? Will you look at this weirdo place? It's almost a whorehouse I tell you! And who the hell is this crank in a dress?"

His immediate subordinate offers enlightened him, "Uh sir, I think it must be a Hindu religious swami burning incense. Do you think we ought to do a raid? It might make the papers and we could get a commendation letter and a $100 bonus!"

As Rednick eyed all the round waterbeds, massage tables, murals, and photographs of voluptuous naked ladies and hunky Hollywood males he winked, lowered his voice, elbowed his subordinate's ribs, and answered his own question. "Ya'll play fo mighty small stakes, Yankee Boy!" bellowed Chief Rednick. "If this makes the papers guess who's screwed, blewed, and tattooed, huh? Upper management that's who. And it wouldn't surprise me one damn bit if the director is running this. A she's a former "lady of the house," you know." He winked. "Might mean a big promotion for us and a little hush money if we sit on it a spell and play a little five card draw with the Ol'Smellyballs herself. Ya'll get the pitcher, boy?"

"Uh, I dunno, chief. That sounds like blackmail."

"So you must like living on GS-9 pay. That right, Yankee Boy? Or you can do it my way and win with Rednick."

Deputy US Marshall Hiram Johnson Fernmayer snapped to and saluted. "Sir, yes sir! Win with Rednick, sir!"

"That's the spirit! Now, ya'll get that weird holy man off the floor and outta here, and grab that turkey off the ledge! Now! He's about ready to leap."

Fernmayer and team grabbed Swami Poontanhgheehr by the edge of his saffron robes, rolled him up, tied him like a Persian carpet, and carried him down the stairwell to the twelfth floor elevator. Then they dropped him off at the nurse's aid station on the second floor where they put him under sedation. While the team carried him off, Swami continued chanting and protesting about his family being most virtuous, and how his four daughters were all virgins. Rednick struck his usual heroic pose and yelled, "Yeehaah," while his Yankee Boy troops did the work.

By some strange coincidence, the Magdalena and Ravi Shankar cassette concluded with the Longhorn Marching Band playing the stirring notes of "Yellow Rose of Texas." How appropriate! The remaining Rednick team members rush the ledge. Deputies Miller, Leyden, Stuhldreyer, and Crowley grab a corner of the INS bunting and pulled Ike Chaiklin to safety, crying and wailing about his miserable life as an Asylum supervisor.

And from combined eyewitness accounts, that's the way it is; September 10, 2007. Steve Melkonian reporting.

Not a bad story for Steve's first day on the new beat! He waited for clearance from the boss before reporting to the Asylum office where John B. would assign him a new supervisor. Two days later, he returned to 1080 North and approached the director's office but stopped abruptly as Mr. Ouine was involved in a heated telephone conversation with Lazarus Longstreet in Washington. Steve overheard part, walked away for ten minutes, and returned when it appeared safe.

"Absolutely not! Over my dead body! He has always had very poor people skills and now has embarrassed US Asylum. You of all people should understand this. Would you like to be in my shoes? I may need to do a press conference."

"No, I don't give a damn that he may attempt suicide again. If he does and succeeds, so much the better for the service."

"Well, admin leave is your call, but I would not give it to him. That's a forty-five-day vacation at taxpayer expense, in addition to his accrued annual and sick leave - pretty soft if you ask me! Yes, I know the regs as well as you do. He is to get counseling and real therapy. That means no more flakey group sessions."

Steve waited for him to finish the conversation then walked in.

"Good afternoon, Mr. Ouine! Sorry to hear about Ike Chaiklin. I understand you want to talk to me about my reassignment to a new team?"

"Don't mention that little bugger's name in front of me. You will be working with Mike Magnesia's team, but I'll warn you now, Mike has no class. He is crude, vulgar, and sometimes nasty, but he is not the kind of head case that Isaac Chaiklin is. Mike is on leave now and won't return for three more weeks, so the rest of the time is yours, good luck."

Steve turned to leave but Ouine gestured and had a final word for him.

"One final request: no more scandal."

That was all that Ouine said; that was all he needed to say.

With another boss to adjust to, Steve would need to polish his diplomatic skills. But a while later, a strange looking Asylum colleague schlepped into his office. Nebbish Asylum Officer, Malcolm Muddleston, shuffled by to tell him that Isaac's long-term domestic partner and now fiancé, Panchito 'Sweet Potato' Navarro was willing to talk – like, good feature copy talk. Impressed with Steve's features, the boss allowed him the some leeway to interview Panchito, but the copy would be held in abeyance until it became expedient to release, i.e. after the Schmelbalz Scandal broke.

Steve located Panchito Navarro at the Sans Souci Lofts condo he and Isaac shared in the Anaheim Old Town section on Broadway and Avalon. They would not talk long. Isaac was recovering at the Dalai Lama Tibetan Transcendental Rehabilitation Center for Emotional Enlightenment. In addition, as much as Steve wanted to learn "the rest of the story" he never felt totally comfortable around gay people, despite his claim to having gay and straight friends. His brand of liberalism was more socio/political not personal - a sort of poor man's Sean Penn. Steve rang the doorbell, Panchito opened the bamboo-paneled door, and the pudgy cherub-faced Hispanic gay guy, in purple toreador pants matched well with chartreuse and purple Caribbean shirt, unbuttoned to the waist, cheerfully greeted him with hands folded in front of his chest.

"Oh, do come in. Welcome to our pad. Would you like a cup of eucalyptus herb tea, or a glass of Beaujolais perhaps? Please make yourself comfortable. My Ikey just bought me this new Ikea sofa. Isn't lovely? Just the kind I always wanted," he moaned dreamily.

Steve tried hard not to roll his eyes.

"You look like such a dear, sweet guy. I'm sorry I didn't get to know you very well before you transferred to Naturalization downtown. But, I understand you also have some connections to the media. Just a rumor, of course, so I was thinking you might be interested in a letter from the pop star Magdalena to my dear sweet Ikey. She is so mean, just look!" With a sob and pressing the back of his right hand to his forehead, Panchito extended his left hand, so Steve could take the letter and read it.

Dear Isaac:

As much as I have enjoyed our channeling sessions at the Monterrey Bay Enlightenment Center and the San Onofre Beach Naked Encounter Center, I implore you to cease spreading rumors about a relationship existing between us. A relationship never existed between us. If a relationship had existed between us, I would have channeled it since I am also a licensed channelist therapist in addition to my titled entity as an existentialist therapist. Now as cruel this may sound and I am going to give you a little tough love here, if you pardon my use of such horrid Dobsonian religious language: 1) I did not run around naked at San Onofre; you and your beloved pudgy little Panchito both did. 2) Neither did I join your gay engagement party there; you and your beloved pudgy Panchito disrupted your channeling assignments by announcing your engagement and crossing the San Onofre boundary to the Camp Pendleton Marine Base. 3) I did not beg you to share a sleeping bag with me at Monterrey Bay & Big Sur Enlightenment Center. As you complained during the mental masturbation component of your existential transcendental awareness session, you were punished by banishment to the Nepenthe Bar and Grill to stay the night and channel the spirits of disgusting dirty old men like Henry Miller and his creepy friends. Please cease these un-New Age attitudinal issues and return to your loving relationship with your beautiful chubby Panchito.

Your devoted Channeller-Person,
Magdalena

With self restraint rising way above and beyond the call of duty, Steve suggested that Magdalena was not mean, but that she understood that Ikey was indulging in a world of fantasy and needed to "re-channel into his inner self."

"Ooh, you are so getting it. But she called me fat and that's mean!"

"No, she just suggested that you are pudgy, meaning adorable. There's a difference."

"Well," Panchito exclaimed, "I never thought about it that way! Oo you are *so* deep."

Hah! As though he ever thought about anything very deep at all except carnal crevices.

"You're such a dear, sweet hunky guy! Guess what? My Ikey called me from the Dalai Lama Center last night and formally proposed over the telephone."

"Uh, didn't Mr. Ouine stipulate that his supervisory reinstatement would be contingent on more conservative therapy?"

"Oo! Don't say a word about that. No one is supposed to know where Ikey is now. I went to our Gay Pride Center Printing Shop and they created special documents from the Pomona Acres Rest and Rehabilitation Center and sent them to Mr. Ouine. And guess what? We are going to be married next month at the San Onofre Naked Beach Parking Lot Wedding Chapel. We are going to have a fully nude wedding, except for my little bow tie. Isn't that fabulous? I must see to it that you get a special invitation, in the front row of course. You have been such a dear, sweet guy! May I have your address? We'd love to keep you informed about our future Gay Pride events too!"

With admirable self-restraint above and beyond the call of duty, Steve could not wait to run for daylight out of the Sans Souci fairyland, but he had the common sense to thank Panchito for his kindness and informed him that he was in the process of moving. He assured him that he would send him an address form once he settled in. Sweet Potato grabbed Steve, and with a big hug showed him to the front door, then got ready to lay on a passionate soulful kiss. With quick thinking, Steve glanced at his Rolex, and with a, "Wow, I am running really late," bolted out into the daylight and took off loping toward his car as quickly as any fast break he had ever done during his UOP basketball days.

Once safely enveloped in that modern suit of armor known as the SUV, Steve thought the Chaiklin feature a total waste in light of the iceberg ahead that might very well sink the titanic that was the Los Angeles Regional Office: the scandal of the 13 floor. The entertainment link to pop/rock star Magdalena might titillate the celebrity groupies among the Riverside County low-end office workers, but would do little to expand the readership, the absolute requirement on which the life of the new *Riverside Times* would come to depend. On the lighter side, it seemed to Steve as though Isaac was making a feeble attempt to go straight. Unfortunately, he chose Magdalena as his straightifier. The following Friday, Steve reported to The Boss, who was in uncharacteristically good humor and chortling over an article he had just read in The Times' sister paper, The Arizona Advocate:

ESTATE OF ADVOCATE PUBLISHER HANNIBAL H. HARDY TO GO TO PROBATE TODAY

MRS. HARDY NOW EXPECTING LATE PUBLISHER'S 50TH CHILD
DNA TESTS CONFIRM

"What a guy! Steve, remember what I told you about Triple H having his last hurrah in Jamaica?"

"Of course! You covered that one yourself."

He pushed the front page of the Advocate toward Steve for a quick glance.

"Now, this has gotta go down in the Guinness Book!" At most it took only three weeks, but he knocked up his child bride before he met his maker."

The boss turned reflective, but only for a moment.

"Wonder what he had to say for himself to the Man upstairs, eaaah! Now, get this. A fight's looming over his estate, with his bride of three weeks due in November, and his 49 other kids that he knows about, 250 grandchildren, 713 great-grandchildren, and 10 great-great grandchildren all battling for a piece of his five billion dollar estate, heh, heh. They don't make giants like that anymore... sad."

He paused and shook his head as he said it, now finally aware that his own style and manner - his way of doing the newspaper business, was fast becoming obsolete and *The Riverside Times and Review* would be his own last hurrah. Or perhaps it was a mild premonition that he might soon confront his own mortality. Not one to indulge in the morbid and with tumbler fully loaded, the boss quickly moved to business at hand.

"Good work on the Chaiklin incident, but it's under wraps until I give you the all-clear. A little bird told me that John B. Ouine might be leaving for greener grass soon, so pigeonhole any freak-feature until after that happens. The Falabenko affair will blow over soon but Karl Keibalski is the original loose cannon so you need to check out anything he tells you, and use caution when you talk to him. Too many people in that office are getting wise as to why you're there. Ouine does not like him, but for better or worse, he knows more than any of our other sources. From now on, use your microchip cell phone to call him, and have him use his too. Ouine will continue to cover for your "temporary voluntary detail" from Asylum while you work the fed. After he leaves, we can go full blast on the other scandals. For the time being Laura SHMEL/balz, (he was careful to articulate with some sarcasm), is our target. The enmity goes back over twenty-five years. She has cut Ouine out of promotions, low-balled him on his efficiency reports, filed affirmative action complaints, slandered him during hearings on the same, and sabotaged his administrative departments with lost files and whistle blower blackmail. In other words, she is a top-of- the-line Grade A bitch and ripe for a takedown!"

He set down his tumbler and smiled thinly.

"This should be more than enough work to keep you occupied and far away from the bottom-of- the-line bitch Hortensia, I hope."

Chapter 5

THE RISE AND FALL OF A DISTRICT DICTATOR

G iving his charge a final pep talk "Citizen Rob" was in rare form.

"Now Steve, the 13 floor aka Hernando's Hideaway, is ablaze with rumors as always. And now it's coming to more than the usual old fart federal judge trysting with his favorite district counsel babe during recess, or raiding the slush fund in the accountant's room that adjoins the bar and brothel area. Everybody who is anybody knows about it, but everybody who is anybody had better not know about it, if you catch my drift. Moreover, what INS employee above GS-13 level isn't on the take? Now, Steve, watch your copy for icebergs ahead. I don't want libel problems or lawsuits unless we're damn sure we can send one of these slimy liberal Immigration judges to the clink for twenty years."

The Boss let his guard down just a bit, a sign that he was ready to take his assistant into full confidence, even when he indulged in inflammatory speech. By those "in the know," The Boss meant those who continued to call it Hernando's even after Da Silva's retirement. Schmelbalz' Hideaway just did not have the same ring after all. After two years as LA District Director she remained an enigma.

No one, not even her immediate GS12-14 subordinates knew much about the professional or personal life of Laura Schmelbalz, even though she had assumed her duties as US INS Director more than two years earlier. She did not readily grant press interviews to forestall a potential scandal. A government-insider type, she was seeking power by efficient networking, attracting little attention and did not like flamboyance. She was also somewhat compulsive. She'd memorized the names of all Los Angeles district employees above the grade level of GS-7. Steve would have challenges ahead of him. Not to worry though. Laura Schmelbalz was not a match for Back Bay Rob even on her best days.

So, Steven Ara Melkonian became Patrick Joseph Robyn, Rob's cousin from South *Bahs*tun, and new deputy editor of *The Riverside Times* pro-tempore. And Steve Melkonian the Asylum officer, continued to be so, but with a much lower profile - no overseas details and no scandals, just another "credible fear roving detail to parts unknown." With new press credentials, Laura Schmelbalz would never be the wiser.

So far as anyone knew, Laura Eugenia Schmelbalz came into the world sometime in the 1940s in Milwaukee, Wisconsin. She was the seventh of nine children born of a Spanish immigrant family. Her father was a prosperous bricklayer who eventually owned his own construction company. She attended local public schools, and attracted little attention in secondary schools, preferring to earn top marks at the expense of a memorable social life. She does not attend class reunions.

At the University of Wisconsin, however, she surpassed any of her classmates with a bachelor's in Public Administration, Summa Cum Laude in 1964. It was followed by over two hundred offers of internships leading to high entry-level federal jobs. She thought about law school; it would have been easy entry with her grades, but she feared that an additional three years study and law degree might restrict her job prospects to legal secretary, as lady lawyers were not recruited or well received by the old boy firms of that era.

A brief marriage in 1965 ended in a quick divorce in 1966. She wanted a career, not marriage and kiddie life. She returned to the University of Wisconsin and in two years took a master's degree, again with honors, in public administration. She was officially trained to be a bureaucrat.

So, with MPA in hand and stout heart in chest, Laura Eugenia Schmelbalz set out on her salubrious career of ripping off her government seven ways to Sunday. Shrewdly, dotting her westward march with off-Broadway stints in Sioux Falls, Fargo, and Omaha, Schmelbalz zigzagged in a deliberate pattern of chess moves to land on the ultimate career nirvana, a west coast district directorship with all the trimmings. Not La La Land or Frisco mind you, but Seattle was not bad as a first assignment for an emergent senior executive, and they make a good cup of joe there. Laura loved the ambience of Seattle - not quite as hoity-toity as San Fran but a lady had to start someplace. The upscale bourgeois liberalism, the misty skies and gales, the great restaurants and bistros, and of course, the scenic Cascade Mountains were made to fit.

Still, it was not top of the line. To find a place in the sun, Her Intrepidness, Madam Schmelbalz would need to find her way to the land of sand, sea, and surf, and most importantly, Hispanic aliens, the bread and butter of INS job creation and promotions. Horizontal moves needed a bit of courage and she was never lacking. If not a direct move, then she would accept the opening for Asylum Director in Anaheim when Joseph B. "Sloppy Joe" Michaelson left for the service center at the Laguna Hills under mysterious circumstances. Rumors were rife that when Supervisor Faggerty was bucking for deputy, he discovered Sloppy Joe with his Filipina girlfriend, Tomasa Toyamagua, a GS-5 clerical assistant, in a compromising position on his US Government grand mahogany executive desktop. Facing investigation, he accepted reassignment and demotion to the service center. So, as Sloppy Joe slipped out, Laura Schmelbalz slipped in, ahead of fifteen other upper mid-level bureaucrats who wanted the job.

She was not happy in Asylum. There were few perks and lots of jerks, especially among the first-line supervisors, none of whom she liked. These people were too shallow and poorly educated to appreciate her prestigious university degrees, excellent professional credentials, and superb administrative competence. They were all conspiring against her, of course, trying to dislodge the first woman to become an Asylum director. Besides, she missed the snob appeal of the Pacific Northwest. But, as the song says, LA is a great big freeway - in a year or two they make you a star!

Now, Laura E. Schmelbalz has her mind set on the 14 floor grand office with a balcony. No one was certain why the District Director needed a balcony, other than architectural whim, as it overlooked beautiful downtown Olvera Street or rather the monstrous edifices that masqueraded what was once beautiful downtown Olvera street. And what a star she would become! Who knew that Hernando Da Silva would choose early retirement rather than remain in office and let the Office of Special Investigations tear his hide away! Once again, the selection committee, the gnomes of the federal government hiring system, chose Laura Schmelbalz over seven other candidates with more seniority. Such a charmed life! Headquarters demanded that everything in LA become airtight - no more embarrassing inquiries or hostile questions in congressional hearing rooms.

Clean up the mess left by the Da Silva administration! That means no backlog of a half million cases pending action, no missing files, no shredded documents, no more ignoring irate telephone calls from congressional staffers, and no scandals. As Casey Stengel might have said it, "Two outta four ain't bad, but it ain't good nieder!" Schmelbalz chose the two and thus went to work doing the major cosmetologist job of appearing to reduce the backlog to just under fifty thousand in one year. She mollified pesky congressional staffers by reassigning a supervisor to the liaison office, one sweet-talking Helen Hu, a Naturalization supervisor known for her sultry speech and luscious libido. Schmelbalz arrived for her first day of work a few weeks after DaSilva's retirement, so he was not there for the traditional changing of the guard, or to show the new director around - really bad form! Perhaps the less she knew about The Hideaway the better, at least until he had the chance to collect all his pension benefits and book a flight to his native Argentina - very clever.

So it was up to the non-descript, deferential, non-person, deputy director of protocol, Lester Yu, to show the new boss around on the cook's tour and deftly steer her from The Hideaway for the time being. He would discern later on whether she would demand a cut of the action and act accordingly. Schmelbalz dutifully greeted all the drones in their cubes and stalls, told them how important they were to the mission, and explained that they should be proud of the part they, the "little people" played in the INS mission…yada, yada, yada. As the elevator passed number thirteen, her keen eyes quickly noticed they were not stopping there and she asked why.

"Uh, Ms. Schmelbalz," the protocol chief replied, a little nervously, "This is a locked floor security area and it seems that Mr. Da Silva took both sets of keys when he retired. As soon as we learn his whereabouts in Argentina, we shall demand their immediate return!"

"That might take months!"

"Ah, yes, months, quite so." Then he broke into a slight sweat.

"I want those keys ASAP! Either Da Silva returns them, or we have the locks changed. Got it? We need to know the status of every active file."

"I shall inquire immediately, but there are no active files here. This is what we call the morgue. The inactive files are stored here pending their transfer to the Records Personnel Center in St. Louis. This floor houses only boxes of obsolete documents and inactive cases. The applicants and their beneficiaries have passed away or are not pursuing their claims. Some now have citizenship. No active cases are kept here."

"I would have expected nothing less."

The irony was that the protocol jockey called it the "morgue" as the bodies that "lay" there are living, not dead, and there were no files kept there of any sort, only credit card receipts for services provided and indulged.

As they got off the elevator on 14, Madam Director appeared to be sufficiently satisfied with her office. Who would not be satisfied with three thousand square feet of office space! As you entered, you first noticed oak paneled walls that featured oil paintings highlighting major events in the history of the old USINS, early life in El Pueblo of Los Angeles, and the portrait of every INS Director since the founding of the service. No one else was worth remembering, after all. Most surprising was the Persian carpeted floor, imprinted with INS logo, then the highly-polished oak wood executive desk with matching high-backed swivel chair, state of the art computer paraphernalia with polished credenza, and finally the private bathroom with steam room and Jacuzzi. You would expect to find these appointments in the office of a higher-level bureaucrat-sub-cabinet level at least. Yet the "previous owner" had most of the perks installed himself. He just left and forgot to take any of them with him, and rightly so as they were purchased with "discretionary funds." Madam Director became curious as she discovered a beautifully oversized jewelry box of elegantly carved mother-of-pearl images of early Los Angeles. She liked the design but thought it strange that someone had fastened it with leather-covered bolts to the paneling of her suit closet and that it was secured by a combination lock. What she did not know was that it contained no jewelry.

In any case, Lester Yu, tasked with retrieving the keys from Hernando's new hideaway, had to find them pretty damn quickly and he did so by contacting consular affairs at US Embassy in Buenos Aires who located Da Silva in the Malbec Region, pleasantly retired and now proud owner of a one hundred thousand acre winery-not bad on a bureaucrat's pension. Former director now vintner, Hernando Hernandez DaSilva-DeSoto cheerfully informed Functionary Yu that the keys were seriously secured in the jewelry box, and that he was most agreeable to provide the combination. Hernando had moved on to greener pastures in every sense of the word and the "accounts receivable" were Laura Schmelbalz' problem now.

Today, more than two years later, Patrick Joseph Robyn, aka Steven Ara Melkonian will present his new credentials to the U.S. District Court side of the fed, and ease his way in with no fanfare, hoping also that no one from Asylum would be there or recognize him. After all, Asylum had recently reassigned him, sort of, so how is it that he shows up at The Federal Building? Are there credible fear interviews scheduled? Why, yes, of course, as there always had been. Why *The Riverside Times* credentials? Uh oh! Better make sure to conceal them unless absolutely needed. Or, try this, instead...

Since everyone everywhere has a double somewhere, he could say, "You know, a few people from your Asylum office tell me that I look just like one of your officers. I can't recall his last name, but I think his first name is Steve." He thought this a reasonable ruse as he turned into the fed parking lot.

Today, the old anecdote about the sex maniac loose in the town was about to materialize in US District Court. One of Asylum's own, Theodore Theophalus Penrod, Esquire, an Asylum officer indicted on charges of sexual assault and extortion under the color of law, was about to stand trial. Sketchy on the details, Steve had to use his clandestine cell phone to contact Karl Keibalski, the only person in Asylum who knew anything about Penrod. Steve hoped Karl would refrain from blowing his usual smoke and mirrors.

"Fuckin' A, I remember him and also how they shit-canned him here! We were in the same FLOTC class together, that's the Federal Law Officer Training Center in Brunswick, Georgia and he was a weir-do even then. I mean, like what kinda guy still wears paisley corduroy bell-bottom pants with a green shirt and purple tie? Anyway, I was nice to him even if he was too much of an oddball to have any real friends. It turned out that he once worked for Don Barfield's old firm. Yeah, the same Barfield who worked here until the duty officer caught him and his girlfriend humping after lockdown hours and reported him the Oz Man who did the actual firing. Now Da Barf was also a senior partner of the Hutzpov, Gonov and Metzschmuck firm in San Pedro. Can you dig that name? I mean, like, it's not what you'd call a winner's firm. Ya know what I'm sayin', right? So, now it seems that the same Barfield and his flunky who washed out of Asylum might both be going to the joint."

"How so?"

O. Don Barfield is involved in so much shit you need a steam shovel to move it. You name a corrupt lawyer's practice and he's been involved in it."

"Such as…"

"Like alien smuggling, tampering with a grand jury, obstruction of justice, extortion, unjust enrichment…"

"And your evidence is…"

"Locked up in the files of that most fortified of all, the Old Boy and now Old Girl Network, California Bar Counsel whose job it is to investigate, expose, and punish attorney misconduct."

"So has he been disciplined?"

"Da Barf has been suspended from the practice of law for one year. Only one frickin' year! Like, can you believe it, dude? They should have disbarred him for life but the California Bar always protects its own, so they put a damper on the AG's efforts to do just that - ethics be damned! I'm sure as an ex-attorney you've heard about the case. Until six months ago when the case finally broke, he used to come in here and rub our noses in it!"

"I don't get your drift."

"Like I said, Da Barf worked here only a short time until Hinkel fired him. Then, he goes to Rolling Heights, opens a sole practice storefront law office, and soon after, he's driving up in a silver-toned James Dean Porsche wearing five thousand dollar goombah suits and bringing his clients here for their interviews. Like whoa, how does he get that kind of money? No one here had balls enough to check it out, that's what I mean!"

"So what is he doing now?"

"He reopened his practice as an immigration consulting service and hired another lawyer to do his legwork. As the sole practitioner, it's technically the lawyer's firm, but Barfield, as the beneficiary of a trusteeship, calls the shots while working as the paralegal. That's how he beats the system!"

"What a shenshun arnik!"

"A what?"

"Oh, it's an Armenian expression, it means, son of a dog, or shrewd businessman, so it can be a grievous insult or a high compliment. It depends on how you use it.

"So, there's a difference, right?"

"In his case, not a hell of a lot, and thanks for the heads-up. But you still haven't told me much about the indictment or why the DOJ is so hell-bent to send a seemingly ineffectual Immigration official like Penrod up the river. Why not just fire him?"

"Like I said, Penrod was one of these guys who just slipped through life's cracks. But the Devil is in the details, my friend; the Devil is in the details. He never made the grade at anything he had ever done in life and that included his short career at Barfield's old law firm. Two due diligence malpractice lawsuits, three sex harassment charges, and they drummed him out fast. Even Da Barf couldn't save his job and I don't know why he would want to. He's an embarrassment to the law firm of Hutzpov, Gonov and Metzschmuck, the California Bar, and the INS. Still. ya gotta feel sorry for such a poor soul."

The more left-brained Steven A. Melkonian, Attorney-at-Law par-excellence winced at such an application of schmaltz, and made a quick excuse to cut off the conversation. "I need to get to the courthouse fast. This case is about to break."

"Remember, you heard it all here first!"

"All right, I owe you one."

"That's what I like to hear – gratitude. I don't get any of that in my office."

Steve Wrote:
Oyez! Oyez, Oyez! In the matter of the US v. Theodore Theophalus Penrod, the Honorable Judge Matthew Brady Dumone presiding, rather he was supposed to be presiding, however, the trial has been postponed indefinitely. Details are lacking pending a full investigation. The trial of former Los Angeles Asylum Officer, Theodore Penrod was supposed to begin this morning. Today, however, there is trouble in tinsel town. The US District court judge scheduled to preside resigned two days ago and is believed to have fled to his vacation villa in Merida, Mexico to evade charges of embezzlement and sexual misconduct in the US. Meanwhile, Mexican authorities have promised to cooperate with the US Marshals who began the negotiations for extradition this past Friday. Mathew B. Dumone, US District Court Judge since 1963 is eighty-five years old and now slightly dippy. A lifelong amateur photographer he began this hobby as an aerial reconnaissance officer with the US Army Air Force during the Burma and India Campaign of World War II.

Over the years, Dumone acquired a vast collection of photographic and video equipment that takes up about four thousand square feet of his palatial Brentwood home and includes two darkrooms. The collections of photos that go back to his air corps days would do any historical museum proud. He has housed them all in his personal photo-library. What is not widely known is that his film library contains a collection of female nudes that cover roughly the same period to the present. This reporter has seen the eight by ten glossy photos that evoke memories of World War II nostalgia and take the viewer on an erotic journey to the present. The earlier photos reveal stunning long-stemmed American beauties sporting Bess Myerson batwing hairdos, high-heeled pumps, and overstated costume jewelry that so typified the era. Unfortunately for the judge, they wore nothing else. Not quite Sotheby's material, but downscale collectable.

The more recent collections however, include digital prints of hip LA professional women to include those of a few prominent INS district counsels. It might have been written off as a harmless indulgence for a life-long bachelor and mildly demented dirty old man, except that this collection included digitals of young, hot young trial attorneys who had represented clients in his courtroom - not cool! Still, the bar counsels and later the courts must obtain substantial evidence to even discipline a federal judge on ethics violations, notwithstanding removal from office and indictment on criminal charges. Before he resigned, Judge Dumone told one of his "ladies" a half-truth.

A Hollywood mogul acquaintance, and fellow camera buff, was in need of a good strong lawyer. He had violated US Immigration and labor laws and was in danger of exposure for both. The director had just finished filming *From Here to Immortality*, a poignant story about a wealthy Seattle real estate developer, champion surfer, ski bum, and licensed Taoist monk who leaves his materialistic life in the Pacific Northwest to journey to Tibet, and for the remainder of his life finds enlightenment as a monk in the Shallow Loon Temple. Nominated for seven academy awards including best picture, it looks like a sure Academy Award winner if there ever was one. The young mogul however picked a fine time to pull a Roman Polanski - right before his breakout year! Under investigation for alleged sexual abuse of his fifteen-year-old undocumented Mexican housekeeper, he also failed to secure proper work permits for her, and to pay her even the minimum wage. These damn feds - picky, picky, picky! Now he has to make it all go away so he can get on with his beautiful life.

Enter Jean Garbahdjian the hot babe defense attorney who would make it all go away - for a price, of course. Five-foot-eleven, a competitive tri-athlete, lithe with espresso-ebony two-foot-long hair, and soulful eyes, Ms. Garbahdjian, a Judge Dumone "favorite" longed to become a high-end fashion model. Why the blazes the liberated flamboyant Ms. Garbahdjian would want this is beyond any sane person's comprehension. She maintained a straight four point GPA at UC Davis, the same at UCLA College of Law, and could easily have started at the Wilshire Boulevard law firm where her father Aesheck Garbahdjian was one of the founding partners. She chose instead a federal judicial internship, clerking under the Honorable Judge Matthew Brady Dumone. He became the lover, friend, confessor, and all-around Big Daddy for the first year of her professional life. They continued their relationship off and on after she went to private practice at her father's firm. She appeared to entertain no other men in her life. During law school, however, she dated a younger guy, All-America football running back, Teddy Tush. He is now All-Pro with the new NFL franchise Bakersfield Bashers, but they broke off the relationship about six months after he broke her cherry.

The ubiquitous Ms. Garbahdjian appeared in Judge Dumone's court with her client, Roland Q. Mendosa IV, last of the Latin lovers, scion of an old Hollywood family whose great-grandfather Roland Q. Mendosa I was the first of the Latin lovers; the very first. RQM IV could trace his roots to the old conquistador haciendados, those whose families owned an original charter signed by the King of Spain. Today, however, his root was the source of his legal problems, rather than the source of his family pride. It took all of ten minutes for the glamorous Ms. Garbahdjian and the crotchety Judge Dumone to reach a compromise and all went away happy, including Carlotta La Hotta, the maid.

The Court will dismiss charges against Roland Q. Mendosa IV. On the record: The Court granted Carlotta immigrant status and work documents. In exchange, the mogul will repay two years compensatory wages with interest, provide medical and dental benefits to be determined by the Court, and provide separate quarters for Carlotta to be supervised by the Court. Mendosa shall obey a cease and desist order during La Hotta's duty hours and a restraining order during non-duty hours. La Hotta, now in her first trimester, will receive child support upon the birth of her baby if DNA tests prove Roland to be the father, as they probably will.

Off the record: Roland Quixote Mendosa IV will pay the court $100,000 to make the whole matter go away with expungement from the records and provide a list of available aspiring starlets that might want to double as photo-models while on their way up. Why the hundred grand? For the maintenance of the Bar & Brothel, of course. With Hernando's retirement and relocation nearing two years in the past, renovation is long overdue on the Hideaway, the thirteenth floor B & B now sparsely maintained by District Director Laura Schmelbalz and Judge Mathew B. Dumone. But this will all soon change. Director Schmelbalz ordered new carpeting, paneling, bar, grill, and brothel for the good judge to entertain his "ladies." Like Party Dolls in Pomona it is run like a private club; only the DD and deputy, a few other discreet federal judges, and one or two senior trial lawyers get keys. Selected special guests use the facilities by invitation with the exception of one. National Director of US Asylum, Lazarus Longstreet, has a standing invitation, but carries no key - a discretionary issue that affords him plausible deniability. The facilities include an opulent lounge area, five modestly furnished rooms for a quick get-away, and a revolving wet bar camouflaged as a law library. As though the facades were not enough, the boxes of files that somehow never made it to RPC are stacked in front of the bookcases, all to conceal the real activities going on there.

Good evening Mr. and Mrs. California and all the boats in the harbors, FLASH:
The arraignment of US District Court Judge Mathew B. Dumone expected today has been postponed due to allegations that the judge has fled the US to evade arraignment.

US Customs and Immigration officials are conferring with the Mexican Federales to initiate extradition. Dumone appears to have fled to his Merida villa in the Yucatan to avoid detection. Apparently, he has maintained a vacation villa there for many years. Where he got the money to afford a ten-thousand-square foot villa with guest quarters, on a federal judge's salary is a source of the controversy that has led to an investigation into the judge's financial affairs. The judge has not been seen at his Brentwood manor home in ten days, and neither his maid nor his butler will comment about his whereabouts or speculate on a possible return date.

Attention to the indiscretions of Judge Dumone came as the result of a lengthy investigation into the sexual misconduct of the judge with female trial lawyers, court interpreters, and reporters, as explicit digital photos of the alleged misconduct appeared on various internet websites after one trial attorney ended a relationship with the judge. Unknown to district counsel Lena La Bamba, the willing subject of Honorable Judge Dumone, clandestine camera work included a nudie photo essay of her, captured by hidden cameras within the walls of The Hideaway, federal property. Off the record: Any way you slice this, Judge Dumone is in deep shit. End of copy. P. J. Robyn reporting.

The Riverside Times would have competition for this salacious end of a federal judge's career, the possible eclipse and demotion of an INS District Director, and the worst kind of embarrassment for Los Angeles Asylum.

Rival papers referred to it as The Immigration and Molestation Service, with the situation becoming increasingly apparent that Theodore Penrod was not the only molester on the federal payroll, and the lechers had even reached the federal bench. The alleged misconduct appeared on various internet websites, too. District Counsel Lena La Bamba hoped for a reassignment. Good luck with that one sister! You are complicit in a compromising situation with a senile US District Court Judge and have violated the ABA Code.

INS Director Laura Schmelbalz, unavailable for comment, promised to hold a press conference detailing the indiscretions that pertained to her officials. The federal bench was beyond her jurisdiction. Boss Robyn continued to hold the bulk of Steve's copy for the future but this was breaking news and it had to be told.

Madam District Director Schmelbalz knew little about *The Riverside Times* and cared even less. It was after all, an "out-county" paper and not worth reading. But the counterpart article, under a different byline threw her into an early morning spaz-attack that caused her to lose yet another cup of morning cappuccino over yet another lady Brooks Brothers suit. Hazardous duty you know - dry cleaning bills to be paid from the "internal fund."

The *LA Times* fleshed out the story with speculation and light facts attributing the Bar & Brothel enterprise to one or two of the previous directors, with sets of keys custom made for themselves and select clients. That Laura Schmelbalz did not receive master sets upon assuming her duties did not absolve her of culpability. If corruption exists anywhere in the district offices, the director should find out about it. As chief custodian of federal property, she had a duty to report and turn over to federal prosecutors, those suspected of malfeasance, especially during the two years since she had assumed director's duties from Da Silva.

There was no time to build a firewall. The Deputy Attorney General was hot on her ass and stormed into LA on official business before Schmelbalz could even hold a damage control mess conference. That was his intention; he wanted her out, or reassigned at least.

She would resign her position and the perkplush megaoffice that went with it, accepting a reassignment as District Director at Miami Asylum - not such a bad demotion when you think about it. Why not join the merrymakers at the fun and games office? All the way from the Too Easy to the Hot Easy in just two years! Of course, it could have been worse. They might have sent her to New Orleans, the Big Easy, but after two years that office was still digging itself out of the sludge, silt, and poop from when the breakwater broke, a catastrophe that occurred due more to southern lazy engineering than any typhoon. So the new Deputy Helen Hu would replace Schmelbalz temporarily. The Attorney General and Secretary of Homeland Security liked her so much that she even got to go on the Homeland Security Honolulu bash that made *60 Minutes*. After two years in the congressional liaison office, she was well versed in stonewalling, subterfuge, and file destruction., The consensus at LA fed was that with her sensual and sultry manner, she could keep the Bush administration macho hounds at bay until a touchy-feely Democratic president might replace them.

Chapter 6

HE FELL IN LOVE
BEFORE SAN PEDRO

The old jingle about the sex maniac loose on the town selling newspapers was about to ring true in the sorry life of Theodore Theophalus Penrod, resident woe-filled weirdo who found his refuge in Los Angeles Asylum. With the manhunt for Judge Dumone in progress, the second part of the breaking news, the arraignment of Theodore T. Penrod was rescheduled with all due haste, and with the US District Court hoping it would defer media attention from the Dumone scandal.

Steve wrote:

What sort of lost soul is Theodore Theophalus Penrod, disgrace to his agency, bane of his office, and disappointment to himself? A lost soul like all lost souls, only a little worse. He came to Los Angeles Asylum ten years ago, and like many of his type, a failed litigation attorney either too lazy or incompetent to succeed in private practice. A ghostly, bedraggled apparition of a dweeb, who shuffled from one law firm to another after his firm's partners fired for him for employee sex harassment, or bar counsel disciplined him for lawyer malpractice, he finally found his refuge in Los Angeles Asylum, or so he thought. Today he will be arraigned in US District Court to answer to twenty counts of misfeasance, malfeasance, nonfeasance, and maybe even tortfeasance under the color of law. Add to that, sexual battery and extortion, and I damn sure would not want to be in his shoes!

What kind of public official was Theodore T. Penrod? A public official like all public officials, only a little worse. Like so many other lawyers who failed in private law practice, he was a weirdo who just could not get a life. Employed by the medium-sized Pomona branch of the litigation firm Hutzpov, Gonov and Metzschmuck, he was fired by his longtime protégé, O. Donald Barfield after two years with the firm, and numerous complaints about his work quality and sexual misconduct. Caught amusing himself on the floor of the ladies' room, the firm's partners unceremoniously and summarily dismissed Penrod. They were not amused. His academic record was equally undistinguished.

Graduating last in his class at California State University at Santa Fe Springs, he finally received acceptance at the non-ABA approved Mahatma Gandhi College of Law and Meditation at La Jolla. There he graduated four hundred ninety-ninth in a class of five hundred students. It took him six years, or twice the normal timeframe, but ironically just ahead of Sean Faggerty, now Los Angeles Deputy Director who graduated five hundredth.

From there Penrod failed his California Bar Exam six times, each time with the lowest score ever recorded, yet he passed on the seventh try under very mysterious circumstances. Reliable sources indicate that prominent Pomona attorney, O. Donald Barfield pulled some strings at the bar examiner's office and that unscrupulous persons there graded his test papers. When Old Barfy took him on as a law clerk following his 1983 bar exam "passage," Penrod started his career as the worst kind of low-end flunky - doing gofer work for the major partners as the lowest paid associate, his billing time a mere $10 per hour. When his mentor, the Big O-Don went before the California Bar Counsel to answer misconduct charges, Penrod jockeyed documents and pleadings at the hearings. Although many of the charges were dismissed, State Attorney General Feather Lockliar initiated disbarment proceedings. After six months of hearings, bar counsel reduced the discipline to a three-year suspension from the practice of law and reinstatement on a two-year probationary basis.

Today, however, the action has shifted to Old Barfy's one-time subordinate. In a sting operation organized by the US Marshall's office, federal agents arrested Penrod at the Dreary Drawers Motel in Monterrey Park where a hidden camera disclosed his attempt to convey US Asylum approval documents to an undisclosed Chinese female applicant in exchange for sexual favors and $2,000 in cash. Tipped off by the woman's attorney, Buster Boomhower, who helped organize the effort, the feds stormed Room 6909 and banged the door down in the nick of time, for Penrod has just pocketed the two grand and was just about to start doing his own banging!

Patrick J. Robyn reporting for *The Riverside Times and Review.*

With these two giant stories breaking, Boss Robyn would finally get the drop on his three nearest competitors: The Orange County Register, the Irvine Upscaler, and the Doheny Bumsurfer. He wanted copy and would gladly clean up the inflammatory language, though he put Steve through the ritual of a good ass-chewing about professional ethics, protecting sources, yellow journalism, slander, and libel, telling him he would fire him if he ever wrote such miserable copy again. Then Robyn gave him "one more chance" with a raise in his pay, "just because I'm a nice guy." Nice guy *my* ass. Steve was the only *Times* reporter who consistently out-scooped the other three OC garbage can liners.

The establishment dailies were clueless as to how he did it; i.e. finding the right source and getting the story in print while the others couldn't get their media people to connect with the "Real Fed." Any cub could locate the judges who would preside, the lawyers who would argue, and the bureaucrats who would lie, but just how do you find out not just the existence of "The Hideaway" but who goes there, who gets the keys, and who does the cover-up. And how did the sixty year bizarre history of Judge Dumone's "Studio and Portrait Gallery" finally come to light?

Steve understood that any hope of a follow-up or any future feature story would require more poop from that most loathsome of the INS moles, the Mr. Go-to Guy himself Karl Kirel Keibalski. After all, who else delivered no-nonsense, straight up-the-middle, full-house Tee OSU red meat news? Steve called on his private cell and suggested they meet that week at Pepe Del Nuevo for an update. It was a good choice. The new Pepe's, a recent upscale Garden Walk bistro, run by the family that began the original, would serve as a perfect deep-throat briefing joint for the downscale Keibalski and the mid-scale Steve. Not very many Asylum office antagonists would go there - too expensive on a federal salary, although he had to look out for a few of the better-paid Bumsurfer and Upscaler types who might drop in for a quick lunch. Steve hoped it would not be an entirely vain effort and Keibalski would spew something besides rehash.

"So Karl, what's been happening in the Ouine Realm since I got put on detail?

"You know what's been happening, so what you want are more horse turds for your brand of interpretive journalism. Am I right or wrong?"

Caught up short by such a base view of post-modern news reporting, Steve stammered for a quick retort. "Well… uh?"

"You know it's true."

True, of course, as truth can be as seen through the prism of the world according to Keibalski, as though there could be any other.

"The Theodore Penrod story has broken, the undergrounds will scurry to do a feature, and the establishments will likely go after the Federal Building and the Dumone scandals. So what I'm thinking is of is an in-depth psychological profile of the negative forces in the desperate life of Theodore Theophalus Penrod that caused a good official to go bad."

Keibalski's smirk grew into a sneer.

"Yeah, right! He lured those two Chinese women into the Dreary Drawers Motel, pawed one and blackmailed another because of the negative forces in his desperate life. Ya gotta love all that psychobabble they taught you at Sensitivity State University, College of Ultraliberal Arts!"

Steve was beginning to get a little bit torqued at this "has been" football jock who after all had no degree beyond a bachelor's. He was always full of himself, sat in an air-conditioned office, and occupied the better part of his US taxpayer-funded workday checking out hot babes on the internet, downloading their nudie photos, and e-mailing the same to all his buddies in Investigations. *How do I get into this man's army?* Steve decided it was time to strike back, if for no other reason than to command some leverage and respect.

"So what's your problem? Are you jealous or just envious of those of us who have had the native intelligence or academic discipline to obtain advanced degrees? Or, perhaps you are just pissed-off because you never made it as a football player anywhere but the Canuck league? And you don't like it because the Cleveland Office, 'as though anything good can ever come out of Cleveland' pigeonholed you into to this woe-ful subculture called *Ass*-y-lum and you want back into Investigations six months ago? Might that be your problem?" Still trim and fit, with black belts in two martial arts. and in better shape than the sedentary Keibalski, dark Armenian eyes blazing, olive skin now red, he was more than ready to kick butt on this ex-footballing Kulak butthead if he had to. So, Karl thought the better of this, stood down, and cut the bullshit, as much as he was able to.

"Well I knew the poor guy as much as anyone in this office was able to get to know him, and also one other poor soul I tried to help, Eduardo San Alfaro, a linguist and classical scholar. He seemed to have so much going for him. Why he checked into in this sad sack joint, I'll never know!" Once again, Steve had the peevish feeling that he was going to be taken for a magic trip to yet another uncharted isle, with guess who as the tour guide - Karl Keibalski, the resident tambourine man. And like Joe Valachi before him he loved to sing.!

"So, did he do something crooked too?"

"No, The San, as we all called him, was a good egg. He even had a couple degrees from the Ivys. Speaks six languages, that's two more than I do!"

Obviously, proud of his achievements, Karl beamed. He was right, factually speaking, if you count English, but one hopes Da Keibals didn't butcher Polish, Ukrainian, and Russian like he did English.

Now The San just wasn't cut out for the job but he had a supervisor who was the biggest loafer in the INS. Dave May, "Do Nothing May" we called him. He liked to take three-hour lunch breaks and two-hour coffee breaks, every damn day! Anyway, The San was a friend and we used to go to lunch together until he got busted. He did all right with his interviews but would never write up his cases because he was a part-time professor at Santa Ana College and used his office time to prepare his lectures. The San had a backlog of five hundred cases that he never finished. Now his supervisor, the do-nothing, protected him with outstanding fitness reports until OSI did an internal audit. After OSI discovered the backlog, it turned out that most of The San's files were discovered in Dave May's office, some even in his portable refrigerator! He never sent them forward or returned them to Eduardo for correction, so you can't blame him. But management got him outta there like shit through a goose. That's when I organized a little street demonstration to try to save his job."

"You did what? Is that lawful?"

Now it was Karl's turn to get snippy. "Ever hear of the First Amendment, counselor? Of course, Ouine didn't like it; management never likes any kind protection for the worker, but at the time I was AFGE local president, so we printed up signs and marched north and south in front of the Asylum Office to attract management's attention.

"Great, but what about Theodore Penrod?"

"I'm getting to that weirdo in a minute. Some of The San's cases were over ten years old and were starting to attract congressional interest. Now that's bad. No INS director wants Congressmen sniffing up his ass. So like, Ouine shit-cans both of them at the same time. Now is that fair?"

"Excuse me, before I left for Saipan, I noticed an aging man always in a windbreaker who seemed to spend the day walking around the building puffing cigarettes. I thought he might be a security agent or CIA type."

"In his dreams! Yeah, that was May all right but he wouldn't have the brains or balls for CIA.

Steve was beginning to get very restless now. He had obtained only filler material about some befuddled, semi-senile philologist on the federal payroll, a wasted afternoon if there ever was one. Karl motioned to the barista for two more megabeers. A simple man, he liked to ramble on, fullhouse -T straight up the middle for six, hauling three linebackers into the end zone with him.

"Okay, so why and how did Penrod fuck up anyway, since you knew him better than anyone else?"

To communicate with this Keibalski, you just had to speak his language!

"Well, as Ronald Reagan used to say shaking his head, nobody really knew him, but if his life story was any clue, he was one totally consumed dude."

As Steve did not have unlimited federal employee downtime, he was just about ready to grab his hidden mini tape recorder and heave it across the room. Best to maintain though, since he didn't let Keibalski know about the "little bug" straightaway.

"I gathered as much, but how about some details, such as do you know anything about his formative years? Like what about his mom and dad? Where did he go to high school? Was he a loner or popular? Did he play any sports? How about college, BMOC, dean's list, gentleman's C-average, Joe Fraternity, nerd, geek, creep, or all-around-freak? What was he?"

Keibalski slurped his second twenty-four ounce brew, nearly chugging it in one gulp. He wiped his mouth on his shirt sleeve and thought for a minute, that being the absolute length of his reflectivity.

"I don't know a helluva lot about his early life. Like, I think he was born in Indianapolis in 1950 and his family moved to California when he was five. His father managed a furniture store in Monterrey Park. There Theodore went to Sierra Mandalon High School. After graduating with a so-so grades he went to CSU Santa Fe Springs, the bottom feeder of the California State University system, and the only place that would have him. And even there at Illegal Alien Tech, where three-quarters of the students don't speak English, the dumbass managed to graduate dead last in his class. Ya gotta be an even bigger meathead than Sean Faggerty to do that! But speak of the Devil - get this! Of all the nerve, he wanted to be a lawyer and so he enrolled at the La Jolla University Mahatma Gandhi Graduate College of Law and Meditation, the only law school that would have him. There he teamed up with the other nitwits who eventually found their way here-O.D. Barfield, Malcolm Muddleston, and Sean Faggerty. Finally, he bests somebody at something. At law school, he finished ahead of Sean Faggerty, our quarterwit deputy director. Like, can you believe it dude? So, after he graduates from college and that dipshit law school, Da Barf took him in as an associate, but he was so bad that he got canned after a year. So he spent years bumming from one firm to another until he finds his refuge in Asylum. Hey, that's pretty good, huh? He finds his refuge in Asylum. Get it? Steve could only roll his eyes and hope that a semi-sloshed Karl Keibalski might divulge some semi-newsworthy material and with no more high fives - against all odds, of course.

"So how did he come to work at Asylum? I mean, what steps led him to it and what steps led to his downfall?"

"Let's start with the Federal Law Officer Training Center. That's in Bumwick, Georgia. It was once a run-down World War II navy base until nerdy national hemorrhoid Jimmy Carter hoodwinked Congress into converting the dump into an expanded federal training center. Just by coincidence, it happened to be in his home state. Gotta keep his fellow yayhoos employed and happy I guess. So, Theodore, he didn't like people calling him Ted, he was strangely formal that way, was in my Asylum officers' class there.   Anyway, he's like kind of in a 1960's time warp. Like, he comes to class in a Beetle haircut wearing paisley bell-bottom trousers. Really gross-looking a on middle-aged a guy with a gut. And get this, he's also got on a green polka dot shirt and purple tie, and he thought he was being hip. Canya believe it, dude? But he was kinda the loner type. Never went on outings with the other officers, and always the same excuse, 'I don't drink or dance, so I don't care for night life.' So the rest of us didn't bother with him after a few weeks. Now I ask you, what kinda regular guy doesn't drink or dance?"

"Well, he doesn't appear to have been a regular guy."

"Fuckin' A," replied Karl, with yet another dreaded high five.

"Oh, a couple more things. One of these snakehead lawyers, you know, like Barfield, except he's not near as rich or successful, but he brings in a lot of Chinese clients and was once Theodore's old high school buddy, probably the only friend he ever had in his entire miserable life. Anyway, this lawyer, his name escapes me, but I can find his business card in my rolodex, and he can tell you some more poop. Like, Penrod was a real loser even then. Never dated, didn't play any sports, had no friends. Oh yeah, the lawyer told me one more thing about him."

"In his sophomore year Theodore gets this crush on the homecoming queen, Sherry Postjean. Like a real beauty, ya know? Yeah, I think she went on to Pasadena City College and became a Rose Bowl princess, or Miss California, something like that. So, Theodore, demented as he is, gets a crush on her and begins stalking. He thinks a dork like himself can attract her. Well, he has no football pin to give her, no personality to speak of, no wealthy family, no decent grades, so like, what do you expect? She's nice and rebuffs him sweetly, like, 'I already have a date for the prom.' So, he follows her around with the usual '"what about next time' line. So, like, she tries to blow him off with a 'well maybe' but the dumbass just couldn't take a hint. He gets totally obsessed and stalks her into the girl's locker room of the gym while the pom pom babes are changing into their costumes for rehearsal. Since a few of them are buck naked, Penrod's in big trouble. Now, this is where this gets really comical. After a lot of yeeking and screeching, the girl's phys-ed coach, a big Janet Reno-looking bull dyke hears the disturbance, storms into locker room, grabs Penrod, beats the living crap out of him, like within an inch of his life, and he's in the hospital a month recovering. And get this, *his* parents, sue Sierra Mandalon High School instead of Sherry's parents, who are willing to make the whole matter go away if the principal rigs the homecoming election and their precious little Sherry makes queen, a true *quid pro quo*. And so, Penrod gets out of the hospital with a restraining order to stay twenty-five feet from any pom pom line member, an academic suspension reduced to time spent in the hospital, and a varsity football letter; SM in the school colors - purple and white. And mommy and daddy drop the lawsuit against the school."

"What? You just said he didn't play any sports and I can't imagine football…"

Keibalski slaps his forehead.

"At five-foot-six and 120 pounds, what do you think? But he wanted the babe magnet football letter and the principal made the coach put him on the team. They just let him manage the equipment, warm benches, and hold the tackling dummy for the real players. Of course, none of the real players liked him and they warned him that if he ever dared come to school wearing a lettermen's sweater, they would tear it off him and give him another pounding, worse than the one the bull dyke coach gave him."

Steve pondered a couple minutes while he took in all this new information, switched off his recorder, and spoke hesitatingly, "It seems that he was just an underachiever with overachiever fantasies and not nearly enough talent to reach any of his goals,"

"Exactly. He lived on his luck until he pressed it too far."

"Yes, but bringing all this up-to-date, couldn't your Asylum office just demote him to a clerk's job instead of letting him become such an embarrassment? In addition, why would a mid-level moderately well paid government official close to retirement blow it all for a two grand bribe and a ten minute feel-job? Might his inability to attract any woman be a reason?"

"You can blame Do-Nothing May for part of it. If he had been on top of Penrod's work, he might have steered him out of trouble. But, like I just told you, he was an awkward strike-out all his life and that led to all his current troubles.

You see, he borrowed this "Catalog of Russian Brides" from the INS marriage fraud unit. It's a 300-page guidebook of the hottest babes from Russia and the Ukraine who want to immigrate to the US with a 'spouse visa.' They get that by having a US resident or citizen file a form of intent to marry a foreign national, present documented evidence of a bona fide relationship, then the intended spouse is granted a K-1 visa, and the couple must marry within ninety days of the person's arrival or this person must leave the US. So, what does Penrod do? He chooses a hot babe from the catalog, brings her here, marries, not once, but twice - the boob. And get this, during his district court arraignment, he claims poverty as an excuse. His alimony payment to the second spouse was so high he could no longer afford the mortgage on his ramshackle trash-heap in Monty Park!

"I don't follow. Did he commit bigamy, too?"

"Nah, he wasn't anywhere near that smart. A few try it and collect a hefty fee from the bride. They marry one or a number of spouses under assumed names, file the petitions, and after two years convert the conditional marriage visa to permanent. After the foreign spouse accrues enough time to maintain permanent residence, the couple then gets a quickie divorce in Nevada or some other sin bin state. First of all though, you need a mountain of well-forged documents, convincing aliases, and the genius to keep fifty steps ahead of the marriage fraud unit and federal crime dicks. Unlike me, not many dudes have that kind of cool."

"If you say so," was Steve's caustic interjection.

"Fuckin' A! But Penrod's case is strictly 'in house' so that makes it a lot worse when he gets caught. So he marries one Russian woman and doesn't even try to collect a bride fee - just horny I guess. After six weeks, she can *so* not stand him that she initiates the divorce, gives up her green card, and moves back to Russia! Can you believe it, dude? So, what does this little jerkoff do, but go back to the bride guide. Only this time he picks out an even hotter babe from the Ukraine. Like, can you imagine any guy butthead enough to fall for the ruse twice? And an Asylum officer no less! I can't!"

Curious about the nature of the bride guide, Steve probed a little more - this time with the recorder switched on.

"How is this Catalog of Russian Brides published and who does it?"

"Most likely the information is downloaded from the internet and compiled into book form, so there are hundreds of copies floating around. The one from the marriage fraud unit was an original print lifted from our man himself, Orenthal Donald Barfied, the Big O-Don!"

Keibalski stretched out the name for emphasis and the incredulous Steve nearly knocked over his Fat Tire Ale.

"Huh?"

"Yeah, you heard me right, and this is how it happened. Ouine hates, I mean absolutely hates, Da Barf, especially when he begins to rake in all this loot from his snakehead cases. So he calls on a couple of his old buddies in Investigations, they get the go-ahead from the Officer In Charge of Adjudications and the dicks do a clandestine raid on the Barfield Immigration Center late at night after the place is closed."

"No warrant? That's unlawful…what had he done there for probable cause?"

"Welcome to the real world of the INS, counselor. And yes, even O-Don has to sleep some sometime, usually with one of his hot babe junior associates. But it turns out, Da Barf covered his tracks very well; probably keeps his incriminating paperwork in an undisclosed warehouse outside county, state, and federal jurisdiction. There are a few of these left. Besides a few 'borderline' documents, the bride book was all the dicks got. My guess is Da Barf probably got wind of the upcoming raid and set these out as decoys - more taxpayer dollars at work, chasing rainbows, aha, ha, ha! Anyway, if you care to check out the bride guide, I can make a couple phone calls and get it sent to my office. I'll bring it here and we can have a good laugh over a few brewskis. Who knows, you might find a couple ladies you might want to hook up with? Being a single again has its advantages," he winked as he said this. "Unless your name is Theodore Theophalus Penrod, ahahaha!"

"Thanks, but I don't need that kind of assistance. And I would not favor the low-end Slavic white slave trade." Obviously irked by even a remote comparison to Penrod, Steve had to add the gratuitous 'Slavic,' as a semi-insult, though not without provocation.

Keibalski returned the volley. "If you prefer low-end Armenian white slave-trade, the bride book has a few of those, but they aren't nearly as hot.

Steve smiled at that. "Thanks but I have enough action already." He glanced at his watch. It was getting late, Steve aka Patrick J. Robyn had stories to file.

"It does seem to be taking a long time for all this to come out. No press releases from your office and only a short feature from the rival Pomona Paparazzo titled 'The Immigration and Extortion Service.' Not bad for a sub-culture rag."

"You think Ouine wants all this shit to hit the fan in his oak-paneled office? Not on his watch and not before he ships out to the S-pore."

Now this was news! As much as Steve tried to hide his incredulousness, it showed through.

"This is the first time I've seen the cynical, ex-lawyer, hard-charging, big city reporter so impressed."

"I thought this was still up in the air? How do you know he's going?"

"Trust me, I have my network. The job title is Director of US Immigration in East Asia and the Pacific, from East Siberia and Korea in the north, to New Zealand in the south, and just about everything in between. Title is Senior Executive Service 1, a grade up from his current GS-15 with a great deal more prestige, a nice plum before his retirement. His wife is from the Philippines. He's building a huge retirement hacienda there and needs the money. So he's hoping for the assignment as his big 'last hurrah' in his old familiar bailiwick, like where he can short hop it to the P.I. and keep an eye on the peasants building his compound.

"And evade all responsibility for the actions of May, Penrod, and San Alfaro I take it?"

"Like I said, The San was a good egg, it was Penrod and May who were the losers. Pierre Ouine is strictly an Investigations man, never really had a handle on benefits, so he just lets the Faggman do his real work while he entertained visiting big shots - worked for him! But get this... off the record and we never had this conversation... Don 'Da Barf' Barfield was also an Asylum officer right here years before the others happened on the scene."

Steve had sketchy details but needed more. Best to let Keibalski rock on and tell more scandal.

"He lasted all of one month before the duty officer for that day caught him and one of his Chinese ladies, like seven in the evening, working his files with his little 'fortune cookie.' She was typing; he was pawing - not cool! Like, she had no security clearance to use our computers, no authorized visitor's pass to enter the building, and no business being here after lockdown. That's three big disciplinary actions. So the duty officer, Oswald Hinkel, who is also his first-line supervisor, fires him on the spot and two days later cuts his paperwork and he's outta there."

"That fast?"

"Hell yeah, that fast. Like you, he was on his probationary first year so management had the right to terminate him without cause, not even a hearing. But, guess who has the laugh, ahahahaa? Orenthal Donald Barfield II, owner of the most corrupt immigration law firm in the great golden bear state of California, and now under investigation by Attorney General Feather Lockliar, herself. But Old Barfy's gonna beat the rap and here's why. The CBA Old Boy Network protects its own; especially against any AG that wears a skirt."

Steve winced at this bit of male chauvinism and did not agree with Keibalski's conclusion about the bar counsel disciplinary committee. Yet Karl was on a roll, offering up material for maybe seven feature stories.

"You see, right now Da Barf has only one more year to go on suspension. I'll give you odds that when he comes up for review bar. counsel restores all privileges. Like the last time I saw him here was about two years ago, right before the suspension. Up until that time he'd drive here in his silver-tone James Dean Porsche wearing five thousand dollar Armani suits with his clients in tow and living large. Poor Ozzie had a nervous breakdown."

"I don't follow, what would be the connection there?"

"Think about it! Oswald Harvey Hinkel, proper loyal company man always does the right thing. Now in walks Da Barf wearing his custom tailored goombah threads and flicking off his Cohiba cigar ash in our driveway. So Hinkel spies him through his binoculars while checking things out from his third floor office window and falls over in a dead faint. Ouine has to send for an ambulance, and grant the Oz the Wizard forty-five days special leave because the incident happened at work. Now, can you imagine what forty-five days special leave for treatment at the Pomona Peaceful Palisades Rest Home might cost the taxpayers?"

"Why there?"

"Because dammit, that is where Ouine sends all his supervisory head cases when they flip out, except Chaiklin, that's why!" Keibalski exclaimed, pounding his empty mug on the table. "And forty-five days is the maximum paid by the government, so it was like a damn vacation for him, except it counts nothing against his leave time. Nada! And they night-trained him outta here on a stretcher with him mumbling something like, 'how does he rate....I have given the best years of my life to the INS.' Like, dude can you believe it? The sups here are *to*-tally clueless! They just can't figure out how the real world works, and why a rich idiot like Da Barf has it all, while they count the days on their government calendar until retirement. Others wait and hope they'll make Deputy Director before that happens or 'blessed day' if or when they move on to almighty headquarters and enjoy the sublime honor of kissing Lazarus Longstreet's ass every Tuesday morning at nine."

"Why nine every Tuesday morning?"

"Longstreet holds his Progressive Enlightened Leaders Meeting at nine every Tuesday morning. To the non-invited it is known as pell-mell and it usually is. The suits at HQ and their resident butt-licks at the Arlington Asylum Office 'brainstorm.' Karl now sneered, obviously proud of his clever witticism, "Now there's an oxymoron to determine how they can make the Asylum system progressively worse - a real challenge!"

"So what do they actually do there?" Steve countered, hoping for a modicum of substance.

"First, they place a giant order of breakfast goodies from an upscale grocer in Georgetown. After these upwardly mobile American peasants have finished gorging themselves like some eighteenth century English lords, they retire to a six-hour bitch session. Here they bemoan their fate as sub sub-cabinet level officials who feel so oppressed by the Bush administration appointees they work for, and hope for the blessed day when they see a Democratic government on the horizon, as though that would make a difference in their miserable lives! Finally, they rail on about how amazing they are as government executives, and how rotten we are as officers. They end it all with an emotional hand-wringing kumbaya circle jerk about what they can do to inspire more loyalty in us. They would do well to try mass suicide! The fault, dear Brutus lies not in our stars but in ourselves… as the saying goes. But don't ask any of these gender-free gnomes to man-up. They need more R & R. That's why they have this Swiss junket planned."

"What the hell?"

"You heard me correctly. Lazarus Longstreet has this mega director's conference planned in Lausanne, Switzerland on Lake Geneva about a year and a half from now, only no one is supposed to get wind of this just yet."

"And just how did you learn about this junket? Your sources are…?" Steve thought this was as good a time as any to reign in Keibalski's stream of consciousness binge, if only to be certain of cross-checking his references and avoiding costly Dan Rather-isms.

"Trust me; I have my network. They keep me posted on the goings-on there. Longstreet has some extra funds he acquired by taking his budget excesses, buying time shares in Maui, cutting the comptroller in on the action to cover his ass, and dumping them fast after modest gains. Then he returned the principal to the comptroller's office before the INS Big Kahuna or Congress was the wiser. Highly illegal of course, but it worked."

"This is really damning."

Karl stuck out his hammy palm. "I'll lay you odds they never bust him but I'm working..." Just then he caught himself and changed the subject. "So it's party time for Longstreet, Deputy Director Kendra Klamato, and the Magnificent Seven. The directors of the seven regional Asylum offices, their spouses, girlfriends or domestic partners, mustn't forget the bum buggers now. Yodel lady who. Ahaha ha!"

Steve did not care for the bugger comment but let it pass. He had gotten more than he had hoped, much more. This was the stuff of which *60 Minutes* episodes are made. And the Asylum director was about to play the poor man's Tom Ridge. A Swiss soiree might prove more costly to the taxpayers than the Homeland Security Secretary's Hawaii scandal. So, Steve and Karl drank another round, shot the bull, and called it a night around eleven-thirty. Steve went back to his apartment to wrap up the Penrod story for Boss Robyn.

He wrote:
The trial of Theodore T. Penrod, a mid-level US government INS official who fell through life's cracks, ended today with convictions on all fourteen counts of malfeasance, misfeasance, and extortion under the color of law. While the pre-trial discovery and arraignment dragged on for eighteen months, the trial in US District Court of Los Angeles lasted a surprisingly short eleven days, with the jury reaching a verdict after five hours deliberation. Judge Vince Tojo pronounced sentence: thirty years in the clink and no parole ever, likely to be the remainder of the poor schmuck's natural life. As soon as the sentence was passed, bailiffs removed his shoes and belt, and led him away to the San Pedro Island Federal Correctional Facility, where he will remain in custody pending appeal. Patrick J. Robyn for *The Riverside Times.*

Chapter 7

THE BLUE MAX LUNCH CLUB - MEMBERS ONLY

Maximilian Van Rumpelsteen, a young man in a hurry knew he had better make first-line supervisor within one year if he hoped to move on to deputy director in the same office, or two years if he planned to make a horizontal move to one of the other six Asylum offices. He found his mojo in the Los Angeles Asylum Office. Those who are serious about moving on to almighty HQ, need to assemble a loyal coterie of sycophants who are willing to tell everyone within earshot what a wonderful boss they have, and how they wouldn't want to work for anyone else. Maximillian Van Rumpelsteen was among the few, the foul, and the fearless. He was on the fast track and but he needed an entourage to establish his presence in the Byzantine culture of Asylum office politics. What had been difficult for him in private practice became easy in the much less competitive govern-ment service. His biggest problem, in his eyes, was that he was to the manner, but not to the manor, born. Actually, he was neither. No scion of upper crust Bay Area snobbery, his father was bricklayer and his mom, a waitress; two life situations that forever screamed wannabe in his upwardly mobile psyche.

Maximilian Van Rumpelsteen, a newly minted U. Cal Berkley (Boalt College of Law) immigration attorney, class valediction as undergrad, he finished tenth in law school, and straight out of law college joined the Oakland branch of the Galvin Bully Law Firm but lacked the family pedigree and contacts to make partner. With a little patience he might have advanced but he preferred to be a big fish in a small pond, the very small pond know as the US Asylum Office. That is why he left Galvin Bully - not to strike out on his own and found his own firm, but to switch to a low-end immigration firm that he immediately disliked as, "a place with not enough class" for a Boalt Law College graduate. After a short stint there, he reluctantly joined LA Asylum for the steady paycheck. Though he tried to hide his resentment, it surfaced in the ruthless manner in which he organized his lunch club, the mother of all cabals, and made his play for advancement while excluding those long-suffering souls who paid their dues, and worked more than their share of cases, but who would never acquire any predatory networking skills.

Maximilian Van Rumpelsteen, an amateur surfer and an even more amateur scuba diver, hung out on the beaches of Maui and Malibu during summer breaks of his undergraduate and law school years, but he couldn't make the championship cut, so he let messianic instincts take over and reinvented himself as a serious power seeker. He would leave the scuba/surf bum life behind him and discover his epiphany, so the bright new Sun of Asylum called three disciples, not by the Sea of Galilee, but close to the dried up Santa Ana River.

Just before his probationary year ended, Max made supervisor, but hearing that Sean Faggerty might move on to almighty HQ, and that Pierre Ouine would get his overseas posting, he knew he would have to move fast to assemble his power cabal. They included Girolamo Fagheletto, an Italian-American sweet guy with greasy hair. His mom was an Adjudications director in the downtown LA Immigration office, nothing like a little nepotism! Audrey Santarello, an Italian-American hot babe lawyer chick with a mysterious past and bulbous nose, and boy what tricks she could do with it! The third, Sylvestorio Strombolio rounded out the Four Horsepersons of the Asylumclipse. Three Italian Americans and a Hollander, not exactly full diversity but they tried!

Actually, only one of them spoke the language of her "ethnicity" fluently, the accomplished and multifaceted Audry Santorello. But what was not so well known was that hot Audrey had an even hotter past. Before she served her stint as deputy DA for Norwalk, California, she served her stint as an exotic dancer for the U Go to Blazes Gentlemen's Club in Westwood, a nudie bar sandwiched between the UCLA campus and the Getty Museum.

Once a month the club held a Blaze Star lookalike contest for their dancers and a drawing for their patrons. Audrey Santorello, who danced under the name Clitoretta La Pasta won the contest a record five times during her two-year career there, the one that paid her way through Pepperdine University Law School. It was a win-win situation. Audrey Santorello paid her way through law school as a straight-A student. The lucky patron who won the drawing got to take Clit La Pasta to the back room for a straight-A good time playing playing "Ol' Uncle" Earl Long with her. O yeah! Small wonder U Go To Blazes was once the most successful skin joint in the Malibu-Ventura recreation zone.

Italian born Audrey came to the US when her parents immigrated. While the name may seem a bit strange, her mom and dad loved Audry Hepburn in *Roman Spring* and named their lovely little bambina in her honor. A week after she was hired, Van Rumpelsteen took a liking to her, and she returned his come-on glances with her impish smiles. They began dating straightaway. She wanted to get intimate after a night on the town. He begged off citing prostate trouble; a somewhat strange condition for one so young, but it rendered him impotent at times.

What is known about the other two is based largely on rumor. The K-man knows all. sees all, hears all, and smells all, especially if something badly stinks. Girolamo Fagheletto, born in Utica, New York attended parochial school there and later Syracuse University, where he received his BA and law degrees. A quiet, studious Catholic boy, he dutifully moved to the west coast after graduation to live with his parents who had relocated there a few years earlier. Now thirtyish, with lightly pomaded thinning hair, mama and papa hoped he would find a nice Italian-American girl, get married, and start a family since he had no inclination for the priesthood. As he was their only son, his parents feared what all Italian parents fear, that he might choose the priesthood. He might well have gravitated to the priesthood for what mama and papa did not know was that he hoped to find a nice Italian-American boy, get married, and start a family. Like everything else in Los Angeles Asylum, no one knows how Keibalski digs up all this dirt. You see, dear reader, in California all dreams come true except for Girolamo Fagheletto and Carrie Prejean. What irony!

Now, Sylvestorio 'Sly' Strombolio, is one of those people who just had to play in a league too fast for him. Also an east coaster, his mediocre grades prevented him from entering Seton Hall, the choice of his family since all his eight siblings were alumni. After high school, Strombolio bummed around a year trying to become a heavy-metal musician, but with no ear for music, his band let him travel as a "roadie" instead, more out of generosity than need. Granted admission to Kuntztown State College in Pennsylvania, his less than sterling undergraduate academic record there would mandate admission to only the lowest end of law schools, Slimy Pond College School of Law in Slimy Pond, Pennsylvania. He graduated with modest grades and by some. miracle passed the Pennsulbania and New Joysey bar exams, duh! Now one thing about Pennsylvania is that it is Da Pitts in the west, Philadumptruck in the east and Alabama in between. Sylvestorio was so dense, however, that no law firm even in the Alabama part would touch this pariah. He did a little ambulance chasing and document jockeying at a couple two-partner law offices in Corleone, New Jersey working as an underpaid associate until he answered a federal register advertisement for Asylum at the Arlington Office.

He appeared to take to Asylum work very well, and after a year joined the quality control team at headquarters teaching Asylum procedures and interviewing. During a detail in Honolulu, however, he coaxed another QC Officer, Frank Folio, an old East Joysey High bud to go scuba diving off Maui during the Memorial Day Weekend. They went down a hundred fifty feet looking for 19 century shipwrecks. Good luck finding any there.

"Now, if dey got shipwrecks here in Joysey, and dey got shipwrecks in Florduh, dey obviously got shipwrecks in Maui too, right? So, like, we go scuba diving and find duh gold we get to keep it right? So we can quit Asylum and go scuba diving every day and find more gold, right?" The world according to Sylvestorio - what an enchanting place! Trouble is, what few shipwrecks there were off the Maui coast, or anywhere off any Hawaiian coast, are likely resting at least a thousand feet deep offshore and had once carried teakwood, tea, and rice, not gold. They didn't teach you about narrow continental shelves at Kuntztown State, did they!

So Sly and, Frank, his Joysey high school bud from way, back went down to 80 feet, but no gold yet, surprise, surprise! Frank, not an experienced a diver as Sly mistakes a tuna for a shark and gets the "bends" when surfacing too quickly and has to be de-pressurized and air-evacuated to the Queen Kamanawanaleyia Hospital on Big Island. Although the incident happened during off-duty hours, because they were on a detail, a legal technicality required HQ to grant forty-five days comp time so they had to rush over a replacement - expensive! Lazarus Longstreet was ready to banish Sly to the typing pool, but with his firmly accrued tenure, it would have been difficult. After a good ass-chewing, Lazarus

Longstreet called him back on the carpet a week later, offered to let bygones be bygones, and suggested that Sly take the new opening at the problematic LA office, the one Longstreet hates above all the others and where, it was hoped, that Sly's career would come to an early end or at least be less of an embarrassment.

"I tell you your chances of making supervisor will be excellent. I tell you, excellent - think excellent! After all, this is your dream - to make supervisor isn't it?" he exclaimed, with a well-concealed sneer. "And your loving Italian mama and papa in New Jersey will be so proud, won't they?"

Sly choked up. "Duh, I don't know what to say. You're so good to me, sob sob!"

"Just say yes. Puleez say yes," the Director grinded his teeth.

Sly took the hint and the transfer.

"Thank heaven the dumb bastard is far away!"

But as events played out, the joke would eventually be on Longstreet. The first meetings took place innocently enough after a typical Wednesday morning training session. Only a week on the job, Deputy Director Faggerty tasked Strombolio to give a lecture on the one-year filing rule and other official procedures. A big mistake.

Sly stumbled over the new sections of Title 8 in the Code of Federal Regulations. He was not up and running on new legislation, and the effect it had on recent changes to the regs, so it soon became apparent that he did not know what he was talking about. And to make matters worse, he begged for mercy pleading that he was just a simple Italian carpenter's son trying to make mama and papa proud. "Da one year filing rule is like dis. Uh, ya gotta file your papers in one year after you get here or you're up shit creek widout a paddle and dat's a fact. But udder tings are important, too. Like dey got extraordinary soycumstances and changed soycumstances if some stuff happens."

Karl Keibalski, in his usual spot in the back row jumped up from his seat hooting, hollering, and fully drowning out Strombolio's voice while leading his colleagues in a chorus of boos and Bronx cheers to the point that poor Sly got flustered, turned jerkily away from the mic, and dashed to the men's room, bawling. Not too good a start for someone who wanted to make soop. but not to worry. Van Rumpelsteen also shared a love of water sports, so they bonded well and only two days later he went to his first clubbers meeting. Six months and five surfing safaris later, he became an official Supervisory Asylum Officer. Now mama and papa could say, "Datsa my boy" not Whatsamatta you!"

Girolamo Fagheletto fared not so well. He had just received a promotion to Temporary Supervisor when, for some strange reason, management assigned him to the San Pedro Federal Detention Facility, not to be confused with the adjacent federal *prison* by the same name, latest residence of Theodore T. Penrod. Giro, sharp hair, sharp Armani suit, and sharp Bruno Magli shoes, let his sharp attitude override any common sense he might have had. Something about the word "supervisor" brought about a change in personality from obedient son and proper subordinate to authoritarian power wielder. He would show 'em he had the power to match his overpriced threads, he would! These non-law school types had better watch who they were messing with.

His first flub occurred during his second week as supervisor. He crossed swords with retired air force sky jock, Colonel Hiram H. Hofwitz IV, a one hundred mission flyboy going back to Nam, Desert Storm, Desert Shield, Desert Palms, the Boer Wars, and the Bush Wars, or whatever. The point is he transferred to Asylum from Investigations, hated his job, and his supervisor. He had poor Giro hitting the ground running in full retreat and it happened like this:

At the San Pedro Detention Center Border Security, personnel were herding to lockup five new busloads of would-be refugees, as they attempted entry into the US without documents or with false documents. A typical lot included a lot of Chinese, a scattering of Russians and Armenians, and a few of the usual cranks from the Balkan republics.

Claiming religious or political persecution based on the Falun Gong cult membership, eminent domain, or one child policy, the Chinese often attempted to lie their way into the US and use the asylum, or credible fear process, to gain quick resident status. It was just one more means to short-circuit the lawful immigration process.

When one of these arrived in their makeshift office at the detention center, of course the old Colonel Hiram H. Hofwitz IV, retired, was more than ready to give 'er the gun - you betcha!

Border Security agents brought in a twenty-year-old Fukien Chinese waif named Xiang Xiangmei from lockup. She supposedly spoke no English, attempted to enter the US without documents, and declared at the customs checkpoint that she sneaked out of Fukien Province without a visa and passport and was afraid to return to her country because of Falun Gong. Taken to secondary for medical examination and interpreter questioning, a full body search revealed that she had stashed valid PRC passport and ID in orifices, plus a slip of paper with the telephone number and address of her "auntie and uncle" in Monterrey Park. As far as sneaking out of her Province, she was already busted with docs at this point. The good colonel attempted to reach auntie and uncle by telephone only to find the number no longer in service. Although it was not necessary, he traced the number and discovered that it most recently belonged to "The Honey Lotus Outcall Service" meaning auntie and uncle were pimps who were likely exploiting the illicit labor of unauthorized Asian immigrants; so busted on point two.

At interview with a telephonic translator, the conversation went thusly:

"Ms. Xiang, good morning. I am Asylum Officer Hiram H. Hofwitz IV, and Colonel in the US Air Forced retired. How are you today?"

"I like it here in America. I want to stay. I am afraid to go back to China."

"Now let's just take this one step at a time. I want you to tell me why you fear going back to your country?"

"Falun Gong."

"Can you tell me what you know about Falun Gong?"

"My daddy say it good for your body."

"How long have you been practicing Falun Gong?"

"No, only my daddy practice."

"Does that mean you do not practice Falun Gong and have never practiced Falun Gong?"

"Only Daddy practice."

"How long has your daddy been practicing Falun Gong?"

"A long time."

"Where is your Daddy now?"

"In China."

"What does he do in China?"

"He go to jail."

"Why did he go to jail?"

"He have problem."

"What was the problem?"

"He make money."

"Is this related to Falun Gong?"

"Oh, no. He go to jail because he manage Sheraton Hotel in Guangzhou, take money, go to Hong Kong, open bank account. Send money to Singapore."

"How long will he be in jail?"

"Long time. So I come to America, make money, and pay Public Security Bureau. He get out of jail."

"How is that so?"

"Auntie and uncle very rich; take good care of me. Find me a job doing social work. Make a lot of money. I like it here in America"

"Well, God bless the good ol' USA! Now here is what is going to happen. You will go back to detention but in one week, you will have an additional interview before the Immigration judge. He will decide whether you can stay. If the judge decides you can stay, you must have adequate, legitimate means of support and lodgings. Do you understand?"

"I understand. Me love you long time."

"That is not how this process works!" Then offside to another employee, "Security, return Ms. Xiang to her quarters, immediately!"

Flustered and disgusted by what he had just heard, Colonel Hiram H. Hofwitz IV, retired, wrote up his report of the interview as non-credible testimony with no nexus. That means Xiang Xiangmei did not offer credible testimony, nor did she give evidence of any kind of harm related to a protected characteristic, a basic requirement for further consideration. He faxed his report to Giro Fagheletto, who in turn went totally ballistic. Giro then iPhones the good retired colonel immediately.

"When I assign interviews, I, Girolamo Patricio Fagheletto, expect them to be completed. Is that understood!"

"Exactly what is it that you allege that I did not complete?"

"You know that without a nexus, the case cannot proceed to the Immigration court and I must forward the case to HQ for review instead, and I am not going to do that. Headquarters absolutely refuses to review credible fear cases. This is Director Longstreet's policy and has been for a very long time and you should know this."

"Well if that's true, then Director Longstreet is in violation of US Immigration law. But this process raises the question, too. What am I supposed to do about nexus? If you read the report, and I presume you did, she has none."

"Who are you to question Director Longstreet's knowledge of the law? You are not even an attorney. You are only retired military, not an important person at all! As for a nexus - find one! If you do not find one, I will pull you off this easy detail. Would you like that?"

"Don't get bitchy with me you little Italian queer. I flew bombing missions in Nam while you were crapping your diapers. You wouldn't be enjoying the soft life, cushy job, and easy money you get now if it weren't for real men and you'll never be one. Do you read me you little faggot!"

"Screech! You are a horrible beast, fascist pig, sexist homophobe! How dare you offend me! I will personally call Director Longstreet and have you fired," Giro blubbered through sobs."

"As though I give a damn about Longstreet and the rest of the HQ pansies."

"Screech!" I hope they put you in jail for fascism and homophobia."

Poor Giro! He could handle no more. Sobbing uncontrollably, he let his $10,000 custom made iPhone, equipped with palm pilot and digital camera that played romantic music from Pokeback Mountain, slip from his hand. But it landed safely onto the plush chartreuse-carpeted floor of his temporary office in The Federal Building, the one Ms. Schmelbalz had installed at the far east end of the thirteenth floor for her "special guys" to use as a quick rendezvous getaway. He ran down the back stairs to his mama's office on the twelfth Floor and wailing into her lap, he broke down completely.

"Sob, horrible beast, sob, sob. So offensive! Why is he allowed to live? What shall I do? Sob, sob!"

"There, there, Mama loves you," she said, while stroking his pomaded hair, yiich!

"Don't mind ugly Anglo-Saxon. You find nice Italian girl and get married, we can have grandchildren; Mama and Papa be so proud"

What Mama Fagheletto meant by this string of non-sequiturs is uncertain, but Giro's response was predictable, and so was Mama's - her stroking turned to slapping.

"Whaaaaa! I want a nice Italian boy, instead, whaaaa!"

"Eh, whatsamatta you? I raised a finnocchio? Mama and Papa give you a good life, have you confirmed, send you to college, buy you new Ferrari. Shame on you! You disgrace, you get out." Slap slap.

And so, Giro ran all the way down to the first floor, with Mama Fagheletto hot on his tail, kicking his butt all the way to the street. And yes, Pierre Ouine had to explain to HQ the incapacitation of yet one more Asylum supervisor and admission to the Pomona Peaceful Palisades Rest and Recovery Home. So they put him on enough goof-balls to keep him from suicidal tendencies, and with therapy sessions and letters to Director Longstreet, he took a turn for the better once he learned his promotion to permanent supervisor was safe. Van Rumpelsteen put in a word to HQ to give him another chance, and the good one hundred-mission Colonel now about to be dispatched to Florence, Arizona to interview Latino gang-bangers, had already resigned in disgust.

Following Giro's return to work, the Lunch Club Cabal reconvened in force. Next on the agenda, Audry Santorello needed to make soop so VR could take his team to higher levels. Springtime came early and the clubbers migrated to a lawn table and beach umbrella outside, near the parking lot where they ate lunch and excluded everyone else, even though all employees were supposed to share usage of the canopy. Their extended lunch breaks kept others from using it. One afternoon, VR signaled the now recovered Giro and Sly to leave early while he consulted with Audry.

VR informed her that he was fully aware of her previous life from a centerfold of a Clitoretta La Pasta in the July 1994 issue of Hothouse Magazine. It gave the name and bio that listed her achievements as a one-time nursing major before she switched to pre-law. Aggressive UCB lawyer that Max was, he showed her the issue and hinted that others might learn about her past, but that he would make it go away if she cooperated. And so Max did, in exchange for a little therapy on his prostate condition. Carrying "brown nosing" to new levels, they made an afternoon reservation at the Anaheim Ayres Hotel and there she used her schnoz as a rudder and reduced Max down to healthful size. Two more therapy sessions, each a week apart, and the title of Supervisor was hers, too. So the cabal was complete; match, set, and game point. Maximilian Van Rumpelsteen had his team and was on his way to deputy director.

Sad to say, however, he indiscreetly left the Hothouse Mag with the La Pasta centerfold on his desk, and when Mike Magnesia was duty officer one night, he discovered it while checking out the building before lockup. The next day he brought it to lunch so he and two of his buddies, Gehrhard Van Mietsukker and Drew Valentine, could indulge in a drooling session at a nearby Philly steak and cheese joint where they were free from snoops and could get their jollies mocking Audrey Santorello and her past career at Blaze's.

While the other two could have a laugh and forget about it, Mike Magnesia developed a bit of an obsession. Magnesia, a former Agriculture

International Development worker in Somalia often told those who would listen, that he supervised two middle school construction projects. He was actually a paper-shuffling clerk. On a two-year assignment, the project manager nevertheless sent Magnesia home when he discovered he had committed, "an impropriety with two nubile Somali girls, tsk, tsk." Mike offered to sneak the porno mag back into Van Rumpelsteen's office before he could discover it was missing. The other two were too afraid. Actually, Magnesia delayed the return for a couple days, stashing the mag in the restroom of his basement workshop where he could use it for his own recreation and where no one else might find it - no one but his thirteen-year-old son that is. Caught red-handed, literally, Pop dragged him off the crapper and slapped the poor embarrassed crying kid around, cussed him out like a Dutch uncle, and then took off his belt and whipped the poor kid's bare butt.

"Shame on you! What's the matter with you? You know you can get retarded doing that? When I was your age, I never did anything like that (yeah, sure). Wait till your mother hears about this and your sisters, how about that bub?" Whack, whack.

"No, sob, sob, sob, please not my sisters, please!"

"Let this be a lesson for you. If I catch you doing this again, we're going to send you to a mentally handicapped school! Would you like that, bub?"

"No, please, I'll be a good boy."

"You better be!"

It was obvious that Michael Magnesia, Jr., now in the full bloom of puberty, had already soiled the July 1994 centerfold of Audrey Santorello aka Clitoretta La Pasta, and thus bore the brunt of Pop's anger. So Mike

Sr. labored mightily two evenings using his best tools, climate control, air-brushing, and retouching. It was easy enough of a job, and with the original colors fading fast, who would know? He could sneak the masterpiece back during his next duty day and Max VR would never know the difference.

From that time on Mike was often seen visiting Audrey's office asking "pertinent" questions about asylum law until she got tired and disgusted of the ugly creep. But what about the smirks from Mietsukker and Valentine, and of course, the K-man? The K-man knows all-sees all-after all! She put in for a transfer to HQ and was gone within the month. With the lunch club now down to two, Max needed to recruit a new member though no one dared tell this puzzled power seeker why Audrey wanted to leave the cabal so soon.

Steve was at *The Times*' office wrapping up on the Judge Dumone and Penrod features when he received an unexpected cell phone call from Karl Keibalski. In his inimical style, he had sourced another scoop, and this one just might conjure up a fitting conclusion.

"Get this: Theodore Penrod is gone. Offed himself in his cell yesterday morning around nine. Hanged himself from some bars on the window with a makeshift noose from his jockey shorts, just like the Unibomber tried to do only Penrod succeeded." He followed his slight pause with a typical Keibalski witticism. "Looks like this was the only thing he ever succeeded at."

Steve thought it a bit harsh, but was of course more interested in learning more details and a confirmation. "Do you know the details for certain? Who are the sources?"

"How does Hortensia Falabenko grab you, ha, ha? She e-mailed the news to everyone in the office this morning. No condolences just the facts. I'll forward a copy to you."

Another pause then he summed all up. "What a bitch! But you already know that. Oh, one more thing. It's safe to come back here again and assume your real identity. Ouine isn't mad anymore."

"Why is that?"

"Because his Singapore transfer is about to come through and he sees you as a means of leaving the next director holding the bag, if you get my drift. So, he's ready to take you back and you'll be working for Mike Magnesia. But I'll warn you now - he's crude.

"Thanks for the heads up. I owe you one."

"Fuckin' A, and then some!"

Chapter 8

EVERYBODY SUES THESE PRICKS

I f your case is strong on the law, argue the law, if your case is strong on the facts, argue the facts. If it is neither, pound the table.

Judge Learned Hand, 10th Circuit
US Court of Appeals

Hortensia's e-mail read:

To all interested persons –

Yesterday morning prison officials discovered the corpse of Theodore T. Penrod in his cell at the San Pedro Island Federal Penitentiary. An apparent suicide, the cause of death was due to hanging by a noose made from personal undergarments. No further information is available at this time. If anyone has a claim against the estate of Mr. Penrod, do not hesitate to consult the INS legal affairs officer.

Steve pondered the e-mail copy from Keibalski for about ten minutes then called at his office. Both had the same thought at the same time and drew the same conclusion.

"Poor bugger owed me $300 but why press it? It's not likely he had even that much in his estate. Penrod did not have much to live for, and he once told me that he would off himself rather than become a "wife," but that doesn't mean he would do it. I mean, it takes some balls to off yourself and he didn't have any. If I were you, I'd check it out and see if it was really suicide."

"Do you mean to suggest that someone might have …"

"Who knows? What I *do* know is he was a big embarrassment to US Asylum, and that certain people at HQ, and maybe this office, might have wanted him out of the way."

"Yes, but in his case twenty years might well be a life sentence, so…"

"Just a thought, that's all. These HQ folks are nothing if not proud, and vengeance is a great motivator. Anyway, Penrod's gone now and bigger things are shakin'."

"Well, like what?"

"Like Sean Faggerty might move on to HQ right after our transition from DOJ to Homeland Security. He's even willing to take a demotion from deputy to supervisor just to be there in the divine presence of the Great Him. Some people would go there if they had to live in trees just to butt-lick their way to power. Also you might remember that flat top dyke from the dinner at Torquemada's?

"Vaguely, real surly type, just stared into her drink right?"

"Fuckin A, that's her. Harriet McCornnell, once on the fast track to deputy director, Schmelbalz loved her but Ouine hated her. It came to a head about then, and a week after that she quit. So now I'll tell you the rest of the story.

Like she was always rubbing her law degree from Stanford, and immigration firm experience, in his face. Two really stupid moves, especially since Ouine hates immigration lawyers and just about anybody with an advanced degree in anything. Worse yet, she organized Wednesday morning whack-job diversity training modules playing 'new age facilitator,' delaying real work for half a day, and pissing everyone off with touchy-feely awareness sessions. Emotional Masturbation 101. Ouine told her not to do any more sessions because the officers might better use the time to review country-conditions updates but she wouldn't listen.

They had words. Then she put in for a couple plush overseas details in Rome and Vienna but her requests got returned as 'disapproved.' Harriet suspected he had a hand in it, not true of course, and she demanded an explanation. He fell back on the old, "another supervisor was better qualified" line. Like what else could he say? It was HQ's decision. Now, when he blocked her promotion to Deputy Director, over which he did have some authority, she quit in disgust and opened her own immigration law office. It wasn't much of a practice, just herself and a go-for paralegal, a real hole-in-the wall operation. Now she comes here with her gay and lezzy clients. Hey, how's that for a pun? A real hole-in-the-wall operation - get it?"

The moment's silence at Steve's end concluded with his request for more depth and substance. They agreed to meet right after Steve's return to work.

The briefing from Magnesia consisted of little more than the usual poop about the requirement to get the cases in on time, do thorough interviews, and be non-adversarial, routine boilerplate. Also, Mike had personally covered for him during the rumored "firing" that wasn't. He was on a temporary detail to Fresno, interviewing Armenian refugees, a passable alibi with an implied "you owe me one." As he had been told earlier, Mike had no class.

Steve was pleased that it took no more than ten minutes, with plenty of time get a more "in depth" briefing from the K-man.

They did the usual high five then Steve opened with the probing question that was on his mind when Karl broke the news about the promotions and McCornnell's rumored lawsuit.

"I should think that a graduate of Stanford University Law College might pursue a more challenging career, not low-end immigration stuff or government service?"

"Like I said, she's an airhead who didn't get the best law school grades either. Daddy, who also went to Stanford has money - owns some investment banks in the Bay Area."

"So, you're saying that 'money talks' got her an easy seat at law school?"

"Yeah and up there, it's a religion, too!"

"Yes, but I'd like to know where you're going with this since it does seem that these events happened over a very short time frame? Since the Torquemada dinner she resigned from Asylum and has started her own firm. Do you know much more about her current activities?"

"Oh, you mean, where's the beef? Well, try this twenty-four ounce porterhouse. A Salvadoran gay guy came here and had an outstanding arrest warrant for heroin smuggling. Lack of good moral character straightaway since he had three drug busts and a rap sheet for petty theft and burglary as long as my cock. Like, the best he could have gotten from us would have been withholding of removal. But Ouine calls up his buds in Investigations, they send over the federal marshals, the feds grab him from the waiting room, clap him in cuffs, and deport him. Turns out he was one of McCornnell's pro-bonehead clients, so she goes into a hissy fit and is now suing Ouine, Faggerty, and Falabenko, the three big pricks in this office."

"I can understand Ouine and Faggerty but why Falabenko?"

"Falabenko was the interviewing officer's supervisor and may move on to better things soon. I'll tell you more later. Now get this, she wants the Court to grant two million punitive, and eight million compensatory, damages for assault and battery, pain and suffering, defamation of character, psycho-harm, and five counts of some other shit. She'll never get it. Like, once the case reaches discovery, the INS super lawyer team will rally and defend the deep pockets of the service. You know that and she should, too."

Keibalski paused for a breath then let his male chauvinism show. "Must be a menopause thing, even a dumbass dyke lawyer should know better." Then the Oracle of Columbus shook his head and let loose with another Keibalski-ism. "Too bad the feds didn't just waste him with a 9mm on the trip home and toss his carcass from the plane. That's what I would have done."

Not without sympathy, Steve chuckled his mild disagreement. "For an Asylum officer and a truly humanitarian guy, you have a strange sense of due process of law."

"Well, I call my shots as I see 'em, and if a vegetarian eats vegetables what does a humanitarian eat? Ahahaha! Of course, I've never been one of those high-salary civil liberties lawyers like you, but I have always done my job with pride, integrity, and guts. Not like the other liberal assholes in this office that grant every case. And you might not know this yet, but there's an opening in the United Nations headquarters in Geneva and I'm going to put in for it."

True enough, he had worked a year doing refugee processing as an NGO official in Paris between his years in pro-football and INS Investigations. He had also had maintained his European contacts through the years but *Karl Keibalski at the UN?* The very thought of it was the stuff for *Saturday Nite Live.*

"And what would you do at the United Nations in *Geneva,*" Steve snickered the location for effect.

"The same shit I'm doing here, what else?"

"When they fly you there for an interview with the High Commissioner for Refugees, and she asks what you would do for the UN, I do hope you say 'the same shit I did at Los Angeles Asylum.' You'll do just fine."

"You think you're pretty funny, don't you?"

Quick with a stinging retort, Steve did the unimaginable and turned the tables on Karl with some piecemeal knowledge of a 'highlight' in Karl's career that he would just as soon have forgotten and hoped that others would have done the same. Karl's mention of the name Harriet McCornnell tweaked his mind of an incident Boss Robyn told him about that occurred a couple or three months earlier but had been hushed up.

"Well, you must admit I have a very good teacher. And since we are discussing the life and times of Harriet McCornnell, is it true that she was once your supervisor here? And is it also true that she kicked your ass in a barroom brawl after work? Hmm?"

"Who told you that? Whoever the asshole was, they got their facts entirely wrong and she did not kick my ass."

"So, she was in fact, your supervisor here, and there was such an incident, and more than one party observed the said incident, are these not facts?" Steve was beginning to play the courtroom shark and the K-man did not like it one bit.

"No, but I will tell you how it really happened. First, on my way home from work, I stopped to have a brew in the bar at the Namaste Pootahngheehr Hotel on Lime Street, on the north side of the 91 Freeway, when McCornnell walks in with one of her fellow butches. Now, I'm at one end of the bar, minding my own business, when just by coincidence Harry-*et* and her butch stomp in, grab a table in the middle of the barroom, and begin to badmouth me and other Investigations people. Like, it was fascist this, bigot that, and Neanderthal someone else. And 'there is one sitting at the end of the bar,' she said this while pointing her finger toward me. She starts belittling me so everyone in the bar can hear it; railing about how my work product is the worst of her team, and she would fire me if I weren't protected by the old boy network, and that of course is her big all-time boogeyman. And like, she was swaying and probably had a few brewskis before she arrived, so already she's talking too damn loud."

"I had had enough so I walked over to where she and her butch were sitting and told her to shut her liberal flytrap or I would shut it for her. So next thing, she mumbles something about free speech then swings a left hook that catches me above the right eyebrow and draws a trickle of blood. Now mind you, she can't really hit that hard, but I've been in my share of fights, so I've got this scar tissue from when I boxed golden gloves as a kid and it opens up again easy. Well, she's no lady, and she swung first, so I had no qualms about taking down the fat dyke and I did. I grabbed her shoulders, spun her around, put her in a full nelson, and dumped her on the floor. Then I do a cross-face and go for the pin but guess what? Her plug-ugly butch comes over and dumps a pitcher of beer in my face. So I fall down and can't see, and then the butch starts kicking me in the ribs. Now that's two against one but I'm still a lot stronger than the two of them, so even with beer in my eyes I jump up, make a grab for the butch and barely catch her black cycle jacket. As best I can with beer in my eyes, I toss her across the bar ass-over-head. Honest, I hoped I had snapped her neck, or at least damaged her for life. But no such luck, she's built like an old-time telephone pole."

"Now with the butch out of the fight, I can go to work on McCornnell big time. I mean, make her face even uglier that it was then, if that was possible. So, I grabbed the empty pitcher, smashed it on the bar and told her I'm going to do a 'facial' on her that her fairy-boy plastic surgeon won't be able to fix if she doesn't back off. She has one, you know, but he sure doesn't earn his pay! Now, she's not so brave and turns to run. By this time though, the Indian holy man's dumb brother Jawaharlal has called the cops, so she dashes right into the arms of one of four of 'Anaheim's finest' when they showed up. That is, if you can call anything in low-end Ana*slime* 'finest.' Ahahaha!"

Bourgeois liberal Steve was again taken aback by Keibalski's vitriol, but was beginning to understand it, even if he could not yet sympathize. "You mentioned an Indian holy man; who is this? Don't you mean the owner? How is he a holy man?"

"Pabu Punjah Punjahbih Pootahngheehr is employed by the INS, believe it or not. In Customs and Immigration at the San Diego Harbor Authority. That night, his brother Jawaharlal Siddhartha Nirvana Pootahngheehr was 'owner on duty.' but instead of trying to help me,

he cowers behind the action, trying to revive the butch with seltzer water and tapping her hand after I dump her ass over the bar. Just by
coincidence, Pabu also works with Ike Chaiklin as his 'spirit guide,' so
no wonder he's so fucked-up in the head! Of all the rotten gin joints
in Anaheim. I had to walk into his. Only I didn't know it at the time.
Ahahaha! So how would it look to you, as an underpaid city cop with an
attitude? McCornnell runs to the cop sobbing about, "the big man tried
to rape me and hurt my friend." I'm standing there with blood and beer
running down my face and a broken pitcher in my hand with a cracked
rib beginning to throb, so it doesn't take a rocket scientist to figure out
they're going to haul me away and let the dykes go. And that's exactly
what happened. Now Pootahngheehr starts to freak out and begins to
plead with the cops. You see, he was hoping it would all go away and the
last thing he wanted was any more trouble with law enforcement."

"This does not make sense. You just said he called the cops."

"Because they raided the place six months earlier and busted the
brothers for pimping and obscenity."

"What the...?"

"It's true and here is how it happened. You know these Indians could
take an outhouse in Mongolia and turn it into a profitable motel, so converting a run-down 'burlesque theater and progressive bookstore' is a
cakewalk for them, and that's exactly what the Pootahngheehr brothers
did. They opened for business before the restoration was complete, so
they had a magazine rack left by the previous owner. Trouble was, it was
full of porno mags on full display. They did not stash it in the management office or at least under the counter while the banging and sawing
was going on. Unfortunately, there was a different kind of banging going on during the construction, so the Anaheim Heat got wind and paid
a little visit."

"So, they walked in while Jawaharlal was arguing with one of the happytime hotties for a 40% cut of her solicitation earnings. He was threatening to call in his goons from Artesia's Little India to collect. She 'overstayed' her hourly rate by fourfold, so he had a good case, after all. Now Jawaharlal is like fresh off the boat, not like his brother who's been here over twenty years. He *doesn't* know all this shit is illegal in the US, so if you're going to do it, you had better do it on the sly. He does anything but, and calls his goons - dumb move. So guess what!"

"Now the Anaheim cops *and* the Artesia Indian goons show up at the Namaste Pootahngheehr at the same time and what a three-ring circus that was! So the Anaheim Heat is packing full riot gear and the outgunned goons scatter in all directions fast. Now Pabu, who has just returned from the airport pleads with the police, sobbing something about his family being high-caste and virtuous and all four of his daughters are still virgins. Hard to say whether he was bragging or complaining. So the cops, thinking they have some head cases on their hands strait jacket and paddy wagon them over to the county hospital loony ward. Poor Jawaharlal - they charge him with the pimping, obscenity, disorderly conduct, racketeering, and get this, *disturbing* the peace. So they hold Pabu for forty-eight hour observation and he gets a pass, but Jawaharlal gets a deportation hearing for moral turpitude."

"Now get this! They make it all go away when their hot babe attorney Megawati Kamasutri cuts a deal with Judge Matthew B. Dumone. Officially, Jawaharlal gets deported for ten years. Unofficially he camps out in TJ for a year, comes back under an assumed name, the Pootahngheehr brothers agree to keep Kamasutri on indefinite retainer for a cool hundred grand per year, Judge Dumone gets Kamasutri as a new "photo subject," and everything's cool. And that's why the last thing Pabu needs is another disturbance. He won't get off so easy this time."

"This is all very confusing, but did I hear you say Judge Dumone? How is that you know about him?"

"Where have *you* been since the since Grant took Richmond? Everybody in the INS knows about Judge Dum*one* and his hot babe lawyer sexcapades!"

"So, he's pretty much common knowledge then? But this Pabu sounds like a real character. How might I contact him?"

"He alternates between the harbor authority and the hotel where you can find him minding the store three nights a week. Just call and find out his schedule, but don't tell him I sent you. He's very paranoid."

"I wonder why! But tell me, were there any repercussions for you? After all, you did try to defend yourself with a broken beer pitcher, which is a potentially lethal weapon."

Karl seemed a little flustered and evaded the question. "It never entered into any of it. I think I tossed it back behind the bar by that time and they never made an issue of it. I went to the police station, signed an affidavit, and that was it. Oh yeah, one more thing; I called my wife on my cell phone. She arrived at the police station crying about those horrible, immoral, un-Christian lesbians. It made my evening! What can I say?"

Steve's cell phone rang and Boss Robyn could not have called at a better time. It gave him an excuse to leave and touch bases with the Big Kahuna. What he really needed was time enough to get Pabu's side of the story before he turned any copy in to the boss. This was big stuff. An Investigations officer on loan to Asylum does a political wig-out and threatens a supervisor with a potentially lethal weapon. And what a story it might become!

Pabu was cautious at first but Steve assured him that the Asylum office might protect him. So that made him mildly willing to present his version of what happened. Steve called Pabu and arranged to meet him on one of his owner-on-duty nights. He had not, however, given full details of this feature to the boss straightaway and he should have.

When Steve arrived Pabu was cross-legged in a semi-trance, replete with saffron robes and Ravi Shankar tapes. He picked a bad time to visit, but his "liberal cool" returned and he did the multi-cultural right thing with the palm press. But this time, he dared not let on that he was in any manner connected to the media, but instead was an official of the INS exploring the legal issues raised by the altercation.

"Peace and good karma, I am Steven Melkonian, a legal official with the INS. Would you be willing to help us in our fact gathering efforts concerning the altercation between two of our Officers, Mr. Keibalski and Ms. McCornnell? Let me first emphasize that this is only an investigation, not a deposition. You are not under oath and are not required to answer any or all questions if you choose not to do so. Do you understand what I have said?"

"Peace and good karma," he said, pressing his palms. "You are understood."

"Good. Shall, we proceed? What is your point of view concerning the events of the evening of the altercation?"

"An evening most unfortuitous as it was unenlightened."

"So, in your opinion, what happened between the two?"

"It is written in the Bhagavad Gita that such a question does not transcend the most unfortuitous encounter of Keibalski Sahib and McCornnell Sahib."

"Yes, but could you at least confirm that the events of the evening conform to the affidavits both parties signed?"

"Omm," he replied, with lights blinking and sitar music playing softly.

"What about Sahib Keibalski? What role did he play during the disturbance?"

"He was of great countenance and fair to look upon."

"Are you being facetious?"

"He was found to be endowed as the Great Bull of the Bhramaputra Uppu-Chuta, the God of Hunga Humunga."

"Yeah, I just bet he gave you his usual humunga line of bull, too!"

"Omm!"

Steve's peevishness began to show, most unHindulike - not cool! But how could he get viable copy instead of a lot of evasive Hindustani hokum, especially with the boss on his ass for immediate copy of any INS scandal?

"Exactly what did he do?"

"It was most unvirtuous and unchivalrous deportment for an official of the Immigration and Naturalization Service."

Now, Pabu the Swami was pointing his finger skyward, like a high-caste Hindu might have done when talking down to an untouchable during the bad old days of the British viceroyalty.

"Yes but….?"

"An official of the Immigration and Naturalization Service should not perform such bad karma."

"Please get to the point."

"Before McCornnell Sahib and my inestimable patrons he…"

"Yes, I know the, who, where, when, and maybe the how and why, so tell me what the W-H-A-T, was!" What would it take to make this Indu Ah-San stop talking in riddles?

"He took his pants down!" The little owner/swami/customs agent screamed and then fell back into his trance.

"Omm."

"He did what? I don't believe it. He would have been fired!"

"Maybe, I might be of some assistance."

A deux ex machina! The Pootahngheehr business and family attorney, the inestimable Megawati Kamasutri arrived with some court papers for Pabu to sign and to otherwise save the day. *Thank God*, thought Steve, in-more ways than one! Replete with the red-dotted forehead, waist-length ebony hair, beatific smile, and Kardashian sister curves, she was more than a welcome intrusion!

Kamasutri always brought in serious business, so Pabu ditched the weird holy man act, and at her behest went to mind serious hotel matters for his inestimable guests. Steve and Megawati took a table at the back of the lounge and began to discuss Keibalski-McCornnell Los Angeles

Asylum meltdown. Yet, above and beyond official business, a little "chemistry" was beginning to develop between the two. He even kissed her hand as he introduced himself, something he would have once considered a grand pretense, but he was a bit intrigued by her doe-soft eyes that revealed some curiosity, at least, toward this robust, but otherwise atypical-looking, American.

"Good afternoon, I am Steve Melkonian, an attorney at law and employee of the Immigration and Naturalization Service. As this is not a deposition or an interview, you are not under oath, and are not required to answer any or all questions I ask. You agree that the statements you offer are intended only to clarify the events of the evening, that they are given with absolute regard to attorney-client privilege, and that you are under no obligation or oath? Do you understand?"

"Perfectly."

"What do you wish to tell me about the events concerning the incident between Harriet McCornnell and Karl Keibalski, both employees of the Immigration and Naturalization Service, US Asylum in and for the District of Los Angeles?"

"In exchange of a pre-trial settlement of compensatory, but not punitive, damages done toward the Namaste Pootahngheehr Hotel, and to the good reputation of this establishment, and with regard Mr. Pootahngheehr's respected standing in this community, I wish to state that my client has a slightly different version of the events of the evening."

"Please continue."

"Mr. Keibalski appeared to have been drinking when he entered the Namaste Pootahngheehr Hotel, sometime after 7:00 p. m. He was not visibly intoxicated but Mr. Pootahngheehr could smell what appeared to be liquor on his breath. Mr. Keibalski took a seat at the end of the bar and ordered a pitcher of beer. Approximately one half-hour later, Harriet McCornnell walked in with an acquaintance or colleague, I cannot be certain which. They sat down at a small table and began to converse. According to my client, Mr. Keibalski heard Ms. McCornnell mention his name. Perhaps he understood her to say something critical or derogatory, so he left his place at the bar, and with his half-full pitcher in hand he turned, walked to their table and began to raise his voice and act in a belligerent manner. By that I mean he accused her without cause of criticizing his work. My client does not recall their exact words, but Ms. McCornnell asked him to leave her and her friend alone. He refused and dropped the fly on his trousers and yelled, 'Wanna peek?' He seemed proud of himself, though I don't know why. Very juvenile, indeed."

"Your client stated that Mr. Keibalski took his pants down. Did he actually do this?

According to affidavits signed at the police station and during a closed-door hearing at the District Director's office, Mr. Keibalski had not previously buttoned his trouser button. As Mr. Keibalski was staggering, slightly by that time, the pants fell halfway down, at which point he became exposed. My client, now fully aware that this embarrassing predicament had caused his remaining patrons to mumble something like 'gross' or 'disgusting' and leave, feared for his safety and sought refuge behind his bar. As Mr. Keibalski fumbled with his trousers, Ms. McCornnell's friend feared attack and also ducked behind the bar. Ms. McCornnell, who has had some self-defense training, feared a sexual assault on her friend or herself and threw a punch that glanced Mr. Keibalski above the right eye and opened a small cut. He fell back and while he was on the floor, Ms. McCornnell grabbed what was left of the pitcher of beer and poured it on his face to keep him blinded while she and her friend made their escape. As Mr. Keibalski recovered his composure, he reached for the pitcher but knocked it against the side of a table while he was struggling to get up, trying to button his pants at the same time. It fell out of his hand and broke. Mr. Keibalski mumbled something about 'making her face an even bigger mess,' struggled to his feet just as the police arrived, and took control of the situation. Ms. McCornnell showed the Anaheim riot squad her bar card and INS ID and demanded an immediate arrest. As Mr. Keibalski also has INS credentials and a federal investigators badge, the Anaheim Police decide to take statements and turn the matter over to INS Internal Investigations. Ms. McCornnell resigned her Asylum job a month and a half ago over disagreement with INS Asylum management and the parties dropped the matter. As far as I am able to ascertain, that is all. I know of her action against Mr. Ouine, but nothing about the details of the same, and if I did, I should not comment."

"Now," she continued softly, leaning toward Steve, "What about us?"

"We'll always have Anaheim."

Steve answered playfully but Megawati sought more than a flippant answer. "We don't have to leave so quickly, unless you have to get back to *The Times.*"

Steve blanched. Megawati pounced.

"Yes, Mr. Bond, I know about your undercover work, and I find it charming. Shall we retire to the room my client has arranged for us?"

With that most serene of Vishnu beatitudes, she led him to a higher plane of enlightenment. And on the way up to the Kamasutri plane of enlightenment, Steve pondered yet another happenstance of ripe fruit that had fallen from the forbidden tree right into his hands. For sure, he had been set up. For shame, he let it happen again!

"The things I do for *The Riverside Times.*"

Chapter 9

THE "TRUE" STORY OF AH PEE AND KING KONG OF YEREVAN

"**J**ust what the hell are you trying to do to my paper?" the boss thundered at his reprobate deputy editor, while pacing back and forth in his office. This time he had the Jack Daniels bottle in hand, not just his usual tumbler, and of course wearing his ever-present Spuds Turkee hat replete with press pass.

Steve dutifully kept seated as the boss rocked on.

"This is just the kind of slimy trash Charles Manson Wakeley would have printed when he ran *The Times* as his depraved hippie *Roach*." The boss paused, setting the fifth down with a smirk regarding his comment about The Times' previous owner. "Did you know he's in the clink, now? About time I'd say. He was busted by the federal narcs about six months ago for running an unlicensed "weed farm" on his twenty-five acre ranch in Guerneville. He might have beaten that rap, but when the feds broke in, they caught him in the middle of a bum buggery party with neighborhood boys. He'll be in San Quentin for the rest of his miserable life, we hope."

Rambling on he delivered the coup, "And why print the two versions of what happened during a brawl between two dykes and a drunk who should never have been on the government payroll in the first place? Are you trying to run this by me as a poor man's Roshomon? If so, it's not going to play in Peoria, never mind my neighborhood. But that's the least of my problems. A little bird dropped by and told me that we can expect a vacancy in the Asylum Director's office, and maybe even the Deputy Director's office, too. Pierre Ouine looks good for the assignment in Singapore, and the deputy is itching to go to headquarters and sit at the foot of "The Great One.""

The boss spat out the last words as he spoke. He regarded Lazarus Longstreet as just another disloyal American, willing to sell his country out to the highest bidder. Just one more untalented and overpriced bureaucrat who would commit any crime or treason just to keep his job.

"That means you're going back there to work and you will keep your eyes peeled for any scandal, a *real* one this time. And there's no time to waste. When Ouine's out of here, my window on Asylum is closed since Faggerty is clueless."

The boss paused, smiled sardonically and continued, "And Faggerty is also a lightweight and a flake, so it's better he stays clueless. Got it?"

Steve could only agree, but the timing of both departures could make his job easy or hard, depending on who went first, but he'd better be subtle about such a probing.

"Mum's the word. Anyone there know who might depart first?"

"Good question. This time the smart money is on Faggerty leaving first since he's seeking a lower-level job. Ouine's appointment is Senior Executive Service. That type of appointment is sub-cabinet level, so all the security clearances move at a snail's pace. You, however, will report to Mike Magnesia tomorrow morning at nine. One more thing... Keibalski is the original loose cannon, so he's no substitute for a real mole. Be more careful what you tell him from now on, and especially sift out what he tells you."

"Got it."

"And no more low-end scandals this time, only high one's," he winked as we said it.

"Of course."

Steve spent the rest of the afternoon reviewing copy from the junior staff, but pondered the boss' admonition. Problem was the K-Man; knows all, hears all, and sees all, but most important, he tells all. So how to pick his brain without the boss finding out about it? Now that was a tall order.

Within the month of April 2008, events would play out with rapid intensity, at least with more rapidity than anyone employed in LA Asylum had anticipated. The first day Steve got off to a rocky start. Mike Magnesia, his new boss, was duty officer for the day, which meant he was responsible for meeting the day's productivity goals, in addition to managing his team of four officers. There were nagging rumors that Steve, like Keibalski, was assigned to Asylum to do undercover work. And while no one was sure of the nature of his assignment, all were suspicious, especially the first-line supervisors. The suspicion put him at odds with Magnesia who was sufficiently paranoid by nature.

"It's about time you got here. I expect my officers to be timely with their work and you suck at it! You think because you were a lawyer you have it made here. Not on my team you don't."

Steve was going to retort with, "Well, you just plain suck and you're envious, too," but thought the better of it, as he noticed that sandwiched between some papers on his ever-sloppy desk, Mike had stashed a dated copy of Hothouse Magazine folded open to the centerfold of... guess whose photo?

"I see you like to collect vintage porn. Might I have a peek?"

Quickly, Magnesia shuffled the stack, obviously pissed.

"You think you're wise? Well, I've got three cases for you to work today and here's the first one," Mike exclaimed, while tossing rather than handing the folder to Steve. "It's a Chinese case, right up your alley. Get with it! Now! Mike slammed his fist on his desk and motioned for Steve to leave and get cracking on it.

As Steve reviewed the file, it looked more like a straight domestic violence issue as opposed to a matter of any kind of persecution based on religion, ethnicity, or politics. The woman, Ah Pee Yan, apparently left the countryside of Guangxi, China to escape the physical, sexual, and verbal abuse of her husband, a provincial policeman. Her documents, which included a passport and birth records, home registration, and family tree, appeared to contain alterations and counterfeiting. Many of these cases involved Hong Kong residents who claimed persecution in China in order to obtain asylum in the US, and thus evade the slow and tedious process of acquiring legitimate immigrant quota documents and this case appeared to be one of those.

Ah Pee followed Steve into the interview room, accompanied by her lawyer, Isaac Goniv, and her interpreter, Huang Ba Don

"Good morning. I am Officer Steven Melkonian of Los Angeles Asylum and I will be conducting your interview. After I put you and your interpreter under oath, I will ask you questions concerning your claim for asylum in the United States. You must be forthright and the thorough in your answers. Do you understand?"

As Mr. Huang translated, he seemed to take a very long time just to explain to her the oath and the need to give truthful testimony. In addition, Steve noticed that the interpreter used some clandestine hand signals below the interview table. This was a rather common occurrence during these interviews, but many officers were too lazy, or too timid to call them on this. Steve however, had a slight advantage, as he could pick up enough of the dialogue between the two to know something was not right. He heard, "one finger means yes, two fingers no, three fingers I don't understand-please repeat, four fingers I will change your answer for you."

Before making a charge of interpreter misconduct, Steve thought it better to consult with Supervisor and Duty Officer Mike Magnesia. Ah Pee's lawyer might get prickly, and this would avoid a confrontation with him. He made the excuse that he needed to consult with his supervisor, excused himself for fifteen minutes, and headed for Magnesia's office with the claims file and Ah Pee's fake travel documents.

Mike was in his usual foul humor and did not want to be bothered with low-level stuff. As was typical, he grabbed the passport from Steve's hand as he approached and glared at it, got out his little infrared flashlight, grunted, and made an expletive deleted remark.

"Didn't you see this was a fake passport? Just look at this; this passport has one date superimposed on another, the photo is a fake, and this household registry is a phony, too. Did you ask her about that?"

"Well no, but I'm not yet very familiar with the…"

"That's why we have interviews! Now go back and ask her all these questions," thundered Mike, slamming his desk, spilling his coffee, and yelling 'aw shit' at the same time. "Never mind, I'll handle this. Now, pay attention and watch how a real pro does this job."

Steve had no choice but to follow Mike meekly back to the interview room as a scared puppy follows its master.

"Hello. I'm Mike Magnesia, Asylum Supervisor and Duty Officer for the Day. I'm going to ask some questions so I know this interview is done right."

As Mike perused the documents, he noticed that the applicant had dolled herself up a bit and looked little like the Cantonese country peasant in the passport photo. She wore a form fitting black silk cheongsam with imprints of white plum blossoms, the 1920ish Hong Kong seductress-type with slits down both legs. Her espresso black hair was drawn into a tightly lacquered bun and held in place with an expensive mother-of-pearl pin. Completing the ostentatious ensemble was an oversize rose gold bracelet worn on her left wrist. It was inlaid with a circle of rubies and silver trade dollar coins from the Manchu Dynasty. Topped with a necklace that contained too many rows of pearls, she came off as Suzy Wong trying to pass herself off as Madam Chiang Kai-shek, a comedic mishap and a fraudulent asylum case as well!

Right away, Magnesia started in on her, "This passport contains two different dates. Why?" He moved closer to her end of the oval table until he was standing over poor little Ah Pee, who was now too frightened to speak. A short ugly-looking, chrome dome, snarling man, he went into his investigator's' third degree mode, "Is this passport real? Is this visa real? Is this house registry real? Is your hair real?"

"Waaaaah!" Ah Pee broke down in sobs as her outraged lawyer lept to his feet and sputtered with his pointed finger in the air, "Mr. Magnesia, I highly object to this irregular line of adversarial questioning and such bellicose behavior. I shall write to the District Director about this!"

Snarling at the hapless Goniv just like James Cagney in the old gangster movies, Mike rebukes the 'dirty rat.' "Shut up little man. You're a pettifogging shyster ambulance-chasing creep. And everyone here knows you've been suspended from practice three times already!" he shouted, raising three fingers in front of Goniv's face. "And I know enough people to make it a fourth. So sit down already before you fall down. Got it, bub?"

"This is preposterous!"

"Yeah, prostateitis is right! You look like some little jerkoff that hasn't gotten it up in twenty years. So sit down and shut up like I said."

"This is a monumental outrage!" Again with the index finger rocketing in the air. "I have never been so humiliated in my thirty years of legal prac…"

Mike cut him off, "Yeah? Just wait till we have you disbarred." Then he grabbed the lawyer by his coat sleeve, pulled out a chair, and forcefully sat him down.

Huang Ba Don got the lawyer and Ah Pee under control so the interview could continue. Actually, the attorney was a de facto employee of the Huang Ba Don Immigration Consulting Service, so the interpreter could fire him on the spot. His firm Hutzpah, Goniv and Metzschmuck, where his father had been a founding partner, had farmed him out to the consulting services where he would cause fewer problems. With the departure of Barfield and Penrod he was their lousiest lawyer. Isaac Goniv knew he would have to eat crow, so Supervisor Mike left and Steve continued with the interview.

"Tell me what caused you to leave your country and seek the protection of the United States?"

The interpreter began to translate the true Story of Ah Pee.

"My name Ah Pee Yan. I live in a country village in Guangxi Province. It is quiet and peaceful there. I marry policeman when I am eighteen. He tall and handsome. I in love with him. We very happy. But he buy sex tape from Hong Kong and want me do kinky things."

"Could you please clarify 'kinky?'"

"He want me to put his jeejee in my mouth. It disgust me a lot. I don't like, but he say all the Hong Kong couples do it."

"Did he force you to do this?"

"Yes, he even rape my anus. It hurt a lot."

"Did you report him to his superiors?"

"I try, but they only laugh and tell me I am lucky to have such a manly husband."

"Did you consider leaving your spouse and filing for divorce?"

"In China no can do."

"Could you tell me why you are here today?"

"You are handsome and have beautiful dark eyes. Me rub you long time."

Steve could see the interpreter freak out, nudge Ah Pee under the table, flash four fingers, and translate her response quite differently from what she actually said. Steve was able to pick this up before the interpreter changed her answer to, "My spouse became abusive and I had to leave China."

Huang Ba Don signaled to the lawyer that they needed to confer in private with Ah Pee, and Goniv requested thirty minutes to prepare his client for the interview. Apparently, Ah Pee had gotten her testimony confused. Ba Don had rehearsed her with too many details and with so much information overload that she responded with what she was supposed to say at her afternoon interview with the Pasadena Progressive Natural Therapy Spa where Goniv's firm had arranged for her employment as an exotic masseuse.

"Absolutely not, counsel," was Steve's adamant reply. "You, as her attorney, have had sufficient time to represent your client with due diligence and prepare your client for the interview, which it appears you have not done. This office is not obliged to grant you extra time to confer with your client and we will not do so. In addition, I grew up near a Cantonese neighborhood in Fresno and I understand this Chinese dialect. Mr. Huang the interpreter is testifying on behalf of Ms. Yan and he is not permitted to do that."

"Are you trying to tell me how to represent my client? I happen to be an attorney and bar member and..."

"So am I and lawyers like you give the rest of us a bad reputation."

"I will write the District Director, and have your job and the duty officer's too."

"Don't do us any favors! If you do, we might owe you one. I will reschedule the remainder of this interview due to interpreter integrity issues. I intend to write a report and ban Mr. Huang from ever interpreting at this office again. I will call the security guard now who will escort you, Mr. Huang, and Ms. Yan to the entrance. Have a nice day."

On his way out, Mr. Goniv railed against the injustice of the The System," man's inhumanity to woman, denial of basic human rights, fascist pig Asylum duty officers, cold and callous interviewers. He threatened to write outgoing District Director Laura Schmelbalz whom he once knew biblically, newly promoted Deputy Director Helen Hu whom he is trying to know biblically, and Senator Barbara Boxer whom he would like to know biblically, head case that he is! Los Angles Asylum is not just smoke and mirrors, it was fast becoming fun and games.

Magnesia called Steve on the intercom phone after hearing how he dispatched his first case with a second and third pending.

"Not a bad job. Of course I would have handled in differently. I wouldn't have gotten adversarial like you did. But all-in-all, a good first effort on my team. Now this is really your lucky day. I've got another case right up your alley, an Armenian political case especially since you speak the language. Seems that ultra-nationalist Yerkrapah toughs extorted and roughed-up this meat market owner and took his store away from him. You could say they beat his meat, ahaahaaha."

Steve could not see any humor in this, but thought it better to let Mike's crude comment pass. As he briefly glanced over the file, it struck Steve that the storeowner might be a victim of toughs and nothing more.

"I'm seeing thug activity here but no political motive. It doesn't look as though the claimant has much of a case."

"Yeah, they're all a bunch of crooks and lie like hell."

"Who? Do you mean storeowners or something else?" Steve countered, but by putting it this way, creepy Mike thought he had an easy out.

"Uh, yeah, sure, storeowners."

"You mean storeowners like my father and my grandfather? Is that it?"

Knowing he had crossed the prejudice line, especially for an Asylum official. Mike answered nervously, "Of course I meant nothing against your family." He paused, "No hard feelings right? No hard feelings right?"

Although he was not particularly sensitive about slurs against Armenians, or the social snobbery his grocer family once endured, Steve could not let this good opportunity pass. From Steve's reasoning, his family had already proven themselves worthy citizens, so the Odar, or non-Armenians are just jealous, after all. Now that he had Mangy Mike on the defensive however, and he could exploit this to his advantage and keep the ugly little bastard off his back.

He returned to his office and greeted, in Armenian, an attractive young female interpreter, Baba Ganooshyan, and her clients, an elderly gentleman, Kevork Tebakyan and his wife Hasmit, and their son, Aram with a brief *inch passess*. It was obvious that Aram was really a *sarsok esh*; the son was just not all there. A big strapping young man with a shaved head, scarred face, and burly build, he appeared mildly retarded. Steve put the three under oath and examined their travel documents. The family was a bit comical. He found the photos of Kevork and Hasmit to be in order. But not that of Aram. He looked nothing like the passport image; which showed a delicate sensitive-looking young man with longish hair, not a bruiser. Steve tried to call Mike on the intercom, but he had gone home early due to exhaustion and left the "recovered" Isaac Chaiklin to complete his duty officer shift.

Steve grabbed the file and documents then walked toward his door. As soon he did, the younger Tebakyan leapt over the interview table, sat down in Steve's chair, whipped out a cigarette, and began puffing away. Further behavioral evidence that he was a little, or maybe even a lot off. Not a document expert or an expert of anything other than humbuggery, Chaiklin's advice would likely complicate the simple and it certainly did.

"This claimant's photo does not match his facial features and from my personal observation of his demeanor he appears to have some mental problems," Steve related, hoping for a modicum of cooperation rather than psychobabble. Nice try!

"How do you know he has mental problems? Do you have a degree in abnormal psychology? I do," Isaac pontificated proudly.

"I've been a newsman and an attorney long enough to know people, so I don't need your Piled Higher and Deeper degree psychobabble," retorted Steve. "Just take a look at him."

As they opened the door to Steve's office, Aram Tebakyan took a look at Isaac Chaiklin's ugly hatchet-face with creepy pencil moustache, JC Penney threads, and sparsely-cropped haircut and did not like what he saw. He jumped up and bolted out the door, cigarette and all, down the back stairwell and out the main door to the new city hall annex fifty yards to the east. The guard called up to Steve's office to come to the first floor immediately, as there was some crank smoking a cigarette and grunting strange noises.

"He should not smoke in the building!" the security guard chimed. "He is a danger to himself and others."

Like-big deal! Aram Tebakyan was now climbing King Kong style up the side of the Anaheim City Hall annex. Tucked under his arm was the voluptuous Rita Rincon, a newly minted Asylum officer, USC law school graduate, and fresh from her FLOTC class where she had been class president. Once Aram approached the plush picture window office of Mayor Willi Von Prinkel, he gently placed Big Mama Rita, who was becoming a bit weighty, on the extra-wide second story ledge where His Honor sent for security to pull her inside with many tears, hugs, and kisses for Anaheim's finest.

Mayor Von Prinkel, however, was not amused. The mustached little martinet flew instead into a serious rage after Deputy Faggerty phoned ahead and warned him that Asylum had a head case headed his way. Relations between the two had always been testy and this incident did not help in the least. The mayor wanted Asylum out of 1080 North Avalon which the city also owned, and he demanded more rent money, or better still a more "Aryan tenant." Negotiations had broken down and this latest incident gave the mayor a valid excuse to cancel their lease. What no one in the know even knew, was that the city of Anaheim had its own "Air Force" that consisted of four late model crop duster Piper Cubs, and two imitation aircraft modeled after the World War I original tri-wing Fokker, the one flown by the Red Baron himself, and an English Sopwith Camel, the one flown by *Snoopy* himself.

As Anaheim had no municipal hangar, Von Prinkel docked his planes at the Pomona City Airport under a secret agreement with the Pomona Mayor Venezio Manicotti which involved an under the table cash only rental fee for the use of hanger space. The money came out of the City of Anaheim General Fund, and nobody but nobody knew how much it cost. The vice mayor suspected something was amiss and attempted an audit but Von Prinkel had the funds carefully laundered through the Anaheim Muni Bond Fund to a Mexican bank, and from there to the Pomona General Fund recreational budget. No one knew the wiser!

Von Prinkel's Flying Circus stood ready for His Honor's orders to scramble and bring down this misunderstood miscreant refugee. With the best of der Fuehrer tantrums, the mayor told Deputy Faggerty that he would not permit a 9-11 in Anaheim, and he would call in his Luftwaffe to bring down the terrorist *untermensch.* Add a few special effects and aerial photography, and the scenario could have played out as *The Aviator* done as a poor man's Gilbert and Sullivan. This could have His Honor's big chance. Why, he might go on to be governor, a job he really wanted, after all. Vun goot Cherman Governor deserves another - jawohl! He would show that uppity Kugel family who the real Germans were.

Vice Mayor Karl Kugel, scion of one Anaheim's oldest aristocratic families had other ideas. Convinced that His Honor was indeed off his rocker, he convened an emergency clandestine meeting of the twelve city council members to invoke the sanity clause, have the mayor declared incapacitated, and then have himself installed as the provisional mayor of Anaheim, pending special election. Of the pro-Von Prinkel group two members, Helmut Kohl Von Prinkel and Heinrich Himmler Von Prinkel were cousins of the mayor. The three others might cast the swing votes, but they saw this as a raw power grab and would not commit without a psychological evaluation. This would take time and likely require a court order, so the five could block the motion as it required a two-thirds vote.

Vice mayor Kugel got a bright idea and said, "Vy don't ve adchourn for luncheon at ze Siegfried Line und ve kome up mit compromise, ja!"

And adjourn they did, to the Siegfried Line Hofbrau House, Anaheim's first and foremost German Restaurant, just past the 57

Freeway at the intersection of Mickey Mouse Road and Kaiser Wilhelm Boulevard. When they got there they were unprepared for the spectacle that had assembled. A group of neo-Nazis and a few paleo-Nazis in gray World War II uniforms and armbands had commandeered the "Line" in the name of the "fatherland" and were holding their annual "putsch."

"Vat zeh devil are zey doink anyvay?" demanded Vice Mayor Kugel. "Zey vill be arrested!" It sort of resembled a scene from Rick's Café in *Casablanca.* All the Germans were singing, most were drunk. Some wore iron crosses and swastika armbands. Others sported *Prinz Friedrich Von Anhalt for Governor* buttons. Above a gigantic oaken fireplace glared the portrait of, guess who? Of course! April 20, Der Fuehrer's birthday! The big *scheisskopf,* not the little schnook in the city hall. What a blasted day the Anaheim City Council picked to go to a German restaurant, just when these old lunatics took over the place!

> "Lieb Vaterland lasst ruhig sein.
> Fest steht und treu die Wacht am Rhein,
> Fest steht und treu die Wacht, die Wacht am Rhein!
> Ein Hunderttausand Helder steht, die Wacht am Rhein!"

"More sauerbraten and more beer!" was the call.

"Vy don't you zing mit us? Vot kind of Chermans are you, anyvay?" der Kommandant leader demanded.

"Boss let's get out of here fast," advised one of the more civilized council members. "If the press finds out we attended this lunatic Hitler rally, we're screwed, blewed and tattooed. And probably impeached, too!"

"Ja, I dink zo doo," responded Kugel. "Und tell ze chauffeur to bring ze car around now."

"Jeez, we came here in the mayor's limousine, too. Of all things, a black Mercedes Benz. Now they'll think we're one of them! I know the owner and I can't understand why he would rent out his place to these dumb bastards!"

"But ve are all goot Republicans und ve vote for Arnold Schwarzenegger, ja?"

"That helps, a lot doesn't it?" was the councilman's sarcastic reply.

What the city hall conspirators did not know was that Herr Von Prinkel's Flying Circus had just taxied off the Pomona runway and were headed south to the Anaheim City Hall in migratory formation with the Red Baron leading the way. Kaiser Bill's *Batman* would have been proud! What further added to the comic effect was that the aircraft weapons contained no bullets but a lot of *guano*.

Under a secret agreement with Von Prinkel, Mayor Manicotti sub-leased the crop dusters for a piece of the action, to a colony of hippies camped out on outlying city property who were growing a little "weed" there. The dusters were armed with anti-insect spray to kill bugs, and the Fokker and Sopwith Camel flew with a load of *guano* to grow the marijuana, but Mayor Von Prinkel did not know all this. Only five minutes by air, they approached the city hall shortly after the council members had adjourned to the Siegfried Line. His Honor, in all his glory, was wearing his new double-breasted swastika gold-buttoned brown I.G. Farbe gabardine blazer. He goose-stepped across his California redwood-paneled office, carpet decorated in the colors of the German flag, and leaned out the window to bark orders as soon as he saw the formation coming to his "rescue."

"*Helder von dem vierten Reich* (Heroes of the Fourth Reich,)!" he bellowed. "Your mission today ist to exterminate ziss *untermensch* und save the Aryan people of Anaheim. Zhoot ziss terrorist down und I, your Fuehrer, vill personally decorate mit iron cross. Today Anaheim-tomorrow ze vorlt!"

Unfortunately, for the City Hall Fuehrer, Seps Schlikting, pilot of the lead plane, the Neo-Red Baron himself, fired his bazooka toward the climber but the canister hit the window ledge, grazing off the buff brick, striking der Fuehrer in the shoulder, knocking him back on his carpet, and totally covering Von Prinkel, his I.G. Farbe blazer, fifty thousand dollar carpet and ruining it all with a load of *Vogelscheiss*(guano). None hit poor Aram Tebakyan, the targeted terrorist untermensch. Mayor Von Prinkel dashed to the window shaking his fist at the lead plane and the *dummkopf* flying it. "Schweinhund!" he yelled. "You vill be court-martialed, zhot, und zent to zeh Russian front!"

Fortunately, the long-suffering huge Samoan security guard, Hutu Mahalotutu, probably the only sane person in the building, had the common sense to summon the city police and fire department to coax the Armenian crank down off the ledge by the back stairs. But the crank saw some cops through the open window, pushed the mayor aside and ran downstairs. At the first floor entrance, Mahalotutu, a former football defensive end at Brigham Young University hit Tebakian with a fierce flying tackle, hog-tied him with hand and foot cuffs, and notified Deputy Faggerty that this Asylum head case was no long under City jurisdiction. The city would only fine him for disturbing the peace and endangering public safety *after* his asylum application was approved or referred to the Immigration court. The crop dusters and the Sopwith Camel and Tri-wing Fokker quickly fled south of the border to an undesignated airfield near Puertocitos, Baja California where no one would ever find them and it was good that they did. Air Route Traffic Control and the Anaheim City Police were getting ready to call the Federal Aeronautics Administration, as the *Anaheimer Luftwaffe* had taken off without a flight plan.

The vice mayor and council members returned to the city complex and by voice vote, without opposition, immediately declared Mayor Von Prinkel nuts and issued a proclamation designating Karl Kugel, Mayor Pro Tempore of Anaheim. He was the eighty-third mayor which was just about one for every two years since the German-American pioneers founded the city in 1857. That's a lot of mayors; some went to jail, many went nuts, a few even deserted to the axis powers in both world wars, and a couple were impeached and later got jobs as tour guides at Disneyland regaling tourists with stories of how Walt Disney and other conspirators smeared their good name and bilked the city out of millions of acres of prime agricultural land. Needless to say, they did not keep their jobs as tour guides very long either. For his first order of business, Mayor Pro Tem Kugel ordered Anaheim's finest to go to the second floor and arrest the "former mayor" and send him to observation at the Anaheim City Behavioral Facility. Yet mysteriously, the former mayor had vanished.

His old buddy, Mayor Venezio Manicotti, had sent SWAT up the fire escape and spirited Von Prinkel away to an undisclosed location in Pomona. Manicotti issued a secret decree granting him "political asylum" and the undisclosed location was...you guessed it, the Pomona Palisades Rest and Recovery Spa. While there he regaled the other patients with stories of how he would solve the state's problems when he became governor. The FAA was not amused. They sent a fact-finding team to Mayor Manicotti's office to learn the meaning of the "unidentified flying objects" that had menaced the Anaheim City Hall annex.

When the team approached the mayor's office, Manicotti, a striking, stocky, barrel-chested, bald-headed man was rehearsing his speech on the balcony he had built at his Pomona City Hall office. Clearly, he did not want any feds snooping around his domain.

"Whatsmatta you?" the mayor demanded. "You guys see any UFO's in my hangar? So taka look. You guys see any crop dusters, or dose odder tings from the World War dey write about in duh papers? Dese are all rumors about me and my good friend Mayor Von Prinkel."

"Where is the former mayor? We would like to talk to him."

"How shoulda I know? I tink he went on a vacation somaplace in Alaska."

"Oh yeah! Where in Alaska?"

"Uppa US, thatsa where."

The FAA team returned to Washington, DC after their full-week junket at taxpayers' expense and falsified their reports to make it look like they labored mightily, but that due to the obstinacy and resistance of the local authorities, they were unable to bring forth even a mouse, much less a comic neo-Nazi.

Steve reported all this to Boss Robyn who agreed that it would indeed be the Anaheim story of the decade, if not the century, but that *The Times* would have to hold it awhile longer, at least, until Ouine made his big move out. They owed him that much.

The following Wednesday, Steve touched bases with Karl Keibalski. Enjoying a huge laugh over the events of the previous week, they boasted how none of the other six Asylum offices could top this for excitement. Since it was a Wednesday, the light day, they went next door to Kugel's Bar and Grill (yes the same Kugel), to swap jokes about Der Anaheimer Fuehrer. Actually, Karl wanted a chance to leave the office and swap gossip about the future of Los Angeles Asylum, as he saw it, of course.

They spent two hours hoisting brews, and laughing and swapping stories about America's early twenty-first century "diversity" culture, if you could call it a culture.

"As I see it, three things are going to happen soon. When Faggerty leaves, Falabenko moves up to deputy." Karl paused and glanced into his beer collecting his thoughts for his next words, "After Ouine goes to Singapore, Falabenko finally makes Director and promotes his good little flunky Max Van Rumpelsteen as the new deputy."

"So soon? I can't believe it. He just made soop a few months ago and had just barely completed his proby year as an officer!"

Karl held out his enormous paw as it to shake on a wager. "Bet on it. They've been grooming smarty-pants for the job from the time he checked in here."

"I only bet on things that interest me and Van Rumpelsteen doesn't, but I'll treat you to a pitcher if this plays out. Now how the devil is HQ going to circumvent the regulations?"

Karl took another long slurp of ale and snorted, "As though dodging the regs has ever been an issue for Longstreet. He'll find a way but it could happen like this; He shuts down the federal advertisement after one week, having accepted a sufficient number of applications. Actually there was only one under serious consideration, Falabenko, even though at least two other people in the office applied."

"Who were they?"

"Mike Magnesia and Regina Skankfield."

"You can't be serious? Who would hire those two buttheads?"

"Exactly. So no matter how many applied nationwide, Longstreet has the alibi that he chose the most qualified, and compared to those two losers that is surely true."

"Yes, but how would he rationalize the rejection of those who applied nationwide and who might be eminently qualified?"

"He keeps the process secretive. I can't quite get a handle on it, but my guess is that he has his clerks fudge the figures so it appears that most of the others applied too late, then he discloses ever so discreetly that it was Skankfield and Magnesia who had applied timely and were therefore under the closest scrutiny."

"How will he move Van Rumpelsteen up?"

"He'll wait until Ouine leaves for Singapore. That could take six months due to the clearances. By that time, Rumpy will have nine months as a first-line soop. And with his UCB Law and private practice credentials, Longstreet can easily claim he is the most qualified and jump him above the other applicants."

"This is hideous," Steve countered.

"No, this is just Asylum," Karl reminded him with a smirk.

Steve reviewed his questions and they decided to probe a little more about Faggerty. "Exactly what will he do in Arlington?"

"Faggerty will likely get his precious job at HQ but he will have to take a temporary demotion in exchange for his coveted lateral move. He'll be a supervisor at the Arlington regional office. As he could not successfully renegotiate our lease with Mayor Von Prinkel that put a damper on his selection to the national office, so no GS-14 National Deputy for him, just yet!"

"You mean, because he could not out-negotiate a crank like Willi Von Prinkel? I've heard he was taken to a rest home for observation and that Karl Kruger is the new mayor. Will the negations continue?"

"Kruger is the provisional mayor. After forty-five days he must revert to vice mayor if the mayor is capable of resuming his duties. And, I happen to know that he just got a clean bill of health from the rest home and will return to duties within two weeks."

Steve could not believe what he had just heard. "How the hell did you find this out?"

"I can't say, but trust me on this. Von Prinkel will be back on the job quicker than anyone expected, and he will be a hard-ass about the lease. And Falabenko, who has major health issues, is not in good enough shape to carry out lengthy negotiations. So it looks like we are going to move."

"Do you know where?"

"Not just yet. But Gehrhard Van Mietsukker is working on it and he's looking at commercial property about a mile from Disneyland on Kugel Street, an old whorehouse."

"You mean 'warehouse' don't you?"

"Back in the day, like the 1920s, there was active Ku Klux Klan in Anaheim, in addition to their paleo-Nazi party. The Klan brought in hookers from the deep South and named the ramshackle building

Savannah Inn. It was to service members only. You could say they made double use of their white sheets, ahahaha."

"Oh, yiich!"

"My sentiments entirely, but Anaheim has always had a bordello culture."

They finished their brews and returned to the office. Awaiting them on e-mail was terse correspondence from Sean Faggerty, telling them to report to his office immediately and that the matter was urgent.

When they entered his office, Faggerty did his usual sneer and directed his verbal attack first to Karl. "Do you and Steve know how long you took for lunch? Two hours!" he screeched, "that's how long! I saw you leave and return from my window. If you take two hours for lunch every day for one month, you will have stolen a paycheck from the government. Do you understand that? And you missed all the festivities."

The "festivities" were the second anniversary of the transfer and redesignation of the INS under the Department of Justice to the CIS under the Department of Homeland Security. It was no great cause for a celebration, but it gave Faggerty an excuse to expend extra funds for his own "farewell party," which just by coincidence occurred at almost the same date. So why not combine the two?

Steve deferred and Karl spoke first. "In all fairness to Steve, he was not aware of the significance of this anniversary, and he is a quiet fellow who is a bit nervous with festivities. So, the two-hour lunch was my idea and I take full responsibility. I'm sure I speak with Steve in our willingness to give up an hour's leave time as compensation."

Having been a union president, Karl was partly right in this, and aware of the flexibility of extra leave for personal issues or emergencies.

Karl went into a bald-faced lie that he was often able to do with a good poker face.

"His his daughter is having some academic difficulties during her first year at Stanford, so Steve wanted to ask for my advice since I also have a daughter in college. Is that okay?"

Faggerty responded grudgingly, "I will approve the leave, but you should have requested it before the fact."

Karl responded with solemn gratitude, "We appreciate this and we won't forget all you have done for Asylum."

Blouse your boots, it's getting deep as they say in the army, but one more bald-faced lie had just worked. After they left and walked the hallway to Karl's office, they joked about the ruse and wondered whether Faggerty would have a watch-window in his new Arlington office.

"Now, you *know* what a first-class prick he is!"

"That was quick thinking, Karl, but my daughter is still in her sophomore year at CSU Rio Linda Journalism School, and is doing quite well. But I guess Stanford sounds more impressive. I suppose it's the thought that counts."

Karl gave his infamous Keibalski grin. "Fuckin' A! And just for the record my daughter is in her senior year of high school but has just received an acceptance letter from Vassar, no less. I'm so proud of her."

"I hope she can be proud of you!"

"You think you're wise don't you?"

Chapter 10

ONE MILE FROM THE HAPPIEST PLACE ON EARTH IS SHAM-A- LOT

Just as Karl predicted, the Federal Register advertisement for the GS-14 Asylum Regional Office Deputy Director opened and closed within the week. Falabenko, Skankfield, and Magnesia made their case during a telephone conference with Lazarus Longstreet, but Falabenko, as expected got the promotion to Deputy Director. He moved into the deputy's office within two days and with three orders of business on his plate.

The first order of business would be to renegotiate the lease with the "restored" Mayor Von Prinkel. The docs gave Der Anaheimer Fuehrer a lot of downers so he proved to be more than a formidable negotiator. He had secured a new tenant and Asylum would have to move. The new tenant, Fabrizio Manicotti, the Pomona mayor's younger brother from Italy wanted the space to start a genuine Italian bistro at 1080 North Avalon. "Give duh corner property a little more class," as big brother would say.

The second order of business involved Hortensia. As an Asylum supervisor, her reporting official was the Deputy Director. As Izzy

Falabenko was her spouse, he cannot also be her reporting official. The Hatch Act and many other federal employee regulations prohibit this kind of nepotism. Even almighty Longstreet himself cannot break these regulations, but he can and would bend them all to hell to suit his purposes and ego-driven personality. It happened like this; Izzy would write her yearly efficiency reports and send them on to Longstreet via his private e-mail. Longstreet would "rubber stamp" with his electronic signature so they would enter records as his report. No one would know the wiser. Everything was cool - everyone was happy. Ah, the joys of Asylum hypocrisy!

The third order involved the time of Director Ouine's departure, and Max Van Rumpelsteen's promotion to deputy. But most important would be the final apotheosis of Isadore Finkelstone Falabenko to Los Angeles Asylum Director so Hortensia could become LA Asylum's first "lady." Don't let it be forgot, that at Anaheim was a spot, that for one brief shining moment, was known as Sham-A-Lot!"

The timing had to be perfect and the process airtight, so the American Federation of Government Employees could not sustain a grievance and have the federal courts overrule the promotions. It had to look as though every qualified applicant received due consideration and opportunity to advance instead of the pure humbuggery that it was.

Events continued to move with surprising swiftness. Instead of six months, Organization of Special Investigations cleared Pierre Ouine within six weeks, and his farewell party followed within the next week. A farewell party for an Asylum director is the one where the peasantry, i.e. the clerks and officers, the grunts who do the real work were only required to sign his farewell card and wish him well, as most did. The disgruntled aristocrats, that is, the first-line supervisors, were the ones hit up for the farewell dinner and they had better pay up. It was a quiet affair with much less hoopla than the grandstanding Faggerty demanded and got. Once Ouine left for Hong Kong, Longstreet made his stealth moves. Falabenko moved up to Director, bad ticker and all. Van Rumpelsteen got deputy - right on the money - just as Keibalski said. How was this done, you ask?

An unexplainable and unexpected (of course it was unexpected), power surge affected twenty percent of the computer files in Director Longstreet's office. A successful rumor was circulated that a virus, planted by a "cyberpirate," deleted sensitive and classified information and many CIS stations were "infected." Among the lost files were three applications from highly qualified supervisors and directors of the regional offices who wanted the job. When the "bugs" were located and exterminated, more than a month had passed, so it was impossible to consider those people after the fact, as Falabenko had already be assigned the slot.

Now that Van Rumpelsteen has progressed in quick succession from officer to supervisor to deputy director, he needed to find another nymphet for his lucky lunch cabal club so he quickly replaced Audrey Santorello with who else, but Rita Rincon. Better in the body department than the brain department, among the lunch clubbers, Rita would least likely make supervisor but she did have other assets.

Keibalski was partly right at least. The means of moving smarty-pants Maximillian up the promo ladder were right on the mark with the time requirement removed by "executive discretionary waiver," but the process Longstreet used to exclude all other applicants required more sophisticated and legerdemain. No matter, it worked. Steve owed Karl a pitcher!

Torquemada was now without part of his network, the one that secured employment based preferences for his club associates and service persons. Bureaucrat Falabenko was not likely approachable - too straight. No longer could Da Torque count on a Pierre Ouine, or even a Laura Schmelbalz, type to engineer I-130 petitions in his favor. His best bet appeared to be Helen Hu, little Ms. Sultry Speech and luscious libido herself. But she was not in the "pipeline" as Schmelbalz had been. No great matter for Da Torque as a little extortion always goes a long way!

Like Hortensia's Colombian "extended family," for whom I-130's were secured. Some were straight family members, other were distant relatives granted "employment" with Torquemada Enterprises. They received visas under mysterious circumstances. Although Colombia was "over-subscribed" for visas, Hortensia's family managed to secure their visas pronto.

With Ouine out of Asylum, the boss also had to find a means of protecting Steve's job. He consulted his morgue files and came up with this juicy little tidbit from the Wakeley era that immediately got promoted to the rolltop. The Torquemada, Ouine, Robyn axis might continue after the fact, even if Falabenko could not be entirely trusted.

Tomasa Toyamagua and Pupa Luz star at Party Dolls
5 for 1 Blackout Lap Dances Monday Nites

Remembering an old rumor about a Tomasa Toyamagua and the previous Asylum Director prior to Laura Schmelbalz, "Sloppy Joe" Michelson, Boss Robyn reached for his cell phone. He did not like it and rarely used it but this was a bit of an emergency, so he dialed Da Torque.

"Leilo, Old Buddy, what have you been up to these days?"

Leilo took the call at his cavernous office at the far end of the El Malecon, discreetly opposite the "sister" enterprise. "Ah, my old friend Rob Robyn! It is what I have been 'down to' that counts, doesn't it? What a coincidence that you should call, or perhaps not such a coincidence, now that our friend John Beauregard Ouine has gone to greener pastures, no?"

"That he has gone on to greener pastures, yes. Bt you and I have not, and that means we need to be pretty damn quick about protecting our interests from the power freaks running LA Asylum office now. Get my drift?"

"Yes, yes, of course. You need to protect Mr. Melkonian's undercover assignment and I need to document and protect my employees. One hand washes the other. I'm always willing to help my old friend from our days on the docks."

"What I need to know is what your dealings were, if any, with the previous Asylum Director, Joseph Michelson?"

"The one they called 'Sloppy Joe' whose desk was always a mess? But we shan't say the reason, now shall we? Giyahahaha. Why of course I do. Everyone remembers Sloppy Joe."

"Well, I have this little tidbit left over from when Wakeley ran this paper with your name, your establishment, and two of your employees mentioned in the article."

"Tell me who they were, so I can place them."

"Tomasa Toyamagua, and Pupa Luz."

"Oh yes, of course, Tomasa was Sloppy Joe's Filipina mistress when his wife Imelda wasn't in town. Did you know that Imelda Michelson is Director of the Riverside Auxiliary Office? You didn't know that did you? Also a very good friend of Regina Skankfield. Actually, she promoted Regina to supervisor despite her innate incompetence."

"How's that?"

"Why, it is very simple actually. Imelda Michelson stole her Sloppy Joe away from Regina and her conscience bothered her, so Imelda promoted her to supervisor as a consolation prize, that's all."

"Some consolation prize - losing Sloppy Joe to Imelda. It seems Regina won big for a loser!"

Actually, Robyn did not know this bit of Asylum scuttlebutt, either. He was vaguely aware of who Joseph Michelson was, and that there was an Imelda Michelson who ran the Riverside annex office, but he either did not make the connection or did not consider it newsworthy. Now it might be... it just might be! Robyn must now probe this without revealing what a big scoop Leilo had just given him.

"All right, so how did Tomasa end up at your joint?"

"Imelda learned about the relationship between Sloppy Joe and Tomasa. All you had to do was walk into the Director's office and notice stacks of new and, pardon me, used 'devices' and lingerie strewn about to know that something was up, no pun intended. Imelda, being a hot Filipina herself, was going to expose him, no pun intended, if he didn't clean up his act and fire Tomasa, and come home early at night. Two out of three are not bad, no?"

"Leilo, just where the devil are you going with this?"

"You see, our beloved Sloppy Joe could not give up his sweet little caramel doll. So, he took care of the I-130 and I hired her as one of my dancers with her schedule subject his discreet 'visits' to Party Dolls VIP Lounge, you see."

"So Michelson was doing your I-130's even before Ouine got in on the action?"

"El Senor Ouine as deputy, covered for Michelson, by keeping OSI off his ass, no easy job, let me tell you."

"Speaking about deputies, how can I keep Steve doing undercover at Asylum? I don't see Izzy Falabenko as sympathetic and he may call in the federal prosecutors on this, don't you agree?"

"Ah, my good friend Boss Robyn from South Boston, so straight-up in dealing with people, no?" the Torque said cheerily.

"I don't follow," the Boss replied suspiciously.

"Perhaps you did not know that Pupa Luz was also the first cousin of Hortensia Luz-Falabenko, did you?" Again, the Mephistophelian laugh, "Giahahaha."

"Great Caesar's ghost! Do you mean to say that Izzy and his old lady are in on this too? I don't believe it! I can't believe it!" he exclaimed, evoking the ghost of Perry White in addition to that of Julius Caesar.

Leilo chuckled, "I would not call her 'old' or say 'in on this.' Rather they sought out the advice and good counsel of Jean Pierre Beauregard Ouine in securing documentation for Hortensia's extended family which also included Little Pupa and she is still in our employ as is Tomasa. Full time I might add, giahahaha!"

"Leilo, are you implying that Pierre secured documents for *additional* relatives of Hortensia?"

"Oh, yes, quite a number."

"Well, if what you say is true, Izzy Falabenko and his Hortensia are in this shit as deep as any of us, even though they pretend to be holier than thou."

"Ah, my good friend Roberto, what a way you have with words, and always the cynical newspaperman!"

"Holy mother of God!"

"Yes, indeed, my sentiments entirely. And just for you my good friend, I shall reserve two free tickets to tonight's show. Tomasa Toyamagua and Pupa Luz are dancing, you know! And, as a bonus, I will add to it the use of the VIP Lounge, especially since we go back a long way. I guarantee a heavenly time, giyahahhh."

He was needling his friend, of course. He knew Rob did not go for that kind of entertainment, but Rob could not contain a discreet chuckle at Leilo's shameless shenanigans. If Leilo were not the Devil incarnate, he certainly gave Ol' Lucifer a run for his money!

"Leilo, if I take you up on your heavenly offer, I'll be lucky to make purgatory, you know that. But thanks just the same."

"Just call on me if you need anything else."

"I would never hesitate, so long and thanks."

Thanks, was an understatement. It was more like game, set, and match point. With Falabenko neutralized, Steve could have the run of LA Asylum to do more features, Leilo would have a fresh supply of I-130's if needed, and even OSI might back off for a time.

The boss might just bring back *The Riverside Times and Review* as morning and evening dailies, just like in the halcyon days of the press.

Now however, there was more mundane business at hand. Falabenko assigned surly, somewhat-demented Gehrhard Van Mietsukker to oversee the move now that the Faggerty/Von Prinkel negotiations had broken down for good, and Los Angeles Asylum would have to move from 1080 North Avalon Drive. Mietsukker selected the "warehouse property" at 101 West Kugel Street, about two city blocks from Disneyland. He employed an assortment of contracted undocumented alien laborers through the underground networks and thus kept any worker complaints a non-issue and the union movers out of the action. Now, the ex-warehouse, one mile from Disneyland, would become, to paraphrase Walt Disney, "the Unhappiest Place on Earth."

After one month of reconfiguring the warehouse with the usual banging, sawing, mortaring, and de-rodenting (four-legged), the new office was ready for the move, but more importantly it was ready to receive the official visit, the Papal Blessing, and the Consecration of the Great Him from HQ.

Lazarus Longstreet, Esq, BS and JD (from Hahvaahd, of course), would dedicate the new LA office in person, not by video camera in the manner that he often did at his Potemkin site visits.

To Asylum corporate embarrassment, management did not anticipate that Bertha De Baggerey, AFGE union steward and pest-at-large, would rain big time on their orchestrated feel good parade. De Baggerey, tried her best to promote LA Asylum's reputation as *l'enfant terrible* of the seven offices, but succeeded only at making a fool of herself. Big Bertha, the happy, plump, and frumpy AFGE local president, i.e. the office "union mama," who even wore union underwear, liked to grandstand at all-hands meetings" and believed she had real power.

Although she didn't like her job as an Asylum officer, and tried her best to circumvent her duties with the union activities permitted by law, like many employees in decline, she stayed because she needed the money.

It would have been better for her to wear standard business attire, give a short welcoming speech like the rest of the office leadership, and save the employee/management issues for a private meeting with Longstreet later in the day. But she chose instead, to confront the Great Him, not a good move.

The Asylum headquarters directorship basked pompously in its authority - its basic leadership style was cheap. It had no sense of genuine *noblesse oblige*. Rather than any concern for the rights and welfare of the oppressed in other lands, a love of bureaucratic power drove the national director, deputy director, district directors, and their immediate subordinates. Employees, especially the interviewing officers, ranked behind the claimants, and even the senior clerks. Thus, the national system had become a national sham, but if nothing else Bertha loved delusion.

Izzy and Hortensia were out of town at a New Age Encounter seminar somewhere in the back woods of Mendecino by the Sea, getting juiced up for their next power play, or so they hoped. It fell on Max Van Rumpelsteen to introduce The Great One. Lazarus Longstreet was about as communicative as a turtle, but a master manipulator need not say very much. Van Rumpelsteen rocked on for ten minutes blabbering about how honored and pleasured he was to be a local deputy director and praising the Great Him for his contributions to international human rights. Van Rumpelsteen was more accustomed to the Audrey Santarello sort of pleasuring, but bureaucratic empowerment evoked its own eroticism. Mietsukker officially welcomed the national director to the new LA Asylum office with his usual prose, obtuse and monosyllabic, then turned the mic over to the Great Him for ever-increasing ennui.

Containing his remarks to Mietsukker's good choice of a location and building contractors, Longstreet spoke only five minutes reiterating his numerical goals for Asylum case adjudications with his digital graphic pointer and beloved pie charts. He talked low, slow and did not say much; he never did. Then he called for employee concerns and questions. Bertha De Baggery immediately leaps to her feet - all 220 pounds of her, rudely cut off those who had patiently raised their hands, and proceeded to gusty oration of her ten-point grievance list. O.H. Hinkel, fresh from the Pomona Palisades had warned Longstreet ahead of time that she would cause trouble but he thought Herr Direktor could handle it, so Longstreet put on his best condescending face.

Bertha was a bit of a comic sight, for certain. Wearing a well-worn 1940's vintage print granny dress and Bella Abzug style flowered hat, her workman's boots covered the bottoms of her union suit and thus completed the dreadful ensemble. As soon as Bertha stood, she un-crumpled her grievance list and began to fire rapid Gatling Gun statements at El Supremo, who was already rolling his eyes. He could not quite believing his lucky stars that she would make such a jenny-ass of herself in front of her co-workers.

"Mr. Longstreet, even though we welcome you to our new Los Angeles Asylum Office, understand that you haven't been very nice to us," she scolded, shaking a finger. "So we, the members of AFGE Local 6909 come to grieve and demand great improvement in the working conditions of the Los Angeles Asylum office personnel."

"First and foremost, since we became part of Homeland Security you have not given us a new contract that protects us from your unfair treatment."

That should convince him to return to the bargaining table, shouldn't it?

"Second, we have too much work to do. Sixteen interviews per week has us all frazzled, you know. And that gives us only four hours to work each case."

Good luck here, sister, as though employee workload complaints are a novelty! In addition, when Longstreet had the job of Asylum officer, he finished a case on the average of every two hours and a half, so don't expect much sympathy on this point.

"Third, we only have half an hour to eat lunch, and we have to give up our morning and afternoon breaks to complete our workload, and that just is not right."

There she goes with the finger again, as though malnutrition were an issue for her!

"Fourth, we officers who have years of seniority, should be promoted to supervisor first, and this just isn't happening. Can you explain why?"

Like, could this be a competence issue or one of style, or perhaps even both; do you think, do you think?

Ozzie wasn't exactly fidgeting but his usual poker face betrayed an uncharacteristically worried expression. The union mama's whole countenance and demeanor was decidedly unprofessional, un-Asylum, and worse still "uncool."

"Fifth, it is about time this job is upgraded to GS-13, especially for us senior officers who have given so much of ourselves to this office."

Yeah, sister, you have given *so* much of yourself to this office that you're about to shrivel up and blow away, aren't you?

"Sixth, we get too much abuse from the immigration lawyers and this shouldn't be. Do something!" she screeched.

Bertha would not finish her magnus opus. O. H. Hinkel, who could take no more of the fat lady's one woman circus, stood and cut her off abruptly. "Ms. De Baggery, you had better sit down before you flip out and do something in your ever-expanding union suit. Otherwise I shall be impelled to summon the paramedics. "

Hinkel then pronounced a high mass of Asylum dull liturgy and boilerplate. "I would remind you that the Asylum officer controls the interview process," he intoned with received catechism. "In addition, we have established procedures to address attorney misconduct. Moreover, during last week's meeting with Mr. Falabenko, you and the other AFGE local officials agreed to address grievances at a separate meeting just for this purpose. Let the other officers present have a chance to raise their concerns to the Director."

Flustered that Hinkel learned about her sartorial eccentricities, Big Bertha fumed and stomped her boots with sunflower shaking madly on her silly hat crown.

"You haven't heard the end of this! Mr. Oswald Harvey-pooh, I am going to write the AFGE national president. He has friends in high plac-es - you'll see!"

"It is Mr. Hinkel not Mr. Oswald or Mr. Harvey," he glared as he spoke, not quite at the level of a relapse but almost.

"Wait! I'm not finished."

"Yes you are, Ms. De Baggery. Sit down now!"

Sitting in the back row of seats in the auditorium, Karl Keibalski sneered madly, as always. Steve Melkonian wrote madly, as always.

Karl elbowed him lightly in the ribs. "I hope you got all that. It's not every day the union big mama gets a smack down but I'm not surprised. Congress has allowed government management to rig all the rules to keep us from ever having a real union, like the one I tried to get for Eduardo and poor Penrod. You know I believe in two tenets."

"Oh," already expecting a punch line, Steve was ready with a sardonic response. "And they might be?"

"Tenet one: There is not justice. Tenet two: The world is run by assholes."

"And if we just let Karl Keibalski run the world, what a beautiful place it would be, right?"

"Fuckin' A!"

Chapter 11

THE TATTOOED LADY AND I – INSIDE THE ANTI-FRAUD UNIT

O swald Harvey Hinkel needed a moral victory big time. Smacking down the union mama was not big league, or even Triple-A bush league, but his rescue impressed Longstreet and that was everything that mattered. Hinkel had become burnt-out as a supervisor and tired of his job. He needed and wanted a break, and his actions at the Longstreet visit would provide one for him.

With the increase in case volume following the relaxation of Asylum standards, claimant fraud had become an ever-increasing problem, hence the need arose to create a special unit that handled fraudulent claims exclusively. The anti-fraud officer and his assistant held GS-14 and 13 slots respectively, so Hinkel applied for, and received the top spot, and the promotion that came with it. It turned out to be a good move, the new fraud officer job would become a cushy one with high pay and little work. It was much better than having to report to a petty little tyrant like Max Van Rumpelsteen.

Hinkel, an extremely self-contained individual did not socialize. And few, if any knew much about his personal life. Best known as "the supervisor who fired O. Don Barfield," pluperfect company man, twenty-five year government bureaucrat, but an average networker, he nonetheless had an instinct for being at the right place at the right time.

As little was known about his personal life, Steve, acting on the sly, touched bases with the "source who would always be with him, Karl Kirel Keibalski. Like, who else?

After he finished his casework for the day, Steve moseyed on down to Karl's office to get a little input, like, "What do you know about Oswald H. Hinkel and when did you know it?"

"Well Steve, I guess I know as much about Ozzie as anybody in this office, which isn't a hell of a lot. Same as with Penrod, may he rest in peace. Now, you *know* he's not exactly Mr. Personality Plus, so it's hard to get to know him. But I'll tell you what I know from the three years I've been assigned here plus a detail in Moscow."

Now Steve's interest was piqued. Moscow? Who would have known? Oz never said very much about his past; recent or distant.

"Moscow? You mentioned that a couple times previously. So he was there too?"

Karl smiled thinly at the question. "In the physical sense of the word, yes. That is, he went through the mechanistic motions of refugee interviews, but emotionally and mentally he withdrew into himself, more so than he usually did."

"How so?"

"We were there during the Russian winter and had a wonderful time."

"A wonderful time?" Steve countered facetiously., "In the middle of the Russian winter? How is it that you succeeded where Napoleon and the German Wehrmacht failed?"

"You know me, I have a way with women, especially Russian women. I speak the language, you know."

"Oh, I get it, it was a matter of the boudoir. The taxpayers funded your Club Med a la Winter Slav excursion. Now, there's a scoop. Can't wait to file this one with the boss. But how does Oswald Hinkel fit into this wonderful time frame?"

"Glad you asked that question. You see, there are two things you can do during the Moscow winter. You can sit alone in your hotel room and brood, or you can go out and party. Guess which one he did? You know which one I did!"

"Maybe he just preferred it that way."

"Well, yeah, I guess he did. I mean, like, there was a group of ten of us doing refugee processing and we invited him to go with us bar-hopping but he just didn't seem interested. He said it was too cold, which it was at forty below. But Stoli is always good for that and I drank my share. That and the big-breasted Russian women, my favorite."

Steve winced as it seemed that Keibalski could think of nothing else but 'hiding the Kielbasa," i.e. Russian slang for sexual intercourse.

"How long were you there?"

"Six weeks, the usual refugee detail. And except to go to the UN compound where we did the interviews and return to his hotel room,

Oz never went anywhere else. Not even sightseeing or shopping which most of us do."

"What about his family life? Maybe he is a *loyal* husband?"

Steve meant loyal as a dig, but it didn't rattle Keibalski in the slightest with his usual crocodile skin about his peccadilloes.

"Nah, he no longer has a wife. He *was* married years ago and has a couple teenage offspring, but Mrs. Hinkel wigged out years ago and he divorced her."

"Wigged out? Do you mean she had mental problems? Might Oz have been the cause of them?"

"Exactly, you catch on quick," Karl exclaimed with a trifle of condescension. "Afterwards, he tried dating a couple of female soops in the office but couldn't make a go of it. The affairs didn't last." Keibalski leaned over his desk and put his hand to his mouth as if to whisper, "Steve, be careful who you tell this to, but Oswald Harvey Hinkel is staunchly impotent."

Steve could not get Keibalski's drift on "staunch impotence" but let it pass to obtain relevant details. "And your source is?"

Karl countered with his all-knowing arrogance, "His ex-wife and two supervisor girlfriends here tipped me off. That's why he can't keep any woman for very long."

"How is it that you became acquainted with them to the point that they would take you into such confidence and share such details?"

"Two out of three ain't bad I always say. And that's how I know."

"So, which two were they?"

"Believe it or not, one was the ex-wife. She used to come in here now and then to shoot the bull. The other was Lucia Sanchez, a former supervisor here, now in Guatemala. He dated her about two months and failed to get it up even once, so she gave up on him and put in for Latin America. She's been running US Immigration in Guatemala. A 'permanent temporary detail' for seven years with all that extra pay." Shaking his head in disgust, Karl mumbled with more than a trace of bitterness, "They even maintain an office for her here in case she wants to come back. Must be nice to be an 'oppressed minority female' and get those perks!"

Steve took Keibalski's sarcasm for the envy it was, but pressed on to find more details, objective reporter that he was. "So how do you fit into all of this? Like, I'm surprised they tell you these things, unless it's hearsay."

"You know me, I've never had a problem talking to women. A lot of guys do."

"I already know about your legendary super self-confidence, but when, where, and why would they reveal the details of such an intimate relationship? You did say that the ex-Mrs. Hinkel would come in and shoot the bull."

At this point Keibalski had to back off a bit, or at least come clean about what he genuinely knew.

"I didn't say she came in and talked to me. She said these things to a few of the female officers here who were her close friends, and they just repeated them to me, and that's all. But Lucia Sanchez was different," he quickly added, gaining some leverage and credibility.

"Every afternoon for two months!" Karl exclaimed pounding the desk for emphasis, "she came to my office giving me a play by play description of her love life with Ozzie, or the lack of it rather. Actually, Lucia wasn't too bad looking and she *was* dropping a few hits in my direction, but my wife was just back from one of her Euro-spending-sprees and when she found out about it, she began watching me like a spy."

Across town at the very moment that Steve and Karl were speaking, Oswald H. Hinkel was trying to "earn his bones" or rather re-earn them, as surely as Keibalski had done his best to take them away.

He travelled to Rolling Hills, fully armed with Yashica camera and tripod in hand to do a little reconnaissance and take photos of O. Don Barfield's "remodeled" immigration service office. Its poster size Chinese character-covered signs offered guaranteed successful processing of claims for asylum, permanent residence, or citizenship, for a small fee, that would develop into a big fee, of course. Falabenko knew Attorney General Feather Lockliar well enough to cooperate on her effort to bust Da Barf and put him away big time - not just disbarment. This time it would be the Johnny Cash Room at Folsom Prison.

Asylum's wizard, Oz, parked his Volvo SB 80 about a half-block away, notified police on his cell phone that there might be a confrontation, and then cased the building for best shots. He set up his tripod and began to shoot. He moved, circled, and got all angles, so that every Chinese sign or placard was included. He intended to consult with bilingual Chinese-speaking bar counselors to determine whether Barfield might be violating his suspension from law practice. After fifteen minutes, there was a small confrontation, but one big enough for him to use as office leverage. Huang Ba Duh, younger brother of Huang Ba Don, dashed outside the O-Don Building and charged at poor Ozzie. Larger than most Chinese men at six feet tall, and slightly obese, he tried but failed to win by intimidation.

"I demand that you immediately cease and desist this invasion of privacy and trespassing on private property." He tried a Genghis Khan snarl but it did not work.

Ozzie to his credit drew up to his six-foot-three height, ignored the threats of Barfy's Chinese flunky, and just kept on shooting. He was, after all, on public, not private property and could take photos of any surroundings. Frustrated, Ba Duh stomped back inside. As Barfield had once been an Asylum officer, he was being watched by old his boss plus Lockliar and her minions, but Ba Duh did not know this.

Ozzie returned with his five hundred-plus photos to a hero's welcome and a commendation from Falabenko for "valor above and beyond the call of duty." Sergeant York would have been proud, too. More than a commendation and kudos, he was given the selection of an assistant for the newly created anti-fraud unit. No problem there - it would be Rita Redonda Rincon. Falabenko winced, but he *did* promise and he would not go back on his word. Rumpelsteen fumed. Now he would have to recruit yet another lunch-clubber with the requisite "potential."

A celebratory bash was held at the Village Inn Booze, Bump and Grind Beer Burger Parlor (VIBB&GBBP) on East Katella, a much happier place two miles east of Disneyland. All his team members were there. Ozzie and the recently upgraded Rita Rincon, looked up adoringly at Ozzie, not yet aware of his delicate condition, but she might soon find out. Never mind the booze, bring on the Viagra instead! There were her close friends too, i.e. Officers Lupita Lopez, Hector Peron, Malcolm Muddleston, Ozzie's nondescript go-fer, the ever diligent Documents Director Bich Hoar (pronounced bik-ho)Tang, loyal and tryst-worthy (as all the male clerks have trysted with her) Vietnam chick from the clerical unit, and the ever ubiquitous Karl Keibalski, always ready to regale with All-America tales from OSU. New to the office was a rousing, burley Irish-American who might just upstage him, a transferee from the

Chicago office and University of Notre Dame Law College graduate, Sean Patrick McSlade, a charming Irish bruiser if there ever was one, and a one-time All-America football player to boot!

Speaking of boots, Oz still has his camera equipment in the boot of his Volvo. Tonight it would come in especially handy as the burly boys from the steel mills had to do the heavy metal lifting. "Easy on the equipment, you guys. It's very expensive, you know. Why can't people take care of things the way I do?"

So the big blokes set everything up, put the Village Inn tables together and got ready for a big evening of merriment. Keibalski ordered his usual four pitchers of Bud for a start, and McSlade called him and raised him one, making his five, but chose Guinness instead. Steve did his usual mojito, Lupita and Hector liked their margaritas with a Cadillac, a mai-tai for Bich Hoar, Ozzie always proper with his Shirley Temple, and Malcolm would have whatever Ozzie was having. Rita, not surprisingly, ordered "sex-on-the beach," one of her many places for it. The server delivered the drinks.

Having set up equipment for photos of the "winners circle," the two "other victors," kindred spirits Keibalski and McSlade, did not take long to upstage everyone else at the BBP. Swapping stories of their gridiron glory days and all the legends they knew, you might have thought their playing days went clear back to the Four Horsemen at the 1925 Rose Bowl, at least they made it seem this way.

Oz was becoming peeved and it showed. Fancying himself a classical scholar, Renaissance man, and under-appreciated bon vivant living on a pittance of a federal salary, he came off as a comic "poor man's" William Buckley. His colleagues mocked him accordingly given his penchant for flicking his tongue, lifting his nose in the air as he spoke, and especially for his habitual verbal masturbation. Who *were* these barbarians, after all, to rain on *his* parade? Oh but it would soon get worse, much worse. For Rita, the epitomic party girl could never, ever, hold her liquor. One drink was all it took and her sunburst smile would light on her "catch" for the night. Tonight it happened be the original Irish Rover himself, Sean Patrick McSlade, or so she hoped.

Rita had recently acquired a new tattoo. In addition to "artwork" on both breasts, and a little purple, gold, and black butterfly soaring joyously above her anal orifice, she had now acquired a new one; this one on her right butt cheek approximately two feet below her right breast, the way the crow flies. A striking scarlet and navy likeness of Saint Elmo, patron saint of all the sailors. She was so proud of it, for after all, Rita loved all the sailors!

So proud that after five cocktails, many pitchers for Steve and Karl, and Ozzie's fifth (tsk, tsk) Shirley Temple, Rita dropped trou and exposed her new tattoo to the delectation of one and all present, including those not party to the Asylum party!

"Hoot, hoot, hoot, eat your heart out Hooters, your chicks can't drop trou, nyah nyah nyah nyah nyah!" The rousing cheer from the total BBP patrons now having out hooted Hooters, Karl took photos, Steve took notes, Hinkel took a hike, and Sean took Rita - later that evening, of course.

After four hours of Asylum-style revelry, the party broke up in the parking lot with Rita hanging on to Sean as he fumbled for the keys to his maroon late model Mercury. Karl had some freebee coupons for the real Hooters, so he nodded to Steve to adjourn there for a few more deep throatisms.

Hector invited the others to his new two-story condo with a two-hundred-square foot balcony off the master bedroom, where later that evening he would bed Lupita and Bich in a ménage a trois after Lupita's tipsy but stirring balconic denunciation of the US Asylum and the unfairness of her "non-selection" as supervisor to any who cared to listen. Welcome to Casa Rosada north!

Actually, the fun and games had begun the previous Monday morning when Hortensia discovered Sean's hand up Rita's mini as she walked into her office to discuss a case. "I am shocked to see such unprofessional conduct on the part of my team members. This is beyond unprofessional and the Director will hear about this." And so, virtuous Supervisor Hortensia Luz Martinez de Falabenko wrote the incident up as a critique of Rita's scandalous deportment and suggestive apparel in a report to hubby, Director Isadore. For shame, Rita for shame!

In any case, the Asylum banqueters were all lucky not to be cited for disturbing the peace. So as Hector's party broke up around 2:00 a. m. Ozzie Hinkel was seen sobbing on the hood of his 1990ish boxy marine-blue SB 80 Volvo with Malcolm Muddleston trying to console him by citing his mentor's unique contributions to the anti-fraud unit. So lie a little, already!

"This isn't right! It just isn't right! She should have been mine. She should have been mine!"

Sorry Ozzie, but in a match between the Lord Jeffs and Fighting Irish, Amherst College is just no match for Notre Dame!

Chapter 12

EVERYBODY LOVE S A DRUNKEN IRISHMAN

Come all ye rogue rousers
And hear my tirade
Of our bold Irish bruiser Sean Patrick McSlade
He drank up the barrels of Six Seal Beach Pubs
No bloke was his equal at slurping the suds!

He hadn't been there even a month, but already he was adjusting nicely and making good friends, as he had always done. A weekend earlier, he located Seal Beach, the quaint Irish-American village just inside the Orange County line and enjoyed his second weekend of mellow folk music - his favorite kind. Tonight was special, though. They were playing all his favorites: *Patriot Game, Whiskey in the Jar,* and the haunting *Suzanne,* so the new transfer, Sean Patrick McSlade, would soon make his mark and his bones in a manner that was as surprising as it was surreal, for no one expected that he would take a passion to politics.

Sean hailed from Chicago, that most political of all US cities. Sean senior, had been a labor leader, Democratic Party official, sometime national convention delegate, and unsuccessful candidate for Congress. Sean junior thought his father's way of upward mobility was old-fashioned, and felt that entering a respected profession was a more effective path to dignity and respect. At his favorite pub, Sean would listen to all his favorite Irish folk ballads and the voice of the haunting, lilting tenor Brendon Shamus Egan who had memorized all of them. It was Sean's way of chilling out after a day's work at Asylum and all the backbiting that usually went with it. He would sit for hours stroking a twenty-three ounce black and tan, perhaps brooding a bit with the melancholy of all true Irish - the longing for Auld Sod.

He especially loved *Suzanne,* a mellow 60ish chanson about Suzanne Verdal, a Quebecoise free spirit who welcomed all artists and musicians to her pad beside the St. Lawrence River. Some musicians read more into it than was there, comparing the spiritual quality of a drug high to an epiphany of straight religion. Those more familiar with the area knew the Cathedral contained the crucified image of Jesus guarding the fate of the passing sailors. *Susanne Takes You Down to that Place Beside the Harbor. You Can See the Boats Go by You Can Sit and Watch Forever....* Suzanne as sung by folksinger Leonard Cohen in1966, and sometimes Judy Collins, was not of Sean's era, but it did not matter to him as he listened to what he liked above all.

Perhaps Sean reflected on the remarkable prestige he and his family had acquired as second generation Irish-Americans. While he stroked his half and half (Guinness Stout blended with Harp or Bass Ale), the local beach babes flocked to stroke him. He was an over six-foot-tall raven-haired Celtic hunk, but when he went into one of these "moods," he sulked at the thought of still more pussy. Instead, he would abruptly excuse himself and leave his table to take a shuffle through the bracing Seal Beach evening chill toward the anglers pier and Ruby's burger joint at the very end of the wharf. Sean loved to gaze into the surf that smashed into the pier, waves crashing into the pylons, but never knocking the pier over as had happened in Ventura years earlier. Now and then, he would stop briefly to talk with the Latino fisherman using his limited Spanish. He loved the way they cursed their fate and fortune when one of them hooked a stingray instead of a marlin. Most of the wharf walkers saw him as a brawny young man with striking features but a somber demeanor, as though he was one who had not quite thought through his mission in life and it bothered him that he had not.

This all changed when the popular local folk singer, balladeer, and lyrical bartender made a short vacation to Galway to attend a family christening. Loved by all patrons for his classic Celtic style, and now married to a local beach chick, he had a six-week-old son, and so a genuine American family. All would have gone well for him had he not taken that short vacation back to Galway to attend his nephew's christening.

For Brendon Shamus Egan, balladeer, crooner, and folk singer was also Edwin Shamus Egan, accused IRA terrorist and assassin. He gunned down two British army officers near Londonderry in 1982, then disappeared off the charts as far as British Intelligence or Scotland Yard could determine. He emigrated to the United States and went as far into the continental US as he could. Go any further than Seal Beach and you're in the ocean.

During the summer of 1982 he bummed about the beach towns, strumming his twelve-string from Mendecino to Otay Mesa. He found Seal Beach much to his liking for its many Irish pubs plus the third generation Irish girls. After many years of crooning and charming, he married one and became sufficiently confident to believe his troubled past had disappeared behind him; at least enough to risk a trip home. It was a bad choice.

He came up on an Interpol hit and Customs and Immigration sent him to San Pedro Detention Center awaiting extradition to the British authorities in Northern Ireland. The local papers carried the story in the evening editions of course, but more important all seven INS offices had been briefed a priori so Sean knew about it already. At the nearby Mimi's Café, where he and Karl and Steve grabbed a quick lunch that day (every INS lunch is a quick one, if you get to eat at all), Karl hinted that he had heard about a fund drive his friends planned to hold at the local pubs to post bail for the celebrated balladeer. Sean stared into his wine glass, looked up at him, and nonchalantly announced, "I'm way ahead of you on this one and this weekend many of Ed's friends are holding a rally for this same purpose."

"Are you sure you want to be there? You *are* an Asylum officer after all, and as straight as Hinkel is, he might not be favorable to your getting involved in a sensitive issue, especially one that involves a terrorist. You *do* need his recommendation for that fraud officer job in Chi-town you put in for!

"Be there? Who the devil do you think organized it all? And I did more than just talk about it. I put up thirty grand of my own money against five g's from each of the Seal Beach pubs. I bet them all that I could drink up their beer barrels in one night. When I win, they have to post Ed's bail. And don't call him a terrorist. He is a patriot! And one more thing. I don't need Buttlick Hinkel's recommendation."

He grabbed a letter from his shirt pocket and slapped it down on the countertop so Karl and Steve could see it. "This is official. I already landed the anti-fraud job in Chicago. I leave in three weeks."

Yes, me, poor unfortunate mentor, in just three weeks after he blew into town and one week after he out-foxed Ozzie for the heart, body, and mind (if she has a mind) of Rita Rincon, Sean P. McSlade would indeed become a local icon with the North OC beach-bar crowd.

O'Malley's Dark Guinness
No match for McSlade
With a good Bushmills chaser
To start the parade
And two hundred proud Finnians cheering him on
We'll make bail for our patriot
Fore the evenin's half-gone!

So, on to Ned Kelley's
Bass Ale to be tried
His legend spilled onward
O' the half and half pride
Swell headed surf bums who dared take him on
Were under the table by quarter to one!

Now Seal Beach pub owners all had to pay
And cough up five grand for the bold IRA
So list' to my ballad for it sure can be told
Of our good Irish patriot so drunk and so bold.
So he left for good Chi Town
Thumb at nose all the way
Cause he out-chugged Orange County
One evening in May.

For Sean Patrick McSlade, the luck and pluck of the Irish had once again prevailed. He got the anti-fraud officer job he had always wanted in his beloved Chi-town. OC, after all, was not his style, but the pub owners were left pissed off and pissing. Yep, a few of them dared joined the contest. Oh, has dear reader been wondering about McSlade's conflict of interest? Of course you have. So how are ethical issues a big deal for an Irishman, anyway? Can you say Kennedy, Curley, and Pendergast?

Two weeks later a Hague tribunal ruled on the case of Edwin S. Egan and held that he fell under the amnesty provisions of the agreement signed by British and Irish Catholic diplomats that included representatives from Northern Ireland and some IRA forces. They negotiated a treaty that would protect the religious rights of all persuasions. Signatories were the prime ministers of Great Britain and the Republic of Ireland. It would become the British prime minister's last hurrah before a well-deserved good retirement. The curious provision included an amnesty for freedom fighters accused, but not convicted, of crimes that included political assassinations. So, Customs and Immigration at San Pedro released Edwin S. Egan, now protected under this blanket amendment, and he left for Ireland with the thirty grand tucked away in his luggage.

Peace in Northern Ireland! And peace or perhaps we should say, piece to our Irish Rover, Sean Patrick McSlade. Yep, he did it. He impregnated Rita Rincon just before he left for the Loop. Rita got another papaless baby. And as for Sean, well, you could say that he got off before he went on and that wasn't very nice of him. Before he left, however, the Los Angeles Asylum Office would suffer one more indignity at Sean's hands, and Keibalski quickly cell-phoned Steve about the bizarre incident and its fallout.

Senior Asylum clerk Elvis Presley Snyder, the sometime drinking buddy of Sean, Steve, and Karl Keibalski (who else, after all), and distant cousin of the "King," needed a vintage clunker to attend a Marine Corps reunion of those few, proud, and brave veterans of Pork Chop Hill, Chosun Reservoir, and the Tet. For some, it would be their last hurrah and Elvis wanted to do it right. What else then, but Sean P. McSlade's fully restored 1955 deep-maroon Mercury convertible with white wall tires! Fully restored, except for the brake shoes, for which Sean was saving his next paycheck to bring it up to speed, and to which he duly warned Elvis not to push it beyond 50.

Good American that he was, Sean, could not say no to this fightin' Marine's last chance to hot dog a bit at the Camp Pendleton NCO Club reunion. Eat your heart out Clint Eastwood; who needs your Gran Torino? With the help of a good whalebone corset, and a few belts of Jack Daniels, Master Sergeant Snyder stuffed his corpulence into his old dress blues and headed down the PCH to his reunion in the freshly-polished maroon convertible, chrome and white walls gleaming in the coastal sunset. Just past the San Onofre Naked Beach and Nuke Power Plant, a vision of those great Marine Corps spirits goaded him on to greater glory. Why, he could see Ira Hayes, Chesty Puller, Evans Carlson, John Basilone, and many others! Gung Ho! Go get 'em Marine.

Now, I ask you what kind of real jarhead would put-putt up to the front door of the Camp Pendleton NCO Club doing not more than 50? Hillary Clinton could do that. No sireee, bub! For the Ol' Sarge Snyde was sure that Sean meant not over 50 at Mach II. So that would make it just under 100. Now, that's more like it. To his misfortune, however, the brakes could not Gung Ho at Mach II. Master Sergeant Snyder, restored Mercury convertible, and spiffy uniform, slammed right into the plate glass window of the NCO Club forty yards ahead of a utility car and blaring siren with a squad of angry MP's waving nightsticks and drawing 9mm's. Fortunately, he had not been drinking, so with a few hours in the brig, and a signed agreement to pay the damages to the Club, the base commander let the Old Sarge, the last of the Chosun few join his reunion. Regaling his old buddies with tales and counter tales of the Old Corps he rocked on about his most recent coup; i.e. how he "won" the Mercury in a recent five card draw poker match at San Manuel Casino. Blouse your boots, Marines; it's getting deep. The mercury sustained only minor scratches and a few fender dents. Now, they don't make 'em like they used to.

Sean P. McSlade was not a happy camper. The $2,000 damage to the plate glass window and front entrance was a Marine Corps family matter, but to borrow and pay for the minor re-restoration of the Mercury would set him back about $1,500 - brakes too! Former Marine Master Sergeant and Senior Clerk Snyder offered one of his collected Samurai swords as compensation, a prized Heian Era rare specimen, which Sean graciously accepted. Rare, that is, if it had been genuine. Just before he left for Chicago, Sean took the weapon to the resident expert at the South Coast Cutlery shop to have it cleaned and appraised. It did not take more than a few seconds for the expert, a qualified martial artist, swordsman, and curator to declare it a fake, based on weight, metal quality, balance, and finally, the smudged over lettering that stated that it had been "Made in Bangladesh." Some samurai! Nice try - don't try to match wits with an old Marine Sarge, but don't underestimate the Fighting Irish either! With a plane to catch and no time to confront the stalwart cold warrior, Sean got even the Irish way - with a beer bottle, thus offering *The Times* as colorful tidbit as any to come out of Los Angeles Asylum.

Post dating the story until he returned fully to *The Times and Review*, Steve did it like a mock press release. He wrote:

For Immediate Release-November 1, 2008

Veteran Asylum clerk Elvis P. Snyder was severely injured today when a beer bottle flew through an open door near the guard post he was manning. Snyder was incoherent for several hours following the incident but managed to utter a statement which led investigators to believe the bottle was hurled from a speeding car approaching him on the near side of the parking lot outside the Asylum office.

Further investigation revealed that only minutes before the incident at the entrance, a reportedly "disturbed Asylum officer" had received separation papers and was rumored to have set out in the direction of Snyder's post at high speed in a slightly-damaged Mercury convertible with threadbare brake linings. An immediate search commenced for

Sean P. McSlade, a one-time Asylum superhunk and reputed "ladies man." McSlade, known to have a great affinity for alcohol, was described by a co-worker as, "a nice guy until somebody messes with his Mercury."

An apparently flamboyant careerist, McSlade was discharged to-day after one of the most bizarre careers in INS history. According to Isadore F. Falabenko, who was temporarily relieved of his duties as Asylum Director yesterday, and admitted to the Pomona Acres Rest and Recovery Home for observation, McSlade was "totally adversarial " and "the most reactionary and unprogressive federal officer I have ever come up against even among the miserable lot of the LA office."

A search of McSlade's file revealed that he narrowly escaped legal difficulties recently when he was questioned in connection with an "in-appropriate" relationship with Rita Redonda Rincon, a fellow Asylum officer. Charges were later dropped when Ms. Rincon suddenly withdrew her complaint. Ironically, and despite his recent conflict of interest as an IRA supporter, McSlade became the subject of a late night bidding war among four prominent federal agencies resulting in his receiving a prestigious high-level position with another CIS unit for an undisclosed salary rumored to be in the six figures.

"I'll never understand how he's gotten away with what he's done here," Falabenko continued. "I fell over when I heard about this. It is alarming I tell you, absolutely horrendous," Falabenko concluded as he collapsed on the pavement at the corner Westchester and East Kugel Street just before the medics arrived. And so, dear reader, this is why everybody loves a drunken Irishman!

Chapter 13

THE GNOMES GO TO SWITZERLAND

Pomona Acres released Izzy Falabenko after his forty-five day all ex-pense paid Relaxation and Recovery sojourn with a special "key to the city ceremony" presided over by Mayor Manicotti himself. No sooner had he returned to his Asylum duties than Hortensia began purring in his ear about the need for them to take a "real getaway" l-i-i-ike to the Swiss Alps.

Dear reader, you *know* by now, or at least you should if you've been paying attention, that when Hortensia purrs, men listen! Why the Swiss Alps, you ask? Well, because they are there, that's why. Moreover, they cost money, and the if the Asylum coffers are not spent, the loot es-cheats back to Congress (not the only thing in the Asylum executive office that cheats), and Congress will cut next year's Asylum budget, so an all-Asylum directors conference is just the ticket and yet one more of Hortensia's brilliant ideas.

The press release did not sit well with the boss, however. Pounding his rolltop, Robyn thundered, "Just what kind of horseshit is this? Is

Steve trying to self-destruct as a reporter *and* ruin my paper? This reads like the old *Riverside Roach* not *The Riverside Times and Review*. This is a classy newspaper! You don't see this kind of reporting in the *LA Times*. You don't see this kind of reporting in the *San Francisco Chronicle*. And you damn sure don't see this kind of reporting in the *Riverside Roach*-uh *Review*! *The Riverside Times and Review;* this is a classy newspaper!" the boss exclaimed pounding the table. "What Steve wrote is yellow journalism at its worst. Not something we're going to print here. They would not even print this kind of garbage in The Hope Arkansas Gazette, Bill Clinton's hometown rag. This is a classy newspaper. If he does this again, he's fired without prejudice!"

Boss Robyn was beside himself. He quickly turned to his third man for moral support. George Herbert Walker Wendt, one of his bright young Ivy Leaguers, a blond haired blue-blooded Yalie and truly a *Times* up and comer. And a Skull and Bones member too. Yep! He even jerked-off in a coffin just like George Bush I and George Bush Dubya, too! If it were generationally feasible to cross J. Danforth Quale with Bristol Palin, the offspring created might resemble George H.W.Wendt, the beatific smile and impish expression having blended well to complete the comic effect. Boss Robyn railed, and rocked, and tapped his intern on the arm as he sought solace.

"George, am I right or wrong? This is a classy newspaper! So get on your cell phone for which I paid too damn much and get Steve here five minutes ago!"

That the Edwin S. Egan story would likely reach print was a 50/50 chance, but the Elvis P. Snyder story Boss Robyn would not even file in the morgue for possible fact-checking. So Steve saved a copy of it in his document files anyhow in case something more newsworthy should develop from the incident.

No matter. A real scoop of a story was emerging about Longstreet and his Seven Little Gnomes planning an all-taxpayer expense paid junket to Geneva, and once again the little bird was warbling big time corruption story – awwk, in Boss Robyn's ear.

But who would cover it? Steve, although sufficiently competent was now proving a bit troublesome as a reporter/mole, and besides the splurge was for the elite, not even the deputies would be invited. Sorry Max, just for us All-Pros you know! Who would mole? What few knew and even fewer suspected, was that the promotion of San Francisco Asylum Office Director and Izzy Falabenko's counterpart by the bay, Gaylord Newskum was already a match, set, and game point conclusion. He would be the new National Deputy Director. Longstreet would announce the appointment at the big powwow and with Newskum's high mass immaculation, his local deputy, Margaret Chase Smith Hamlin would move up to acting-director, making her eligible for the trip.

Once an investigator, always an investigator, or so the saying goes, so Margaret Hamlin's low-key balanced personality was sought out as a counterweight to the psycho-neurotics who generally populated the maladjusted subculture of modern Americana. Think of her as a bit of Thorton Wilder, some Norman Rockwell, a smidgen of Grandma Moses, and maybe even a little of Henry David Thoreau, but no Grace Metalious, thank heaven! Who needs a scandal, after all? A descendent of the Mayflower puritans with a computer-like brain, Margaret could visualize a missing file among half-million stored, and perfectly respond to a congressional inquiry. Accordingly, she would be the only non-lawyer among the Magnificent Seven, and the other Magnificent Six would not like it. Aeeah tiz!"

At five-feet-eleven inches tall, with thick flowing blond hair, granite cheekbones, and jawline lean and fit, but not without a measure of feminine softness, her features might do Mount Rushmore well. Sarah Palin, beware! You will not be the next face. You betcha!

An anomaly among the directors, Margaret Chase Smith Hamlin was decidedly "old school. A sturdy Mainer and rock-ribbed Republican lady, one of the last, maybe even the very last of a dying breed, the stoic solid square-jawed New England mama - a little bit Abigail Adams, some Barbara Bush, a little bit Clare Boothe Luce, and a lot like her own namesake, Senator Margaret Chase Smith. Moreover, she was also a great-great-great granddaughter of Abraham Lincoln's first vice-president, Hannibal Hamlin. Her dad was the forty year mayor of Turner, Maine. What was not so well known among the lawyerly self-appointed elite, was that MCSH was an old, old friend, and if rumors were correct, a sometime lover, of Karl Keibalski during their BoPa days down on the Yeehah Texas border. Instant mole! This time a match, set, and game point for the good guys! Hot damn at an Austin fourth of July barbeque! It just doesn't get any better than this. James Dean would have been proud and now so too would Dandy Don Meredith, the most recent resident of Texas Heaven. Of course, Texas is Heaven as Heaven is Texas! Yeeehhhaaa!

She would be the only director who would have a good time on the trip. For the others, it would become a glorified power lunch. Sean Faggerty, quickly promoted from supervisor to Arlington regional office deputy director had just returned from a productive and successful supervisory detail in Africa, or as Keibalski quipped, "He's perfectly safe there. No self-respecting cannibal would eat that shit, aha, haha, ha!"

Faggerty had hoped to make a big enough splash before the summit to leap-frog a move up to HQ and oust the non-descript deputy director rumored to be suffering from uterine cancer. What Faggerty was not counting on was his own upstaging at the hands of the surreptitiously appointed former Director of the San Francisco office, the colorfully flamboyant former trial lawyer, Gaylord Newskum. Is there no justice? No happy camper he!

The power players would have to make the events move fast and they did. Longstreet arranged lodgings at the Hotel Henri Guisan in Lausanne before the House Budgetary Committee on Extraneous Bureaucratic Affairs knew what in hell had happened within this elitist little Immigration subculure. They travelled Swiss Air, first class of course, and the first session commenced in the Grand Ballroom under the austere portrait of the great Swiss patriot, World War II General Guisan with Hotshot Deputy Dick, Gaylord U. Newskum taking over the speaker's dais from the laconic Longstreet who again preferred manipulation to communication.

A syllabus of events and briefing were prepared just to make it look like a real conference instead of the junket, retreat, and high-end vacation that it really was. They would ruminate, remonstrate, and regurgitate, and possibly reflect(assuming any of the directors are capable of even rudimentary reflection), on how wonderful the Magnificent Seven were, as opposed to how rotten, recalcitrant, and revolting the Asylum officers, and most of the supervisors were. Essentially, it would come off as it had been planned to come off: a laudatory, valedictory, pre-emptory, directory new-age mutual ass-kissing kumbaya retreat. Most disturbing and morale busting for the Asylum peons would be the new policy directives.

New England stoicism be damned! Margaret Chase Smith Hamlin had had enough of such comic farce, especially for a proper Maine lady. What would she do? Why, she would call her one-time border patrol compadre and old flame, of course. She excused herself from the conference with a "blood sugar" issue, but instead of taking an insulin shot, she made a beeline for the ladies head, whipped out her Good Old Maine flask and took a couple shots of Black Sea Vodka instead. And, with her transoceanic cell phone she could link up with Karl Keibalski, whom she managed to reach just as he returned from work.

"Well, how's it hangin' Big Guy?"

"Long and loose and full of juice as always. You know that!"

"I might have known, but I also have something that might interest you, or at least your underground "Man in Managua" aka Steve Melkonian, if you get my drift."

"Yeah! I see. Newly minted Deputy Dick from San Fannywhammy is posturing again?"

"You got it. Moreover, INS management would be tragic if it weren't so laughable, but we know that from working in "the system" for so many years. In any case, you have the 'Dick' or rather the 'Dickhead' part of it right, but he's miserable as a deputy already. It has to be all or nothing for him. So instead of initiating a series of programs to address office morale problems and usher in the new procedures under the antiterrorist and alien ID Acts, Newskum has totally wigged out and is now holding court at the executive conference room of the Guisan to expound on alien issues in the Bay Area."

"Such as?"

"Recognition of safe harbor cities, churches, safe houses, clown houses, crack houses, and the like. Anything to protect the downtrodden alien, whether criminal or law abiding."

"My cell phone goes international and so does Steve's. I'll grab him from his office and we can continue this conversation at the BBP, where Van Rumpelsteen and his spooks can't monitor us. Talk to you in five."

Karl and Steve convened for an extended lunch break at the BBP and linked up with Margie for the underground conference call. As she had put her cell phone on high-power recorder mic, she could play back the keynote session for her two rogue subordinates to enjoy.

"So, just what is the Longstreet-Newskum 'New Policy?'"

"It's called the Anchor Baby Reform Act and the Citizenship Advancement for Documentation of Aliens to Bring Reform to America." ABRA-CADABRA"

"Is he serious?"

"Is any civic leader in Frisco serious? They're all liberal potheads up there. You know that."

"Fuckin' A, but we need to know exactly how he pulled it off."

"If he had any talent he could have been a movie actor."

"So…"

"I can't be certain, because I'm not party to the inner workings of the deep bowels of INS headquarters."

"You've got the "deep bowels" part of it right! I'll bet Longstreet's bumbuggers hassled him to make Newskum his deputy but ABRA-CADABRA is too far off the wall and will likely contradict US Immigration policy."

"As it stands now, it surely would. But these people are hoping that President Hilary Clinton will change US policy in 2009. That's all that the lefty polit-junkies talk about in the soops lounge."

"Assuming she's the Demo nominee, and defeats her GOP opponent. I don't think it'll happen, she's too polarizing a figure. That young senator from Illinois might have an outside chance. He sounded impressive at the last convention."

"I think I know who you're talking about. The one with the weird Arab name? He's got a long way to go yet."

"Yeah, and we're getting too far off point. What Steve and I need is more details to flesh out his reports to *The Times*. Off the record, of course."

"It had better be off the record! And Steve, you are to delete this call or lock up your phone, got it?"

"Understood."

"In addition to his ten-thousand dollar Armani ball-buster suits and ball-stroker lifestyle, Newskum has some curious mannerisms when addressing a group, even a formal board meeting."

Steve recorded Margret's synopsis of the weeklong megabuck junket, deleted the message, and hand-delivered the copy to the boss.

He wrote: Deputy Asylum Director Gaylord Newskum speaking at an all-expense paid secret directors' conference in Lausanne, Switzerland outlined three new policies, which if implemented, would run counter to current US Immigration policy.

Consider the acronyms; it appears that for INS Management this was an embarrassing oversight: Anchor Baby Reform Act and the Citizenship Advancement for Documentation of Aliens to Bring

Reform to America. ABRA-CADABRA, a policy to grant immediate citizenship to all relatives of one child born in the US. Works like magic for some! As though this isn't comical enough, there is the policy of the "Safe Harbor Initiative Towns. SHIT, a policy to clandestinely transfer funds from the INS budget to small town treasuries that offer refuge to undocumented aliens by hiding and shielding them from the US Border Patrol agents looking for them. This is a clear case of one part of a Service going to war against another. Clearly unlawful, unconstitutional, and unethical, this policy has been enacted without due process, misappropriates federal funding, violates the separation of powers clause, and amounts to payola on the part of the national director's office. But as Al Jolson used to say at the Winter Garden, 'you ain't seen nothin yet!' To keep Congress at bay, Deputy Director Newskum has created through his very own Frisco Office, the Alien Security System. ASS, a monitoring and tracking early alert and warning system to notify residents of the barrio, safe houses, clown houses, crackhouses, outhouses, and yes, even one or two whorehouses, of any and all impending BoPa raids.

Newskum restated his new "policies" at a black-tie dinner today at the all expense paid mega-junket at the luxury six-star Hotel Henri Guisan in Lausanne, Switzerland. In the oak-paneled convention ballroom he announced his policy directives as Director Longstreet, much less theatrical and much more the straight man, sulked in silence. He had to sit and listen to this dilettante rock on while he was able to say absolutely nothing. Houston Director Maria Valasquez, a former managing partner of a local mid-size law firm, raised administrative and implementation issues. How might we facilitate these new policies given current time limits? This strains time and training resources for our supervisors. Newskum's response was merely to crane his neck in an habitual nervous tick while he rolled his head from side to side while saying, "This is going to happen whether you like it or not."

Margret Hamlin raised the personnel issue. "As you know Mr. Newskum, at San Francisco we are under-staffed and our officers are working over…."

Anticipating her request for more personnel, he cut her off, again craning his neck and gassing out his mouth, "It's going to happen whether the officers like it or not."

"Gaylord, please let's move on to a more pressing matter. We have the funds to upgrade which we would have to return to the Hill if we don't utilize…"

"We had the funds. As of now they have been fully utilized on our directors' conference budget allocation for our symposium and this information is to be held in the strictest confidence," Gaylord paused a moment to secure in his medial lobe a final profound thought before continuing, "because this has happened whether the Hill learns about it or not."

"Yes and if the Hill *does* learn about it, we all go to the federal pen."

"Ms Hamlin, you are a very unprogressive, level-one negative thinker. You need to expand your transcendental consciousness like the rest of us.

The 'official' part of the conference ended the next day, but the final two days were spent on sightseeing and recreation for the directors, their spouses, significant others, domestic partners, or ad hoc bed partners. To humor his regional heads, Director Longstreet offered a "progressive spa package" to make the junket worthy of their collective psyches. At the Wilhelm Tell Recovery Reconstruction and Rehabilitation Meditation Protocol Kurhotel a fifty-thousand Swiss franc package was offered to each participant director, and one other of the above mentioned. Unlike its name-sake, it would not be necessary to shoot a straight arrow.

Located at Interlaken, this delightful little hideaway offers high-end "renewal packages" for distinguished (read: loaded) international personages. So how, you ask, could Longstreet pull this off for relatively common federal bureaucrats at the Kurhotel, a six star resort accustomed to George Soros assets clientele? Simple really. He had the bill printed in German, totaled in Swiss Francs, and his old friend on the House Committee on Discretionary Assets, Congressman Boney Fwaenk appropriate the loot. It was a well-planned and well-executed misappropriation where no auditor would know the wiser. Most members of his committee were not bilingual in any language, and not financially literate. Not planned was the sudden death of a local director.

It was not supposed to happen but it did. You could say it began with a sandwich massage at the Hanging Gardens Progressive Therapy Center at the Kurhotel. Izzy Falabenko was overwrought by the events of the prior six months. Overwrought, as in, the local director with the greatest caseload. Overwrought with the sense that upcoast rival Gaylord Newskum would pull his typical legerdemain in an upstaging effort to appropriate more funds to his former office. Overwrought by the physical demands of a wife thirty-five years his junior. Overwrought due to increasing suspicion that spies were operating at large in his office for reasons which he was generally unaware. And finally, overwrought - thy name is GS-15 federal bureaucrat.

The therapy center, located one hundred yards behind the main building in an unobtrusive area, was separated from the main complex to avoid controversy with the very proper Swiss. Falabenko sneaked out early in the evening while Hortensia was shopping and dining with the other dom-partners. He pulled up the high collar of his Mongolian camel-hair double-breasted overcoat, and adjusted a floppy taupe

Italian fedora down over his forehead so he would not be recognized. He had packed them but had not worn them until this part of the junket. Lacking the panache of Newskum, or the steely countenance of Longstreet, Falabenko at this time in his life looked like a rather seedy KGB agent no longer on top of his game.

The hair was once long and blond with flowing locks, the build lean but muscular, and the moustache/goatee non-existent when he wowed the crowd at Woodstock during their frequent acid breaks. With his thundering lectures on "our rights" at pot-picnic law seminars 101 and 102 on procedural civil disobedience defense, he wowed the Great Unwashed with his profound (profane) treatises on: resistance to arrest, resistance to the draft, and extra-legal seizure of university property from the class enemies. Enemies known as, your dirty rich parents and fellow-travelers who paid for your education, LBJ, President Nixon, Governor Rockefeller, etc. Yep, a 'liberal' Republican is still a Republican to the poets of *this* revolution, but nice try Rocky! And better luck with Meghan Marshak, ya know what I'm sayin'? So Isadore Finkelstone Falabenko, MA, The Hamptons University, JD, Daniel Shays College of Law, pounded the picnic table under the makeshift thatched-roof ramada where he delivered lectures that railed against war, poverty, racism, fascism, capitalism, De Gaulleism, McCarthyism, and whatever ism as long as it was not an ism that appealed to the deconstructionist instincts of the fabulous "now" generation.

Now, semi-balding, gaunt, bent over, with slight paunch, a sad, tired old bureaucrat who had never gotten a partnership in a prestigious corporate law firm, or even an associateship in a not so prestigious criminal law firm, he now trudged his own "green mile" except that his would be "gold." Forget the corner office of the Wall Street corporate law world. You could say that remuneratively speaking he was just a cut above a seasoned senior associate, and this must have weighed on his mind as he approached the Hanging Gardens. This, and the unexpected elevation of Gaylord Newskum. As Falabenko approached the golden pagoda however, his spirits lifted, just as his usual one hundred milligram dose of Viagra would lift other parts. Too bad Hortensia did not also include his digitalis in their travel packet. An oversight perhaps? Not quite the Temple of the Golden Pavilion but a lot more fun, the quaint Asian Edifice of the Alps beckoned all who appreciated the finer pleasures in life.

Speaking with a slight, but not readily distinguishable accent, Madame Helga Von Oberstrasse, a tall, elegant exotic-looking woman met him at the vestibule then ushered him quickly to the parlor area. Likely Eurasian, Von Oberstrasse sported a nostalgic Anna May Wong hairdo replete with teapot bangs. But her full name, corporate world manners, exquisitely-cut dark gray business suit, moderately-heeled mirror-polished black pumps were purposely Western. Incongruous, yes, but the entire room, minimalist but not Spartan, was a bit incongruous. It was a little bit of languid tropical Asia in uptight hyper-efficient Switzerland. Falabenko regarded the Zen of the parlor and felt oneness with the aura. He had taken a Taoism class in the 1960s and thought himself "still into it." A more rational choice, he thought than the Ike Chaiklin's Kumbaya Clique of the LA office. Especially tranquilizing was the natural twenty foot-high waterfall in the far corner of the parlor that might Tao him out to a higher plane of enlightenment. Zonky dory!

With a gentle swaying of her hips, Von Oberstrasse walked to a luxuriously upholstered Victorian sofa and beckoned Izzy saying, *"Machen Sie sich bequem* (make yourself comfortable)." She then crossed the room to remove a leather-bound list of some two hundred therapists from a twenty-foot high oaken bookcase that also contained volumes of classic European homes and estates, international architectural patterns, oriental philosophy, and many classics of Western literature. Today, however, the courtesan collection would supersede Oliver Twist. She removed the volume, and placed it on a tea table table where attendants had set two cups of expensive Darjeeling.

She then pronounced his last name with a slight exaggeration, "Mr. *Falabenko,* an interesting name. Ukrainian, I presume?"

"Well, my grandparents came from Poland and Russia before the Great Proletarian Revolution and…"

"And now you are no longer *great* or *proletarian,* right?"

Not accustomed to such an abrupt cutoff, he glared briefly and stammered a denial. Indeed, in any of their power conversations, even Longstreet would not treat him with such condescension.

"I…I, uh, ahem, I have always identified with the masses against the unjustly privileged and wealthy."

"Is this because you have *not* been very successful in the practice of law?"

"How are my failures…oops, uh… how is my career history related to your services?"

Totally out of class and out of gas, Izzy could only but listen as Madame Von Uberstrasse pronounced his name with suave condescension, "Ah, yes, Mr. *Fala*benko. You may not know that we *are* joint-ventured with the Hotel Guisan, and that we *do* examine the credentials of or guests assiduously. As the services we offer are quite beyond the means of the general populace, we must protect our reputation and that of our clientele with the utmost discretion. I am sure you understand."

A passionate egalitarian and socialist, except for his own salary requirements, Falabenko resented this smoothest of put-downs directed
toward his personage, but lacked the stature to express his displeasure.
Now aware that this was not to be his power network, Izzy obediently
returned to the purpose of his visit. He requested the Around the World
Session of the Progressive Executive Package: a two-therapist three-hour
ecstasy binge with the five major massage styles represented: Swedish,
Chinese, Thai, Deep Tissue, and Hot Stone. $4,000 in all, yet another
off-the-books-expense shell-gamed by Congressman Fwaenk. Now you
see it, now you don't. For another one thou you got a Torta Sandwich
(you supply the meat) with happy ending. With a clandestine congressional compensation package, why not up the ante to five bills and get
the full Montgomery?

Von Uberstrasse clapped her hands and two progressive masseuses
appeared: sensual Saigon Suzi and titillating Tonkin Tina, both extremely attractive medium-height, athletically built Asian women. Dressed in
purple and gold dragon-printed blouses with the Kurhotel logo, and
form-fitting white trousers, they were sufficiently experienced not to
giggle no matter how incongruous the situation or ridiculous looking
the client, but rather to cast dreamy and erotic smiles and beckon him
to unseen, unheard, and previously unfelt pleasures.

Suzi and Tina led him into a the VIP area. Dark and pleasantly san-
dalwooded, this highly secluded lounge was enclosed within the cavern
portion of the spa to assure maximum privacy, security, and above all,
anonymity. Just the ticket for an over-burdened Fed exec. The pair, mul-
tilingual in European and Asian languages, did not do the "me rub you
long time" line. This was a six-star spa, after all. Yet, this would prove
the last massage for all concerned. Having entered Switzerland with
good documents, no easy process in ethno-centric Switzerland, they had
earned enough to pay for residence certificates, and after five years were

now ready to open their own establishment; Suzi and Tina's Sandalwood Therapy Room at Interlaken Will Leave You Rockin!

The pair had poor old Izzy totally denuded and slapped down on the whoopee (not Ms. Goldberg) rack before he knew what would hit him. After kneading, stroking, pounding, pummeling, and pulling to get him fully woodied, an extremely grueling process that took up the better part of three hours, the two stripped down for the torta part of the session. Yet as soon as Suzi and Tina jerked him to his feet for the *Shimmy Shimmy Ko Ko Bop* his heart gave away. You betcha!

Sprawling out on the sandalwood and travertine tile floor, Izzy keeled over bigtime, eyes rolled back into his noggin, as he did the golden parachute belly flop right on Suzi's succulent Oriental charms. No happy ending for Izzy, and certainly no happy landing for Suzi! She yelled the traditional Asian primeval "Aiiyyah" scream that called down the good karma of all her ancestors to counter the bad joss of Izzy. Tina, the tough and smart one, nonchalantly crossed to the changing room totally unclothed, picked up her cell phone from her purse, and calmly called on Madame Von Uberstrasse to summon on-call medics and remove Izzy's bedraggled remains to the on-site morgue. Apparently, this was not the first time something like this had happened. When they anticipated a fatality, as it sometimes happened with elderly clients, Madame called on Tina to direct the massage and usher the corpse to its agreeable journey to the afterworld, but above all, keep the local press from learning about it. Can you say massive myocardial infarction following radical massage therapy?

Chapter 14

IT'S DÉJÀ SILKWOOD
ALL OVER AGAIN

The Asylum Directors Swiss Conference, having ended on such a somber note, and with everyone, or rather almost everyone now safe at home, Lazarus H. Longstreet, Esq. Harvard Law College, JD, National Director US Asylum, and other laurels checked into Bethesda National Naval Medical Center with an undisclosed illness.

Pandemonium had now hit Los Angeles Asylum. Who would have known the director's conference would become Falabenko's Last Stand? Longstreet, who could not attend the funeral, nevertheless declared a day of mourning and sent Deputy Newskum as representative. He might have done so in any situation though, as eulogies or any other official ceremony that involved speaking was not his bag.

With Gaylord Newskum doing the eulogy, Izzy had a funeral that befitted a feudal lord, or at least Lord Senator Wellstone. But this time it would be the third-level bureaucratic "elite" doing the wailing, weeping, foot stomping and teeth gnashing. With a few obscure Latin phrases he had learned as an altar boy praying on his knees. Of course, dear reader, you know that wasn't the only things he did on his knees, the comic effect was a bureaucrat's memoriam done as a hootenanny. The director of the Miami office even brought his twelve--string gui tar and why not? No office parties like the Miami Asylum Office.

Ikey and his fiancé Panchito held hands, hugged, and cried throughout the service. A few "mourners" mumbled words about a vast right-wing conspiracy. O.H. Hinkel even suggested that political commentator Hush Lambug had a hand in it. Izzy martyred by slightly dippy Right Wing Radio Shock-Jock? Now that would have made their day! Dream on, oh progressive warrior. his burial at Forest Lawn East was attended by the "best and brightest" of US Asylum. Okay, so it was a comparatively small group; delusions of grandeur always played into the Asylum psyche. Keibalski and his cohorts sat in the back. He with his broad inimitable smirk on his face cracking nasty jokes about Hortensia. Steve took copious and he hoped, inconspicuous notes about the funeral. With his feature series just about done and not having Pierre Ouine to protect him, it was time to 'officially resign' and head back to The Times. He went the distance. He kept the faith. That was all that Boss Robyn required.

Why Forest Lawn East, you ask? Well, you haven't lived until you die in LA - or at least get buried there. The FL East mortuary was sort of a bastardization of a Las Vegas Wedding Chapel with overtones of Westminster Abbey, the Ponderosa Ranch (dad gummit pawh!), and a low-end Reno blackjack parlor with convenient brothel in the back. All they needed was a "Re-elect Harry Reid" poster, actually the first stiff to be sent back to the Senate.

So Newskum, the Gay Lord, rocked on with his inimitable poor man's Marc Antony oratorio. "Directors, supervisors, plebians, lend me your ears. Today, we celebrate a life rather than…yada, yada, yada."

He never met a cliché he didn't like! The remainder of the hour and a half long paean was dedicated to Gaylord's favorite subject; Newskum and his great life as the 'future' of Asylum and all the reforms he was about to institute provided The Great One would see the wisdom of retirement, now no longer an issue. Just as today we 'honored' its past. Big Bertha De Baggery sat at the back of the room and rubbed her inner thighs together in an erotic free association binge that did not quite reach the level of stream of consciousness - sorry James Joyce, but you've always been a 'sporting' sort of fellow, haven't you? Sorry for the both of you; Newskum *is* a handsome devil, after all!

There was some subdued speculation as to why Longstreet was not present to send one of his hand-picked protégés to greater glory. One bit of gossip suggested that scandals within his directorate did not set well with him and that he also faced the awkward choice of demoting Neswkum to fill the LA void or promoting the Merry Widow herself. More nepotism, anyone? And of Hortensia, what can I say? Absolutely gorgeous in black! What a stylish widow she was: tall, lithe, sensual, athletic, unbelievably stunning, and not at all perturbed by the peccadilloes of her late spouse. She *did* have her own peccadilloes, after all. Rather, make that peckerdilloes. But she graciously accepted the condolences of all well-meaning attendees; as though she had any other choice. Power becomes Hortensia; must be careful not to pull a Jiang Qing though. Best to wait until the office was seeking the woman instead.

Longstreet never made it to rest and recovery though, as he checked out at exhaustion and paranoia. That's right, dear reader, he flipped! Leaving no definite clue, inclination, or suicide note, Longstreet tossed himself from a fourteenth story window and landed on a ninth floor ledge. NCIS ruled out foul play for the time being. Good work special agent Special Agent Gibbs, your crew, and Ducky, too.

Keibalski, always the happy warrior of bad tidings broke the news to Steve first, and then a few of the soops in LA office, with one of his usual unwelcome quips, "Say, you hear that the Asylum Director jumped out of his fourteenth floor window at Bethesda Naval Hospital this morning and landed on the ninth floor ledge? Looks like they'll have to look for a new Asylum Director. Think Smarty-pants (Van Rumpelsteen) will get it? No? Well, maybe Slippery-pants (Newskum) then!"

Oh please, Karl, you can do better than that! Well, uh maybe you can't.

These guesses were as good as any. VR was already Acting Director of LA, the largest volume Asylum office. And with the apparent demise of Longstreet, Newskum moved up to Acting National Director, a job that was likely to become permanent, as he *knows* that it is tailor-made for him. Tough break, Hortensia. Match set but not quite game point just yet. Best to get on the horn to Margaret C.S. Hamlin up in Frisco to find out the real poop.

The irony to those familiar with the history of the Bethesda Naval Medical Center is that during the Truman Administration, the Secretary of the Navy jumped from the same fourteenth floor room, landed on the same ninth floor ledge, with the same history kind of paranoia, and ended up just as dead. Of course, they had to look for a new Secretary of the Navy. Was there a curse on this room going back to the suicide leap of Secretary Forrestal? Might there be other issues instead? It is not uncommon for cloak and dagger speculation to begin within the nebbish culture of the Asylum office, so have a field day, conspiracy theorists!

"Margaret darling, we have been through so much together and now this. It is just too much to bear."

(We have-do tell.)

"And I know that your sorrow for poor old Izzy is as deep as mine."

(That's news.)

"May I ask a big favor for a grieving widow? Would you mind very much feeling out the CIS Director (as though you need any help 'feeling out'), to see if I am under consideration to replace my late lamented husband as Permanent Director of the LA Asylum Office? I know that Max is a wonderful progressive person, but he is really such a boy in the ways of the world. Would you be a sweetie and look into this for me? And please remember our dear friend Gaylord Newskum. He is such a progressive person with a multicultural outlook and he does so deserve permanent director."

(Ah, Madame Hortensia-you give so much and ask so little!)

"Eeaaah! I can contact Director Aguilar and see if he *has* made *definite* plans for permanent appointments, but I cannot promise anything. Those are his decisions."

"Well," she replied, a bit huffily, "understood. Talk to you again, soon, bye."

(Don't make it too soon now, dearest.)

"Eeah, looking forward to it, good-bye and keep well."

Ms. Hamlin would suffer yet one more annoying, inconsiderate phone call, but at least this time it would be "friendly fire."

"Hey, last of the Red Hot Mamas, this is your last of the Big-time Spenders. What's shakin' in that Cesspool by the Bay?"

"Nothing you would understand, and I'm not your 'hot mama' anymore. Now what is it that you really want?"

"I just want to feel you out about…"

"We've been over that for some time. You *know* you *suck* as a lover!"

"But ya gotta admit, I'm damn good as a fighter and that's why I'm calling."

"So what can I do for you? That means, anything that *does not* involve sex?"

"This Asylum job sucks so bad the tide won't go out. I want back in Investigations."

"Well, you will need not wait long, the orders have already been cut. You leave asylum two weeks from today."

"Hot Damn on a Polish ham! So where is my next duty station?"

She hesitated, "I cannot tell you very much except that it is likely to be very close by with some travel required. And you will be working with one other investigator or a small team. That is all."

"That sounds very espionage. Is it?

"You will find out soon enough, in the meantime try not to make too much of a jackass of yourself, good-bye."

A terse hang-up for sure, but Keibalski was nonetheless elated by his return to Investigations, whatever the assignment. He was all packed up and ready to go in fifteen minutes, so he dropped by Steve's office for one last hurrah at Frank and Steins to compare final notes.

"What's shakin' Big Guy? How's your golf game?"

He pounded Steve's desk and extended his hand, not a good sign, as he usually meant he was about to screw somebody: literally, figuratively, or both.

"My golf game is under a ten handicap, how's yours?" Steve replied without looking up from his terminal."

Karl did not want to hear this as his own handicap was much higher and the last time they played, Steve had beaten him by fifteen strokes. Karl quickly retreated to his favorite subject, Karl Keibalski and his great life as an INS investigator.

"Well, I just stopped to say I'm finally outta here dude. And not one day too soon. This job can drive you to drink. My guess is that you'll soon go back to your real job too, so let's go kick back a few brewskis at the BBP or or Pepe's. One last hurrah waddaya say?"

Steve had better say "race you there for the tab" and let Karl win if he knows what's good for him. With a presidential election less than a few months away, and the McCain-Palin ticket seemingly about to go down, Boss Robyn was likely to be in his foulest of moods. He needed Steve to close out his Asylum features and get cracking on Orange and Riverside County congressional races. Steve desperately needed filler to flesh out the sketchy details about the last moments of the life and times of Isadore Finkelstone Falabenko, briefly touch on the Longstreet matter, and the Swiss Luxis Extravagansis, the glorious third act of this immorality play. Yet, there was another issue, a personal issue on his mind.

He had to coax his boss into letting him take at least two days, preferably three, to attend his daughter Rosemary's dedication speech welcoming the ultra-conservative Doctor of Democracy and Great One Himself to the dedication of the Hush Lambug Mass Communications College of the recently chartered California State University at Rio Linda. Chosen for the honor as the Masscom student with the highest GPA, Rosemary Melkonian had also founded, with nine other of the journalism college's best and brightest, the CSURL charter of the Sigma Delta Chi journalism fraternity and served as its first president. Daddy was so proud! A bright future awaited her indeed! All of the Rio Linda undignified dignitaries were present for the dedication including the beloved Publisher and Mayor Hector "Hecky" Horatio Lambug (first cousin and mentor) and the common (very) council. The concurrent homecoming football game and dance that followed was a gala affair truly unmatched in the city's colorful history.

Although the eminent Talent on Loan from God (he thinks he is) took in part in the football game, he left post haste late in the fourth quarter with the Division Four conference CSU Rio Linda Rough Riders trailing the CSU Carmel-by-the Sea Mermaids 69-0. Barreling down the stadium steps, his 290-plus pounds disconcerted the fans more than the lopsided score of which their team was miserably on the business end. Hush begged off, citing a pending debate engagement against Michael Moore at the Hollywood Bowl and he needed a lot of time to prepare. What a smack-down Whale-o-Rama that might have been! Except that there was no record of such an event scheduled at the HB, but no one present at the CSURL Homecoming knew that. Homecoming fans found him visibly embarrassed, as he left. At the dance, there was much speculation as to why. Surely, he could hold his own against St. Michael the Corpulent. Or maybe he was just too shamed by the Rough Riders' lopsided loss during their fourth year of organized football. He *had* railed against the "feminization of the American male" during much of his commentary, and those poor buttheads just had their stuff yanked off and handed to them by the only "chick team" they had ever played, or would ever play, in their now besmirched athletic saga.

No, it appeared that he begged off the ball because the homecoming committee scheduled him for the first dance with homecoming queen Rosemary Melkonian (of course) at center court of the Rough Rider Pavilion, under the big shiny glass ball with everyone watching, no less. The graduates, committee members, honored alumni, mayor and *Rio Linda Republican* publisher and common council waited anxiously for the gala to begin. The two football captains, homecoming king and runner-up ditched the event too. Guess why? No matter. The beautiful, elegant, and poised Ms. Melkonian adjusted to the situation with professional dignity and re-scheduled the welcoming dance with her proud papa. So father and daughter saved the evening with a genteel foxtrot and spared the Masscom College's namesake the embarrassment of tomorrow's probable *Rio Linda Republican* news feature of the event:

Right-winger with Two Left feet Crushes Toes of Lovely CSURL Homecoming Queen.

The crowd had by now, grasped the real reason of The Great One's hasty departure. With gossip and champagne flowing, the party began to take a lively and light-hearted turn, especially with campus security having located the truant team captains sobbing and soothing their bruises in the weight room whirlpool. The humiliation of it all! Threatened with expulsion, they were forcibly monkey-suited and dragged to the ball by the campus cops. They entered the pavilion sheepishly to the laughter, derision, mock applause, and hiss-hiss, hoot-hoot, shame-shame finger pointing by the delighted revelers as they had to settle for the last dance with Rosemary and her runner-up, instead of the first.

The entire family gathered at the event. It was the first time they had been together since the divorce. The joyous mood of the siblings helped ease the awkwardness of the reunion, and her parents spoke civilly to each other, if not warmly for the sake of a daughter in whom they could regard with justifiable pride. So the gala event of the season ended on an upbeat note and a star-studded evening was enjoyed by all. So much for the *Rio Linda Republican* society page and its grandiose clichés.

It was all business once Steve returned to the office. The fedora was still in sight, not far from where the boss could grab it, but the booze bottle was not. Recently, he had been in a somber mood as opposed to his usual cantankerous one. Steve did not notice it so much, after all Robyn was now in his mid-seventies and mellowing just a bit. He had seen this happen to the elders of this own family. To the younger report-ers, the mood shift seemed obvious. He followed the pending election closely and was greatly troubled by its likely outcome. An old-school East Coast Republican, he was a staunch McCain supporter, the candidate whom he considered America's last true patriot. None of the others in the primary or general election from either party had even done one day of real military service, always a plus for him. By now, first term Senator Barack Obama's lead had widened to the point that it could not be overtaken. The boss viewed the Illinois senator as a rank amateur, whose politics and lack of experience in handling executive matters made him the poorest possible choice for the job.

In his lifetime, Boss Robyn had witnessed many of the twentieth cen-tury's conflagrations and had actively participated in one. Though he held most US presidents in reasonable regard, he knew the American people could flub it once in awhile. It appeared that this election would produce one of the flubs. The younger reporters, many who were first-time voters, to a person supported Obama, but not openly. Paychecks came first. Steve, still in the "undecided" column, did not regard ei-ther candidate highly but would follow The Boss' editorial lead with his usual loyal attitude. Today, he seemed a bit more upbeat than usual, and though he would never say this, he was relieved to have Steve back for good. The flakey junior reporters needed the discipline and the boss needed the time to wheel/deal and write anti-Obama editorials.

"I imagine you had a great time at Rio Linda even if the even if 'Prince Charming' didn't make it to Cinderella's ball. The copout artist! Or maybe he was just torqued about the football game. Such an embarrassment. I hear the provost may cancel the program or at least fire the head coach."

"Well, that's the first time I even heard anyone refer to him like that even in jest, but I'm relieved that he wasn't there to stomp on my daughter's feet, or worse yet, cop a feel."

"Good point. He *goes* about three hundred and she *is* very attractive."

The Boss lifted a new quart of JD from his dry bar, and two shot glasses from his rolltop, then publisher and senior editor enjoyed a rare moment of hearty laughter.

"Welcome back to the fight Steve. This time I know our side is going to win," he greeted Steve with conviction and increasing trust knowing that his second in command could and would "bring *The Times and Review* back."

"Now where have I heard that before?"

"It's from Casablanca, Victor Laszlo to Rick Blaine before he flies out of there to freedom, one step ahead of Major Strasser. Before your time of course."

Not to be outdone Steve retorted, "Well, we all have a Major Strasser in our lives, but fortunately I also have an Inspector Renault, too. Asylum Officer Karl Keibalski has been a great mole."

The humor was not lost on The Boss. "Yeah, he is but a poor corrupt official and your copy had better show accounts of the rich ones." More laughter.

"Got thirty CDs right here," he boasted pointing to his well-worn briefcase."

"Seriously, we'll put those on the back burner for now. I'm putting the junior editor is charge of the troops while you cover the local congressional."

He picked up on Steve's slight wince. "Yeah, I know it's grunt work crap, but I need somebody on this job who can do it right. In the meantime, your salary and standing here remain exactly the same!"

From Boss Robyn, this was high praise, so Steve took it at face value and bounced the boondocks with a little more spirit.

At Citizenship and Information Services HQ, however, Director Jaime Aguilar received a terse and somewhat troublesome untraceable cell phone call from Margaret Hamlin.

"Yes, I have scheduled the announcement for tomorrow's press conference and I certainly appreciate that your discretion in the matter. You have remained non-committal toward our two charlatans without appearing to stonewall. I'm sure you understand our situation. Obama is going to win this election and infest this department with his leftist lackeys to the point that the designation 'homeland security' will be rendered facetious. As it is likely to take him six months to install these dregs at the Asylum level, I am making your appointment as Asylum National Director immediate and permanent. "

"Now, don't get angry. I'm double-hatting you as chief of CIS inspections. This is a lot on your plate, but I need someone competent and experienced who can investigate the alleged suicide of Longstreet and the strange circumstances surrounding Falabenko's passing, too. Also, I want an audited account of that 'director's conference' and the budget overruns it caused. I've got congressmen all over my case. This is likely to carry into the next administration, so you need to keep this under wraps, otherwise the new Homeland Security chief will get wise and terminate that part of your appointment, which is on the political side of SES not civil service, got it?"

"Yes, I will accept, but I would like to raise a couple issues. Hortensia wants LA Director."

"Not a chance! Van Rumpelsteen will remain Acting Director until further notice. Hortensia will remain a supervisor and she is lucky to keep that billet pending investigation into what appears to be a fairly healthy scandal. Newskum will return to the San Fran office as the permanent director. Supervisor Mary Weeks will move up as deputy there."

"How do you think Gaylord will react?"

"I don't give a damn how he *or* his boyfriends will react, for that matter. Your appointment is going to happen and he will return to Frisco whether he likes it or not, aha ha ha ha ha!"

"Eeah, understood."

Karl Keibalski could not believe the good news when Margaret phoned him about the "internal coup."

"Serves the bastards right. They've had it coming for a long time."

"Just remember, mum's the word. The Asylum insiders don't know about this yet and we want it to be an unpleasant surprise."

"Got it!"

It did not take long for Keibalski to leap from his desk and give the OSU blood-curdling football yell. Then he stuck a two-hour leave slip under the duty officer's nose. Hot damn on a Polish Ham, he was finally back in Investigations! Luckily, it was Friday and the workload was sparse. He hopped into Steve's semi-restored 1985 Mercedes coupe that they had been working on in Karl's new mega-garage over the past year. With DVD deck playing you-know-what, Karl lit out on the 91 east peeling rubber for his new two-story, three-thousand-square foot luxury home at Nixon Park Acres in Yorba Linda. Fleetwood Mac drowned out the I-91 pre-rush hour hordes.

For such a do-it-yourself kind of guy, there was concrete to lay on his personally-designed backyard basketball court, or even a party-doll to lay at you-know-where if perchance he should take a detour along the way. Oh, he would take a detour all right, but not the kind he would like.

Just before the Nixon Park turnoff, Karl noticed a fast approaching, tinted-window cream-color Iacocca Model 1990 Chrysler Goombah 440 in his rearview mirror. He slowed to take the new I-91 Watergate Avenue exit, the one with the landscaped high knoll and recently-planted young spruce trees, conspicuous among the older palms that pre-dated the construction. Fortunately, he chose this one. Steve's little deuce coupe would prove no match for the klutzmobile bearing down on him fast. But what would the mob have against him anyway?

The last thing Karl noticed about the Chrysler before it rammed him off the freeway exit was its federal plates. At that point he knew it was no mob mobile and this was no accident. It happened too fast for

Karl to make out the numbers as the hit had been well-planned but not so well executed. The knoll kept his coupe from a very dangerous plunge, and the young spruce trees broke in half as he slammed his brakes, skidded, and broadsided. They also prevented his car from rolling and crushing him as they had not yet installed a roll bar. Who might have known this about this car, and if they had, why would they not have tried to force him off the road earlier at one of the more dangerous overpasses or exits? Did they not know about the hundred foot ravine beside the Robert Vesco Road exit where such an "accident" would have surely proved fatal?

Karl walked away from this one but might there be others? Or was Karl even the target of this amateurish assassination attempt? Unsettling questions to be sure. So as soon as Karl flipped the seat belt and hopped out to appraise the damage, he got on his cell phone to place three calls. The first was to Triple A for a wrecker. The second was to his most trusted friend in Investigations, retired Special Agent Brian Conlan, who he affectionately called "The Conman." This time he really needed The Conman's wily instincts. The final one to Margaret Hamlin with a "heads up" about another in-house "mishap." After the wrecker had driven him home and given him an estimate for the repairs, he called his wife who was vacationing at a sister's in Seattle, but gave her only sketchy details about some "crank forcing him off the freeway." He added that the local police were clueless as he did not get a good look at the car or its plates. white lies to be sure, but necessary to allay fears about his safety. Having been alerted, the Conman and Hamlady would use their network to protect him.

Chapter 15

DON'T SPA WITH TARA HOA

Much to his own surprise, Steve Melkonian genuinely enjoyed the congressional assignment. He had finished early and sent his copy to the boss. Focused on the presidential part of the election and not certain where Steve's sympathies were, he did the editorials himself and surprised Steve with a two-week salaried furlough. Steve would have a little time on his hands for the first time in fifteen years. The Lambug Dedication and gala caused Steve to reflect on his life and how he might have lived it better as this kind of thinking was always easier after the fact. He might draw closer to his family, no easy attempt after so many year's neglect. He might do better to quit and retire completely as Boss Robyn would never go for a traditional sabbatical or extended absence. Steve had the means, but he enjoyed his work and did not relish early retirement to go marlin fishing in the gulf or golfing beside the gulf. It was just not his style. He turned in his CD-Rom, shook hands with the boss, and they made brief small talk about the furlough and Steve's trip up north to visit his children and now one grandchild.

"I should give myself two weeks with pay and go up north, too. I've got enough contacts to play a round or two at Pebble Beach." He shook his head. "It's just that this damn election gets my nanny. Why McCain put that ditz on his ticket beats me."

You never want to get Robyn's nanny if you can help it. "You mean Palin?" Steve could barely contain even a little laughter. There were some things about which the boss was decidedly 'old school,' such as a woman's place in the home, not the House or Senate, and certainly not one aged heartbeat away from the Big Kahuna.

"Oh, come now, surely Joe Bi-*dumbdumb* with his murky background does little for the Democratic ticket." Ever so slightly, Steve had just played his hand about his sympathies much to the approval of the boss.

"Good point. Looks like I might leave *The Times* in good hands after all."

"Oh, that reminds me; you took over the editorial department, did features, and pounded the beat like a real "for Boston" guy. That's what I like. I've had my attorney update my trust and will." He took a vinyl notebook from his rolltop and put it in Steve's hand like an old BC quarterback handing off to his left half. "Here, open it. This paper is yours when I die. I just ask that you never let it become a hippie rag again. Cash out and enjoy yourself before you let that happen."

Steve, of course, was flabbergasted (astounded) beyond belief! "I don't know what to say, Boss. What about your family?"

"What *about* my family! My kids don't write, I haven't heard from my daughter in five years, and don't even know what my grandkids look like."

Steve blanched and the boss read his expression, but he also knew that Steve's family had instilled in him some old-fashioned manners. You do not comment or pry into your employer's personal life.

"Like I said; she doesn't write. My son only calls when he wants money."

The boss shook his head more out of sorrow than anger, and then in a moment of candor rare for him, he revealed part of the reason of his estrangement from his family.

"Robert junior never made it to graduation. Got poor grades and dropped out to sell crap at a stall near the Common. Two years of Boston College tuition wasted on him. Yours have done a lot better."

For the boss having his son and namesake flunk out of his alma mater, especially one with the pride and tradition of BC, was tantamount to having a daughter leave a convent and become a prostitute. It hurt. Awkwardly, Steve tried to offer some consolation but the boss was not buying it.

"I understand. I was a disappointment to my father. After college he wanted me as the eldest son to follow him into the wholesale grocery business, but it wasn't for me."

"And if you had followed him into the grocery business your education would have been wasted, and an education is a terrible thing to waste. You did well by becoming a newspaperman."

He became a bit reflective, a rarity for the boss as he despised such gas bagging as "going Cronkite," a term he used for any journalistic humbuggery.

"Newspapers!" the boss thundered. "The backbone of our democracy. It's better to have a press without a government than a government without a press. Jefferson said so himself. The internet can never and should never replace them. Any idiot can write any piece of humbuggery and put it on the internet. With a newspaper, you always have the editor to check and sift out the lies, distortions, and misuse of facts. And don't you forget that!"

Steve was still too overwhelmed to say very much. "This is a very great honor...I don't know to express my gratitude for your confidence..."

"Now, don't you go weepy on me. You know how I hate that. This is a city daily, not the Oscar Awards."

"But what if you outlive me?"

"Trust me, I won't. One more thing before you take off. George Wendt will be handling your editorial duties - rather poorly I'm sure. And the cubs will finish off the Congressionals if anything new breaks. Though I doubt it. Now, get out and enjoy yourself. You may never get another chance."

They shook hands and Steve promised to work in a round of golf somewhere, anywhere. This was the last time they would ever talk.

So certain was the boss of an Obama victory that he had pre-written a couple editorials denouncing the callowness, complacency, and ill-informed character of the American electorate. The modern polling process, Gallup, Roper, and all gave a rather accurate prediction of the outcome even two weeks before the event, so another "Dewey error" was unlikely.

Steve reconnected with his family, awkwardly at first. His children were more receptive, Maria less so. So he put the office behind him and he made sure to get in that round of golf at the Fresno Country Club and touch bases with old colleagues from the "Bugs."

Ten days into the vacation, and during a second round on the course, Steve received an urgent text message from George Wendt to contact the office immediately. He hesitated as he was about to make a crucial putt on the twelfth green. He and his three partners all had "green and game wagers." So far, he was only one stroke behind the leader for the thousand-dollar pot, so he decided to wait finish the full eighteen before responding. George was a nervous little "Yalie" after all.

At LA Asylum, the office had a short subdued farewell party for Karl Keibalski. They were still in semi-official mourning for the director, and the establishment was relieved to get the investigator out of their hair and lair. Van Rumpelsteen did the five-minute speech and appreciation certificate ceremony. Everybody got cake and coffee, and wished him well on his return to Investigations. It was a true win-win situation. Asylum got rid of Mr. Macho, loudmouth, vulgar ex-football jock culture, and Karl gleefully left behind Ms. Girlie-man, dikey-bitch, maladjusto, neurotic, paper-shuffling culture - if you could call either of these phenomena a culture.

Once again he could not wait to blast out the door like he was going off-tackle, toss his personal effects in the back of his other restored vehicle, a 1950 Ford V-8 standard-trany wood-paneled station wagon with custom built DVD deck, for you guessed it, Fleetwood Mac. This time he checked his rearview with a little more suspicion as he exited Watergate Avenue toward his home. "Should I use a different route?" he wondered outloud, "or at least take Deep Throat Boulevard instead? Naw, I guess not. Paranoid schizophrenia is Ike Chaiklin's style. If your time's up, they're going to get you no matter."

Karl relaxed in front to his new widescreen plasma TV to take in the six-thirty news when he heard the OSU Fight Song chimes installed over his six-inch thick double-entry oak paneled doors. "Who the hell could that be?" he wondered, picking up a Beretta 38 from a built-in strongbox inside his coffee table. He quickly loaded two chambers but placed it discreetly hidden on a nearby hallway unit. As Karl checked the peep hole he noticed a uniformed federal courier with an "eyes only" packet. Not to worry, he was expecting to receive his new set of orders and travel documents, but why the courier and "eyes only" just to summon him to HQ? A quick perusal of the fifty page packet clarified the secrecy.

Margaret Hamlin would arrive in Los Angeles by Amtrak in three days and would set up a temporary office in an unobtrusive desert palm and plant enveloped "civic administrative center" behind the Edward R. Roybal Federal Building. Known as the "Little Roybal Building," no one would be the wiser. There would be no flights to and from Washington that might alert possible saboteurs. There would be a clandestine investigation of the recent "demises," meaning off the record and off the books. Forty pages explained the investigation process and rationale for it. He would work with a special investigator of equal rank and experience. He would not have to go to Libland and do an investigation working for superiors from a potentially hostile new administration. The final ten pages were a dossier, resume, and photo of a Tara Hoa (pronounced hwa not ho), his new partner and a more intriguing, brilliant, and able Special Agent one could not find. Slightly resembling the Asian-American actress, Tia Carrere, she was *so* hot looking in addition. Hot damn on a Polish ham. It didn't get any better than that. Yet Karl would need to learn the hard way as he always did. Never spa with Tara Hoa.

Late thirtish, Ms. Hoa came to the US via Malaysia where her Vietnamese family lived for two years at a refugee center awaiting processing for passage to America as political dissidents - real ones. Tran Hoa, the father, a captain in the Republic of Vietnam Navy spent two years at a "reeducation center" but it didn't take. So he went to the harbor, towed the wreckage of a forty-five-foot pleasure boat that an American army general had left behind, dry docked it, and refurbished it Special Agent Gibbs style, piece by piece. Determined to make the trip safely, Hoa spent two years readying the Chris Craft: sanding, caulking, and painting the hull with the appropriate Viet Minh party decals so not to arouse suspicion. The extended family of twelve put to sea in the treacherous South China waters 1200 miles to Malaysia.

Thuy, her mama, a sensitive and romantic French Vietnamese upper-middle class lady saw *Gone with the Wind* as a teenager growing up in Saigon. She gushed over the swashbuckling cavaliers and genteel crinoline ladies and decided to name her eldest of what would become a family of four strong-willed daughters after main character, Scarlett. Papa, however, did not like Occidental "decadent' films or the characters who acted in them, so Scarlett as a name was out. Tara, the name of the O'Hara plantation, was suggested by the family "aunties" as a compromise after a lot of arguing and delay of naming. The parents could not agree, so they bundled up their hot-tempered, aggressive, precocious firstborn and consulted with a "holy lady" and fortune teller. The shaman burned a little incense, brewed a pot of oolong tea, juggled dried lizard bones, snake skins, and tiger gonads in a porcelain bowl, chanted a prayer from her meditation tablet, rang some chimes on her rattan altar, banged a gong on her teakwood altar, and pronounced the child a prodigy (surprise, surprise), predicted a bright future, and declared Tara an auspicious name according to the spirits. She charged the family $500 in US green.

The old shaman mama neglected to tell the family that she had also seen *Gone with the Wind* many times and was familiar with all the characters and loved, absolutely loved, Scarlett O'Hara and saw many of her qualities in little Tara. But it was easier indeed to rip off clients when you convince them that the Eight Immortals (or Immorals!) divine your incantations, without whom you will never receive any emanations. Ah, the mysterious, inscrutable (but not un-screwable) Far East! Even among humanity's most mendacious merchants there is still "one born every minute."

At eighteen months, little Tara was quite strong, not toddling but running about, speaking in complete sentences, fetching construction tools for her father, and sometimes negotiating with the montainards for little pieces of scrap metal. An old monk at the Matsu Temple near the harbor taught her basic martial arts skills and found her motor skills, balance, speed, strength, and coordination to be that of a much older child, but neither old monk nor the young "grasshopper" knew the level to which the skills would become an integral part of her near and distant future. A scrawny montainard who took her papa's money and tried to cheat her out of her scrap metal got taken down with a series of knee-high roundhouse kicks and kung fu punches performed by this little "iron lotus."

The family spent two months on the high seas, dodging storms, typhoons, and pirates while they discreetly pulled into unmapped ports in Mindanao, Sabu, and Sarawak. They traded leftover scrap for good water and fuel - then more sailing, but this time to fairer winds and safer harbors around the Malacca straits to the refugee center outside Kuala Lumpur. Tara grew six inches aboard ship where relatives and hired crew taught her many new card games, the fundamentals of numbers games, and elementary racketeering. Tara's parents marveled at the memory and mental capacity of one so young, and though they had birthed a daughter and not a son, her family nonetheless gained much face with the creation of this auspicious offspring. At the refugee center where she continued to grow healthy and strong, security guards, UN personnel, and refugee officials marveled at Tara's ability to adapt to such a negative environment. She organized her little playmates in the refugee camp of five thousand persons and ran little enterprises, numbers rackets, a small black market (under-priced boat fuels), and a slightly vicious syndicate. The family in the next hutch stole Papa's catch for the day. That family got a ration of crab lice and scabies infestation placed in their bunks - this from a charming little Vietnamese girl not yet five.

Immigration to the United States brought a wealth of new opportunities and many challenges for the Hoa family. One more American success story. They settled into a comfortable middle-class American life in Westminster, California's "Little Saigon." Three more daughters were born but no son. Not to worry. All four girls would mature into gorgeous, successful, bi-cultural young women and kick the world in the ass - at least their part of the world. Two graduated from UCB Magna Cum Laude in business., Tara whose IQ was measured at 170. and her youngest sister, graduated from Stanford Summa Cum Laude in pre-law.

As butt-kicking Asian-American beauties go, Tara was the recognized leader of her generation and Little Saigon. When more cousins arrived from Nam, they had to offer tribute to Tara, the de facto "Little Mayor" of Magnolia Avenue. She breezed through elementary school first in her class, found time to learn the Kayakum for Asian-themed school plays, and in the back alleys of Little Saigon, she continued with her martial arts training from the best and the meanest. Earning eighth degree black belt rating in three different martial arts, Tara became an expert knife thrower and pistol shot as well. Her academic excellence record continued as she graduated from Westminster Nguyen Cao Ky High School as class valedictorian 1990, and best GPA with athletic letters in track and field - javelin and basketball as point guard. Playing on both the girls and boys teams as needed, she made All-America on one and All-State on the other. Fifty-point games were common as she became the first female admitted to the "Letterman's Club," thus causing it to be re-designated the "Letterperson's Club."

Oh, has dear reader been speculating about her dating life? Of course you have! Well, many had tried but none were chosen. All knew better than to pursue the matter. Tara had developed a reputation - more iron than lotus and with a hot temper directed toward any kind of disrespect toward her family. Walking her youngest sister home from school during her junior year, the girls were confronted by the Three Horned Dragons, a notorious Asian youth gang. Four of the Dragons tried to pull them into a small alley partly hidden by a picket fence and adjoining a lightly-wooded park. The leader brandished an open switch-blade while the other three tried to test their prowess at aggressive love-making. Stupid move! The screams, groans, and yells, amid a flurry of kicks, bends, breaks, and cracks caused enough of a disturbance to get the police there just in time to observe the Dragon's "leader" eat the switchblade with a howling groan, as it was now stuck clear through this tongue and protruding through his lower jaw. One more Dragon, slightly gelded, was kneeling on the pavement sobbing and scooping up what was left of his masculinity off the concrete. It seems the switchblade in Tara's lethal hands had done double-quick duty. No panties were jerked off but some jockeys were! That'll teach him to drop trou in public! A third Dragon who had obviously lost control of his bowels and bladder was now choking and twirling on the ground, wearing a not too becoming necklace in the form of a greasy spoke chain Tara had torn from the studs of a nearby bicycle. He got the stiffest sentence of all from the old-fashioned disciplinarian Superior Court Judge John Marshall Bedford. Thirty days in the clink and a hundred hours community service cleaning up not just the mess the Dragons had made on the good streets of Westminster, but sweeping every street and alley for the "good burghers of our fair city." He did all this while wearing a sign in English and Vietnamese stating that he promised to become toilet trained. The fourth was never prosecuted; he is still running. Police investigations cleared the two lovely teenage girls, hailed as heroines in their community and the Three Horned Dragons now deftly dehorned, quickly disbanded.

There seemed to be nothing she could not do! Entrance to the nation's prestigious law colleges would have been a given with her GPA, ethnic minority, and as a female - a slam dunk. But no, she would choose the military instead, of all things! Father would not hear of it. I did not raise my girl to be a soldier! Actually, she wanted the Marine Corps and had passed a battery of intelligence and psychological tests for Special Operations. She cited prior experience and family history.

Her father still had contacts in the Westminster Republic of Vietnam underground and Tara had organized a demonstration against a bookstore owner who was flakey enough to display a poster of Ho Chi Minh in his shop.

Overnight a citizen's brigade five thousand strong camped out, sang patriotic songs, picketed, and made fiery speeches. Although the Westminster police maintained sufficient order, the geeky storeowner, still not convinced of the error of his pinko ways, nonetheless closed and moved on, (but not to dot org.). Tara proudly asserted her willingness to take on the toughest assignments, including organizing a commando force to parachute into the jungles of Tonkin and reorganize resurgent forces there and overthrow the reds.

Major Hannibal H. Beale, chief of the Special Forces recruitment panel rejected her application and made it clear enough, "No cranks in my covert operations unit. Not now, not ever. Dismissed!"

She tried Navy Seals and Army Rangers. Both services were adamant about combat Special Forces - no females, no exceptions. Desperate for training instructors, however, the Army Rangers commissioned Tara as adjunct combat martial arts instructor and weapons anti-detonation expert, a billet she thoroughly loved. When a new trainee class arrived she called out the biggest and dumbest male chauvinist good ol' boy for a little sparring match and just about made a good ol' girl out of him instead. How she especially loved matches against those newbies who mumbled things like "dink," "chick," and "skirt!" Would these 300 pound galoots never learn? This ain't varsity football at Ole Miss, y'all! Although Tara earned outstanding efficiency reports, special commendations, and quick promotions, her training tactics, deemed too "injurious" to new recruits caused her superiors to transfer Captain Hoa to the reserves with promotion to major. Not a bad quid pro quo, and less damaging to "expensive government personnel."

Father hoped she would give up this profession which was not fit for a woman and enroll in law school. Or perhaps she could start a family, if she could find a guy not terrified of her? Now the owner of six businesses including two accounting firms, Mr. Hoa, respected as a community leader and a candidate for mayor of Westminster, could use a good corporate lawyer in the family, as her sister, the family liberal started to drift into criminal defense, of all things. Not a chance. Within two weeks Tara had assembled a computer disc full of career offers, most of them from Defense language and special investigations agencies, but a few lucrative offers came from international banking conglomerates in need of security systems analysts. She chose the Defense Investigative Service with the agreement that she could go "on loan" or TDY as needed with off-the-books compensation. For Margaret Hamlin the selection was a minor coup against the entrenched types. Someone with a history of solid achievement and military service, and a genuine patriot as opposed to another failed liberal lawyer.

It took Karl about an hour and a half to fully read and digest this packet and dossier. Now that he would soon get to know Tara Hoa professionally, he was hoping he could get to know her biblically. He glanced at his watch, 8:30 - too late for the CBS and local news. No matter. He could *not stand* Katie Colonoscopy whether casting news in her tinny tempo, cakewalking an interview over Sarah Palin, or sloppy drinking and dancing at a White House reception, so best to catch the daily highlights from the paper instead. He walked out to his new sprawling front patio to get *The Times*. The headline and bold print were unmistakable and unbelievable.

Riveside Times and Review Publisher Robert W. Robyn Dead at 75.

"Holy mother of God, it can't be!" He said out loud. *Steve touched bases with him right before he left on his trip. He told me he looked well and in good spirits. Better than he had in recent years. Why, I talked to him myself a couple weeks ago!* He quickly read the rest of the article to get the basic details: cause of death, funeral plans and wake, family issues, condolences, etc. *Jeez, this does not read like Steve's writing, it looks like Wendt did the obit. I wonder if Steve even knows about this yet? George should be the first one to tell him, but I wonder about that kid sometimes, he is a bit of a nebbish. I better phone now just to make sure.*

"Yes, Karl, I've been informed. I finally answered my cell at the club-house after a quick shower and cocktail. No, I could not believe it either, but I understand it was a massive heart attack. He was at that age of course and under a lot of pressure to turn *The Times* around, but his doctor at UCLA Medical Center gave him a thorough cardio-pulmonary check six months ago and was amazed to find his arteries like a baby's. He might have been puffing a bit, it was like him, I don't know, it just seems…" Recalling their last conversation Steve's voice broke a bit. The boss had become the father he never really had. "It seems a little strange in light of other recent deaths… like trouble comes in threes.

You could say fours, Keibalski thought to himself, but Steve did not know about the 'Watergate Avenue incident' and Karl was not about to tell him just yet.

"Listen, Karl, I'm at the Monterrey City Airport and my plane back to Riverside leaves in fifteen minutes. They're announcing my flight now, so I need to run. I should be back in three hours, but I want you to know that I'll phone you right after I touch bases with George. I need to go over a lot of matters with him. And believe me, there is something strange happening, and I will press him on these issues."

"Call me if you need anything, even if it's late. Like the song says strange things happen in this world."

"Will do-'bye."

Strange happenings, he mused. *Yeah, that's just what I was thinking.*

Chapter 16

THE INQUEST

The return flight, not quite a red-eye, gave Steve a chance to collect his thoughts and plan for an orderly transition of ownership. He would keep the same format and editorial policy. The Times' lawyers could keep the Robyn "flower children" at bay as he intended that they would get no piece of the action.

Sinister thoughts also entered Steve's mind. *The boss passes on just as he had transferred nearly all his income-earning assets to his senior editor and now executor of his trusteeship and will. The trusteeship would keep the paper out of probate, but would the will be contested? Might the lawyers suspect foul play and demand an inquest? Will I become a "person of interest?" Might the Court demand I surrender my passport? This is madness! Robyn was seventy-five after all and it's fairly common for a man his age to succumb to a heart attack, or is it? Has the coroner made a ruling, or was the heart attack "apparent" as the obit suggested?* There was much to discuss with George. Why, would a man in apparent good health change his will and talk about his demise? Did he have some sort of a premonition or is it just a coincidence. And what about his last remark? "Trust me you won't." *Taken together, it all seems a bit strange.*

Steve was adamant about the content and format. It would remain moderately conservative - no return to the hippie rag of yesteryear. Woodstock was dead - now leave it buried. That left one matter to settle above all others. Steve would fire the aging, bearded, slightly-demented second-line Deputy Editor, D. Delfynk Dobbin, a hack reporter and one time failed lawyer, now the last holdover of the Wakeley era who kept his job only by threatening management with lawsuits. Dobbin, an old queen who could not keep his paws off the young male reporters was a creep who had to go. This would be Steve's first task when he returned to the desk. Steve's attitude: go ahead and sue, I'm a lawyer too.

Steve would also review all George Herbert Walker Wendt editorials, and the follow-up obits of the boss, as he noticed Delfynk's style in the first one, and thought it a bit snide. Mustn't expect any kind of decency, respect, or gratitude from the old, hippie bastard. Worse yet, this Yalie little shit that thinks he's God's gift to journalism but still needs some eyesore old fart's input just to do a simple obit? *I guess that's how Delfynk lasted so long here; George couldn't cut it without him, but maybe, just maybe there is more to it than that? Nothing, I'd want to watch,* he mused to himself."

There were other things going through his mind. Steve had never developed with Kevork, his dad, the professional relationship he had with Robert Robyn, his long overdue mentor. Grandfather Aram, who he genuinely missed, died when he was about fourteen. As colorful a handlebar-moustached *"mets hayr"* (grandfather) as you could ever meet, he spoke in broken English laced with Turkish-Armenian in an enormous booming voice. His fierce countenance was accentuated by his six-foot-five height (gigantic for an Armenian) and unsightly tufts of hair growing out of his ears and nose. Add to that an overbearing scent of Turkish pipe tobacco, lamb, and onions he intimidated all but the bravest or most curious of his Odar (non-Armenian) neighbors. How he loved to sit and tell stories on the front porch of the family's three-story house, one of the few in Fresno, a miracle in itself that it was never flattened during an earthquake!

In spite of the language gap, he tried his best (Kevork did not speak Armenian with his children) to share his love of the "old country' with grandson Steven, Kevork's first born. He would tell ancient warrior tales of the Daredevils of Sassoon, recite poems, sing folksongs, and patiently try to convince his young charge why Armenians were smarter than everyone else. "Remember my grandson, it takes ten Jews to outsmart one Greek, but it takes ten Greeks to outsmart one Armenian! May you grow big and strong and become a true shenshunarnik, *inshallah*! (a shrewd businessman, if God wills it)."

Always happy and gentle when it came to his grandchildren, the one thing that could make him angry was his remembrance of the massacres committed by the Ottoman armies in 1894, 1896, and especially 1915, that final and most horrible, and the one that drove the Melkonian family out of Turkey on their blessed journey to a new land with new hope and a new nationality.

Young Steve listened with rapt attention as Grandfather Aram pulled his well-chewed favorite pipe from his mouth and waved it accusingly in the air, angrily denouncing the government of the new Republic of Turkey for their continued cover-up of an obvious and shameful historical record, and the US State Department's complicity in the same. He knew, for example, that Hollywood had planned to make a movie of Franz Werfel's *The Forty Days of Musa Dagh* with no less a rising star than Clark Gable playing the noble young Lieutenant Gabriel Bagradian, the lead part. The Embassy of the Republic of Turkey protested vigorously and the State Department Nervous Nellies leaned on their Hollywood mogul friends not to do the film. The moguls showed the same lack of principle, scrapped production, and the film has never been reconsidered by any A-list producer or studio exec.

Father and son, however, had a distant relationship at best with his soft, gentle, God-fearing mother, Hasmik ever playing the role of conciliator. The father could never understand why Steve would not want to go into the wholesale grocery business when "everything had been set up for him."

Now it appeared that Steve would inherit a troubled Southern California daily and continue the quixotic effort of breathing life into, not just a medium-sized city daily but a dying medium. Could it be done? Would it be done? Would he do it? Or would *The Riverside Times* become one more dinosaur daily? A statistic for the almanac publishers? Or worse yet, for Wikipedia, a final requiem for the newspaper business, Boss Robyn's "last hurrah." He had a newspaper to run, a business of his own, and heavy responsibility for the first time in his life. Steve's moral lapses aside, why had it taken him this long to find his own life path? An unanswerable question really. Why give it much thought except that it would haunt him now and then.

Lost in his thoughts, Steve ignored the landing announcement.

"Excuse me, sweetie. Fasten your seatbelt please," gushed the flight attendant.

To enjoy such pampering there is nothing like flying business class! Of course, Steve always had a way with women, but she might have merely recognized his name and status from the manifest. Finally home, he could piece together the fragmented details of Robyn's passing. He wanted to go to the office but he knew that Yalie George, an 8 to 5 type would likely have locked up by now. Best to get a good night's rest and pummel him hard in the morning, boola, boola! He did a quick cell phone call but it was obvious from the giggles and sighs on the other end that George was sharing his sleepy time, probably with Chelsea, the new intern.

Steve made the conversation short, "Be at the office at 6:30 a. m. sharp and pass the word to Delfynk, if you can reach him and he isn't zonked out on some chemical."

By five the next morning Steve was in his office reviewing the last ten days' issues and blue-lining new copy. He would need to review the legal documents and rewrite the complete obituary with details about the funeral arrangements, plus correct the addle-headed editorial copy superficially thought out by preppie Wendt and wimpy Dobbin.

Steve had to play catch up. The copy could never make this morning's edition. He would need to run it tomorrow, at latest. The election was yesterday, so any reproof of the American electorate would be dated by further delay. Six-thirty a. m.; the deputy editors should arrive any minute. That would give him a half-hour ass-chewing time before the beats arrived. He took five and regarded what would now become his office and inheritance; the half-empty Jack Daniels quart, the sad-looking Spuds Turkee fedora, the iconic old-time rolltop, and most of all, the 1930 Underwood manual typewriter, all the trappings of Boss Robyn's Time and Life, all from a bygone era. Steve noticed a crow that had perched at the picture window but at his glance it flew away.

As he returned to his typing, Steve heard the two underlings opening the front doors and talking heatedly.

"I'm telling you plain enough we *will* keep the same editorial policies. If you cannot accept that, just type your letter of resignation. The accountant will draw up a month's salary, and you're out of here. Otherwise, get with the program!"

"Why can't we be more loving people?" Delfynk replied, tearing up.

"Stop your habitual whining and get to work, now!"

Wendt reported in to the new boss. Steve handed the editorials to his new first deputy. "George, here are the corrections I want made on the editorial, and the additions to the obituary. I have reread Mr. Robyn's will, and as his executor and beneficiary, I know how he wants this transition done. You have two hours, then I want to see you first for a confidential meeting. It should not take long - you will become the senior editor. In addition, I suggest you start reviewing your new career objectives. You will need to get up to speed quickly on these or we stand a good chance of losing the paper, but I'm confident you will step up to the plate. After we discuss the transition send in *Dull..Fink,*" Steve exaggerated the name for emphasis.

"He's deadwood-the last holdover from the Wakeley era and he's outta here thirty minutes ago, but don't tell him now. I will handle it." As Steve took over for Robert W. Robyn, he handled it all very well, decisively, but with a warning, encouragement, and promotion for his immediate subordinate. He believed in George H.W. Wendt: he was just snobbish and a little arrogant, but these negatives were easily overcome with experience and a sense of commitment.

During the next two hours Steve, now the boss, drew up a new organizational chart and business plan for the New Year that included objectives, goals, and personnel reassignments. George reworked the editorials, extended the obituary, and reviewed his new job requirements. Dobbin, who would be the only reporter terminated, spent the time drinking herb tea and doing his morning mental masturbation, or meditation as he like to call it, or levitation, transubstantiation, cross-fertilization, or anything else to get out of doing real work. When the time came for the changing of the guard, Steve handled it the way Robyn would have liked: brief, precise, no nonsense. As he typed furiously, Steve thought he might reiterate his plans to make certain his new right hand man was fully on board and ready for greater commitment.

"George, as I mentioned this morning, I am asking you to take over as editor because it is a big job and I know you can handle it. As I said, Dobbin is dead wood and must go. We're going to move Ricardo Rios to first deputy."

"Do you think a Dartmouth will play sub to a Yale?"

"I happen to be Fresno State and it's my paper now, so you two had better play ball. Now I want you to call an all-hands meeting and distribute the new organizational chart. Also, and this is off the record, there are many issues about Boss Robyn's death that aren't adding up. I've got contacts that can help me clear this up, but I want a full disclosure and report from you by the end of the day. I want to know who was the last person to see him alive, what emergency treatment he received if any, or who took him to the hospital, and who chose the mortuary. If you did any of these things, please let me know. Something just isn't right about all this. Karl Keibalski will meet with his boss and new partner downtown today and I'll touch bases with him this afternoon and then arrange a meeting where maybe we can put the pieces of the puzzle together. We may have nothing more than a series of remarkable coincidences, or a major expose. Who knows? Now, before you go out to address the troops, send in Dobbin. The sooner he's history, the better I'll feel about the future of this paper."

And so, dear reader, George Herbert Walker Wendt addressed his troops for the first time as the new field commander and then returned to his editorial work. For as Nappy said so well before he got Bone-Aparted at Waterloo, "In every corporal's knapsack is a field marshal's baton."

It did not take long for Steve to deliver the coup de un-grace. The new senior editor's speech took ten minutes and the staff of sixty returned to their desks. Five minutes later George glanced up from his editorials to observe Dumbarton Delfynk Dobbin, decadent scion of a once prominent Maryland family, shuffle out of the office, head down, tears streaming down his greasy matted beard that was gross even before Woodstock '69. He was mumbling something about the 30 best years of his life for the *Roach* and why can't they be more loving people" or some woeful moronic dirge like that. He'd do better to go out to MGM central casting and get a job doing the last years of Karl Marx, except that the part might require some measure of intellect in addition to a pathetic countenance. So with the Fall of the House of Dobbin now completed, we have Edgar Allen Poe to thank.

Whew good riddance and glad that's over, were George's only thoughts as he anticipated his new responsibilities without the dead weight of that old pervert.

Engrossed in his objectives, Steve made arrangements with Keibalski to meet the next afternoon.

They met halfway at the Arte Café, a modestly-priced but charming continental bistro at a town center mall in Cerritos, a sleepy Asian-American small town tucked away in the San Gabriel Valley between Los Angeles and Orange Counties. More famous for its overpriced auto square than anything else, no one would ever think to look for them there, thus a good place to hash out the past month's strange happenings or ditch whatever fedspooks might attempt a trail.

Karl could not stop hyping about how happy he was to be back in Investigations. And how much he was looking forward to his new assignment, "Check out my new partner-what a dish! Don't be too jealous!"

Nice going, Karl, ever hear of something called a security clearance and need to know, or does it matter that you kinkoed classified documents just to impress a bud?

"Believe it or not I am being followed and while I can't prove it, some feds in a tinted-window Chrysler sedan forced me off the road and tried to bump me off for whatever reason. And in your car, no less."

Good move, Karl, that's always nice to hear.

"My Investigations training taught me to note details fast, so when it happened, I picked up on the U.S. Government plates, but I couldn't read the numbers before it merged into left lane traffic. Margaret is checking out the description now. You know model, year, and all that. She's trying to trace it. But if it's a rogue element - fat chance."

"Could they have been fake federal plates?"

"I thought about that but where's the motive? Not the underworld - no connection. Longstreet, Falabenko, and even your boss joined the turf club within three weeks. Can you say Pierre Ouine?"

"I think you're getting a little too old to do broken field running, like you could get benched."

"Ya gotta love a sports fan, but hear me out. The guy's envious, para- noid, and crooked as a ram's horn, so he's got real mental problems and I wouldn't put assassination past him."

"That's interesting. Now where did you take your degree in abnor- mal psychology? Wasn't your major downfield blocking?"

"Naw, it was accounting and Armenian Studies, that way I could learn to chisel all my customers. Now if you've got a better theory, let's hear it. It seems like I've been feeding you prime cut and even risking my life while all you need to do is get out a Mac burger front page on a has-been radrag. And you don't need a Headshrink PhD to know people. A loser like Chaiklin has one and he can't even shrink his own head."

Ignoring the gross ethnic slur, Steve countered, "Now that I control the vault, you could be privy to the locked files the boss collected on Ouine, before and after his stint at Asylum, and the dirt we have on him might fill an outhouse not just a privy - if you behave yourself! In addition, the report George Wendt prepared raises more interesting questions and you may want to relay those to Margaret. So don't accuse me coasting."

Karl blanched at that, "Huh, what sort of questions?"

"Questions l-i-i-i-i-ke, why the Anaheim Pioneer Progressive Hospital pronounced him dead of natural causes, but the coroner has not released his remains to the funeral home for the wake as his parish priest, children, and I have all requested? We keep hearing vague responses and I am about ready to get our lawyers in on it. Also, George was likely the last person to see him alive, he thinks, but not the first person to see him dead. George went home with Chelsea at six that evening, so he's in the clear. The boss rarely went home until ten or eleven. First reports indicate that death occurred around 1:00 a. m. George, Delfynk, and Ricardo arrived about the same time the next morning, 7:00 a. m. and found him slumped over his desk, and a Jack Daniels bottle with about two shots left on the floor next to his chair. I'm going to talk with the coroner at Anaheim Progressive and try to get the boss released for the wake. This delay is just causing agony for his family. I'll bring one of our lawyers, if necessary."

Steve was being charitable. The only agony to his family would be the lack of an inheritance that his children, now on their way from Boston, had anticipated.

"I have another meeting with Ms. Hamlin and Hot Tara Hoa tomorrow. Would you e-mail a copy of George's report? It might work well for us both if I have something this impressive to submit." He smiled a bit. "And she might bend a few rules in your direction a little, too."

Karl checked his watch, a new Rolex, just like the one Kobe Bryant wore. Who knows where in the blazes he got the money to pay for it. "Four o'clock already, can you believe it, dude? Time flies when you're having fun. Gotta get back to my apartment for a quick shit, shower, shave, and shine. Then, I'm meeting Tara for a little after-hours cocktail brainstorming session at the Pootahngheehr around five-thirty for a little poontang there. Ahahaha….pretty witty, huh?"

"Apartment? I thought you just bought a new home in Yorba Linda?"

Karl seemed chagrined. "Well, uh yeah. But my old lady is back from visiting her relatives in Seattle, and I got this little hutch tucked away in The Lofts for any extra action. You know how it is. Tara seemed a little stiff at the meeting today but I can loosen her up. Anyway, I split the rent with The Conman and we use the pad for our quick scores. No one else knows about this, so the next time you see Judy, I went overnight TDY to San Ysidro and stayed at the Border Patrol dorm. Got it?"

Dismayed, Steve glanced up from his mojito and set him straight. "I don't know much about this Tara, except that she's not one to try your horizontal antics with, so I wouldn't go there if I were you. Also, I don't like subterfuge."

"Well, *you're* getting mighty preachy for someone with your reputation. When did you get religion?"

Steve thought about the events of his lifetime that had coalesced within the past month and his response became a glaring retort. "When I began to understand the damage I had done to my family life and professional reputation, some of which I can never repair, that's when!

You've got a teenage son and daughter that you say you are proud of. If you don't look out you might not be part of their lives ever again. Think it over - it's not too late for you."

Shaken, Karl said little before he got up to leave the Arte, except that he hoped that Steve would keep him posted on the developments, especially any persons of interest to a federal jurisdiction.

By six p. m. Tara pondered this low-end assignment over a bourbon and soda at the Pootahngheehr Mountbatten Lounge for "our distinguished patrons," a slightly more upscale watering hole across the main lobby from the No-Tell Lounge. A moderately cool but sunny day by California standards, she wore a lightweight Lady Burberry trench coat that she did not need given her strong constitution, but it had been tailored to secure classified documents. At thirty-eight, she carried a lean and steel-coiled 175 pounds on a shade over six-foot-tall frame, large in bone structure, her torso - a double V curve with vectors, nuclear warhead breasts, and teardrop sinewy hips. With longish legs and arms that were perfectly balanced and muscled, it was rumored that she could do a four-hundred-pound bench press. Dressed in her usual dark blue pantsuit, Tara wore her medium length black hair straight, no perm, so she could easily wrap it into a bun, when the action got rough. Evoking a bit of her French blood, her deep-magenta oval eyes sensually concealed the steel behind them. Completing the visual ensemble were her powerful yet elegant ivory-toned hands, large even for a woman her size. Deceptively smooth skin covered prominent knuckles that had seen lethal action. Jawaharlal noticed all this as he furiously mixed guests' drinks in an expensive cocktail shaker and worried about his "undocumented help" that Pabu kept off the books and underpaid in cash. He excused himself, turned toward the rows of liquor bottles, and nervously cell-phoned his brother speaking in Punjabi about yet another potential "raid", asking him to come immediately and keep things cool.

"You don't *really* pay your undocumented alien workers $2.50 per hour do you?"

"Madam speaks Punjabi?" he flustered.

" Yes, she does. And seven other languages in addition, doesn't everybody?"

"Yes, yes, of course."

Oh, he was beginning to sweat now!

Tara gazed into her drink deep in thought. *Esprit de corps notwithstanding, it's best that I'm just on loan to these turkeys; I would not want to work with such losers for very long. Hell, here comes the densest of the lot - we had to explain everything to him twice this morning. I wish I were back on active duty, I would be a full colonel by now with a line number for brigadier. I volunteered for Iraqi Freedom four times! Always the same damn excuse - the billet is filled already.*

Such bullshit! I rough up a few wimpy rednecks that can't take it and I'm hosed forever. How I hate this digital military! Tara glanced at her lady Omega watch. *This is so damn boring. It's about time that dumb Kulak got here....don't know why he picked this trashy-looking Indu Ah San dive, of all places to discuss security matters. He will likely try to come on to me. They always do. I am so damn tired of clumsy presumptuous males, especially has-been jocks who still think they are God's gift to grateful women. I wish I could avoid another confrontation but these peckerheads never learn.*

Better watch it, Karl. She looks like Madam Butterfly but reacts like General Patton.

"Pardon me," Jawaharlal Pootahngheehr inquired politely. "Would madam like another bourbon and soda? For you it is free."

Tara rarely drank but when she did, she nursed her usual bourbon and soda which she never finished.

"No, she would not! I am waiting to meet a business colleague.

Worried that Keibalski might take his pants down again, the owner screamed in his falsetto Brahmin high pitched voice, "I recognize him as a most troublesome of all patrons - extremely bad karma!"

Tara stared briefly into her drink, mumbled something like, "I can handle it," and waited for the Kulak drunkard to make his move.

Karl had already put away five Budweiser boilermakers and was already way past the eight point level when he barreled into this pseudo-gentry Old Limey Lounge.

"Hey, Tara. How's my favorite fortune cookie? Sweet and crunchy I hope! How about the house favorite, porterhouse steak and ranch fries washed down with your favorite brew? My treat of course. Afterward, we can talk shop at my loft - it's only two blocks from here. Old Pootahngheehr stops playing Hindu when it comes to treating his customers right."

"Actually, I am Vietnamese, not Chinese - also vegetarian. And while I'm not very sweet, I do crunch buttheads like you, so you got that part of it right. Now, as you are thirty minutes late, let's cut the bullshit and get on with the briefing."

"Oh, you can brief me anytime or even de-brief if you like. And then I'd love to pull your knickers off, too, as the Brits say. So let's do a trade.'

"You've already jumped the shark, so the meeting is over and you don't get to leave like a gentleman."

"Well, I hear that they used to call you Old Ironcrotch during your active duty days, and I bet your reputation is well earned. But I can do a hot lube job and remove a little of that rust that you must have by now."

Tara cut him off with a clench and a glare then steeled herself for a takedown. It might not be an easy one; he had the size advantage, sort of. And as sotted as he was, not likely to feel pain - much.

"Stupid, drunk, and boring is no way to go through life. Now, Keibalski, I can break your neck and finish you off before your rogue feds do. Or I can break your back and you get to crap in a bag the rest of your miserable life and never again bed another bimbo stupid enough to shack up with you. Or we can do this the easy way, I can simply kangaroo hop you out of here in a bum's rush that will have you so embarrassed that you will never again show your face in this little swami's passion pit."

Now on the scene, Inestimable Elder Brother Pabu went into his smoke and mirrors liturgy. "Please, madam, please. My hotel is virtuous," the owner implored. "My family is virginal. All my daughters are respectable."

Yeah, swami, a likely story! You just got your adjectives a little mixed up. No matter. It happened too fast even for Karl's running back reflexes.

"Okay, Tara, don't get radical. I'll lea…aaheowhoohoohooey!"

"Good move, Karl, you chose the bum's rush! You just don't get to leave like a gentleman, that's all!"

To the astonishment of the turbaned, handlebar mustached, bronze-faced, monkey-suited, jodhpured, attendant standing outside the Mountbatten, a little bit of Old Malaya in beautiful downtown Anaheim, both doors few open simultaneously. Only it would not be a nose-in-the-air British viceroy exiting to his carriage after brandy and cigars at the club.

I daresay that through these exotic portals flew OSU butthead ex-fullback Karl Keibalski, kangaroo hopped, tossed, and landed at the car hop stand. His dislocated left arm hanging precariously from the shoulder on the cobbled circular driveway, he lay sprawled with two legs over the curb, and a dazed "what hit me" expression on his face. This time it wasn't Michigan's ugly, stocky, nose guard to do the damage, just a modern, superbly self-confident Asian-American beauty. Times had certainly changed, hadn't they, Mr. Heisman Trophy winner - almost? But you haven't. And so, dear reader, our pile-driving, dust clouding, high-testosterone, fifty-yard line wonder, has-been OSU fullback learned the not so easy way not to spa with Tara Hoa.

Straight up the middle (no longer) Karl was caught between the proverbial rock and a hard place. He called on The Conman who, as fortune would have it, happened to be in town and on this evening had no action planned. As Karl was more shamed than badly hurt, The Conman took him to Anaheim Pioneer for treatment and medication, and later to the "hutch" to recover while they called on Steve to drive Keibalski's car from the Pootahngheehr lot to the crash pad. Propped up on pillows, with his favorite brewski just for you-ski, and a lot of valium as painkiller, he did a little channel surfing on The Conman's new plasma screen to pass the time and wig out.

As far as Mrs. Keibalski knew he was out of town on business. Tara thought about ratting him out to his old lady but decided against it as Margaret Hamlin was a straight arrow about such things. He tried to find his favorite porn movie station, but it appeared that Conman had not paid his part of the cable bill in months, so service was cut off and the remote defaulted to Channel 40, CBN, the religious station out of Costa Mesa - just what he wanted to see. Mega-televangelist, faith healer, and religious shakedown artist Barney Hein was giving his usual pitch. "I can heal you with the power of prayer if you subscribe to my newsletter. Only $300 a year. That's all you need to cure your pain, save you from Hell, and assure you your seat in Heaven," he said pointing at Karl through the airways.

"Groovy, I already feel like Hell because of Tara (he still didn't get it), and you want three hundred clams just to cure my pain and walk me down the fire escape past Good Old Pete through the Pearly Gates? You are my pain! Better luck conning little old ladies out of their social security checks. Between him and that terrorist-loving pinko Tommy Crapola, these born-again Christians are giving God a bad name! There must be something better on."

There you go again; always blaming others for your screw-ups. Make sure your cable bill is paid *before* you use the pad. The next day's scheduled meeting was postponed due to Karl's unfortunate mishap. No matter, it was Friday and better to start fresh on a Monday instead.

Tara arrived at the Little Roybal Building Monday at nine and talked with Ms. Hamlin first.

"Off the record, what you did was admirable. And yes, I found out about it, I always do. I'll see to it that you receive a commendation for your slightly eccentric disciplining of a reprobate officer. Mr. Keibalski has always been an aggressive, overbearing, and slightly depraved male who has acted habitually with conduct unbecoming a federal investigator, however his knowledge of the law, fact-finding skills, and uncanny ability to close difficult criminal cases have saved his job more often than I can mention. So when he arrives... and I see the flash on my phone so he must be here, I must present each of you with a letter of counsel that such conduct impedes the mission and is not appropriate conduct for a federal officer, after which I shall file yours in number thirteen. I hope you understand."

"Yes, I understand and I hope you understand that I did not volunteer for this assignment, and I consider it below my level of experience and competence. Mr. Keibalski, on the other hand, seems to be mismatched to the point that he has to cover his insecurity with alcohol and sexual bravado. Moreover, his language was vile and full of salacious innuendo."

"Don't I know that! I have worked with him for twenty-five years and I have saved his job more than once."

The receptionist nodded to Karl that Ms. Hamlin would seen him, so he pranced in, left arm in sling, and head high like a race horse that had just won The Triple Crown. Avoiding Tara's glare, he went straight into his ruse, "A little pick-up basketball with my son, heh, heh. Like, you shoulda seen it, Kobe couldn'ta done it better. Made the lay-up but came down hard on the concrete. Getting a little too old for this sort of thing but Jeffrey needs the off-season practice if he wants to make All-State!"

"You are such a *wonderful* Dad, aren't you? Except I happen to know exactly what happened last Thursday night at that Punjab passion pit, and that your behavior was beyond reproof. It was despicable. You are worse than a common barnyard animal and a disgrace to the service. This is the very last time I am going to save your job."

"Oh, don't believe everything Tara told you," he said winking. "She's always had problems with men and is a well-known les…"

"Want the other arm in a sling too?"

"That's enough, both of you! One more disparaging word about another officer's private life and I *will* fire you! For the record, Ms. Hoa has a fiancé and she did not inform on you. But others aware of your disorderly conduct did. So consider yourself walking a tightrope."

"Who were they? Can I ask?" Karl gasped, incredulously.

"You may not. And you have been warned. I see all, I hear all, and I know all. So if you think you can put one over on me forget it. I have issued you both letters of counsel"

She reached into her desk drawer, took out two sealed envelopes, and handed one to each. "Read and heed. After you have read, please sign. I do not want to have this kind of conversation again. Clear enough?"

Both nodded and Ms. Hamlin regarded another red signal on her desk phone, and answered it by saying, "Yes, send him in." Turning back to her unruly charges, "You will work with a third partner whom I have sworn and deputized a federal marshal to assist you with this investigation. You already know him."

Karl turned and who should be standing there but his cohort in expose, Steven A. Melkonian. "Judas Priest on a Vatican Sunday!"

"Yes, Karl, I know you're surprised but he knows too much not to use his insights, and besides, you have a reputation of sorts of working well together. This time for the good of the service, I hope."

Margaret had a full career history of flying in under the radar. Nonetheless, she must have bent or broken at least fifty federal regulations to make such a direct appointment; no training, no experience, no law enforcement history. Usually, only the President has this kind of appointment power but he was busy today mumbling about bringing *demokersee* to *Eye-rak* or whatever *A*-rab hell hole had caught his attention at the moment.

"Yes, but a U.S. Marshal's badge? I've never had one of those even with all my training."

Tara, who had until this moment looked uncharacteristically down-cast as the "third person out" perked up a bit and sneered, "At your level of competence and efficiency, you could always pick a reasonable facsimile out of your kid's cereal box."

"That's enough, Ms. Hoa. I can assure you that you will have their full cooperation in this enterprise and that they understand the sacrifice you are making."

She now turned slightly in her swivel chair to confront Karl and Steve. "Gentlepersons, and I do expect you to conduct yourselves as such, this is never to be a gender hostile effort. Until further notice all three of you are hereby officially neutered. If I detect a hostile work environment, the person or persons responsible, are off the team with my personal recommendation that you be dismissed from the federal service. Keibalski, I am especially addressing my words to you. I know your daughter has been accepted at Vassar, and tuition is not cheap. So don't do anything to disappoint her. Got it?"

"Yes, Ms. Hamlin, of course." A little formal, perhaps, for one who had been a former lover, but this time there was a genuine look of fear in his eyes.

She glanced at her wall clock. "It is now half past ten. You will proceed directly to Dr. Ishmael Fernwood, Riverside County Coroner who will give you the details of the Robyn inquest. Steve is likely to have the best information on Mr. Robyn's actions and contacts - rely on him. You will jointly prepare a report with documentation of his findings to be submitted by the end of the week, this Friday. Dr. Fernwood has assured me full cooperation with these materials. You will use the unmarked company car which is parked in the third stall behind this building. He is expecting you in one hour. Good luck."

They filed out and Steve spoke first, "We will need a lot of good luck to make sense of vague bits and pieces."

"Yeah," Karl countered, "but you knew him best so this one is your call. I can handle the Asylum and Investigations parts and my own near death experience, and if we can get past my recent bad manners, Tara can be a great help with the Intelligence part. There have got to be some termites in the woodwork." This is as close to humble as Keibalski would ever get so they "shook on it" in the parking lot.

Dr. Fernwood, an ebullient, slightly-undernourished stooped-shoul-dered nebbish of a nerd of medium height with pasted-down gray hair, oversize granny spectacles, doctor's smock, dark brown tie beige shirt, baggy corduroy pants and badly scuffed brown oxford shoes, greeted them cheer-ily in his coroner's office. "I see we have had a little mishap, haven't we?

"Oh, that? It's nothing really. Just a little pickup basketball," Karl sheepishly replied.

Tara, now in a better mood, smiled just little bit. "Yeah, we did a little one on one. I got the lay-up, he got the concrete, but it was all in good fun."

She had out machoed him - again! Uncharacteristically at a loss for words, Karl went into a mini-sulk and the good doctor continued.

"Um, my team and I have completed the inquest and have sent the decedent to the Anaheim Shady River Mortuary, per instructions of the will. Mr. Melkonian, you have indicated that you are the executor of the estate. As executor you may make arrangements with Shady River for the funeral and burial, according to his wishes," he continued nervously.

Just barely concealing his irritation, Karl was beginning to fidget. *Just what is this geek's little problem anyway,"* he thought.

In a moment they would find out what the geek's little problem was. He would lay a forensic whammy on them and it would make it *their* big problem instead.

As his hands shook, Dr. Fernwood handed them each a sealed one-inch thick eight by eleven manila mailer.

"I have prepared the full report of inquest and autopsy…." He had done this many times but this was the first one for the feds. "Also a copy for the local police. As you shall see, Mr. Robyn did not die from natural causes."

"MOTHER TERESA ON A POGO STICK, IT WAS FOUL PLAY! That's three in a row and almost me!"

Brilliant deduction, Sherlock. A not entirely unexpected development and you wanted back in Investigations, after all. You just didn't expect to pursue your own case or anything close to it.

Steve was nonplussed. Head down he wondered why he had been damn fool enough to accept Ms. Hamlin's offer of the deputy marshals badge.

"Well, uh, I can think of maybe one or two who…." He paused. He thought the better of offering a premature opinion. Tara took up the slack.

"Would you elaborate please? We would like input from you before we read the report. Would you speculate on what, or who, killed Robert Robyn?

With a little more sweaty nervousness, he stammered it out, "Uhm, p-p-perhaps you recall the famous British spymaster case from about twenty-five years ago…" Stretching his words for emphasis, Fernwood continued, "uh, th-th-th-thee Soviet Union sent an assassin to, uh, dispatch a prominent Bulgarian dissident expatriate living in London as refugee? It was done with a vial of resin concealed in an umbrella?"

"Oh yeah. That was the Ivan Droopov case. Fascinating. I have the book."

"Ah, yes, Mr. Keibalski, I see that you are right on top of things."

"Fu…uh," he caught himself, as Ms. Hamlin had also warned him about his foul language. "You bet. I usually am."

We definitely ruled out a natural coronary thrombosis once we discovered a massive dose of resin in his circulatory system. Also, the lesion on his right calf above the ankle indicates he was poisoned in much the same matter. Our report will give the sufficient details, I believe."

Team leader Tara thanked the good doctor for his patience and efforts. They stopped briefly at an upscale but subdued Anaheim restaurant, Mr. Fox, for a quick lunch. (not the No Tell lounge) After locating a darkened area absent other guests, they felt it safe to open the envelope and do a quick skim and discuss seventy-five pages before returning to The Little Roybal for consultation with Margaret. Tara and Karl did most of the quick analysis. Deep in thought and a little depressed a somber Steve could not say much.

How? Why? No time to think about these things now. As executor of the estate, it fell on Steve to make the funeral arrangements and contact Boss Robyn's children in Boston. Wendt had informed them of their father's passing already, but they had to come to California for the reading of the will and attend the funeral. Over the telephone, they did not appear to be shocked or very grieved. He would need to "pull back" on his own reporter's instincts out of decency until after the burial. The resin issue could wait.

The family held deeds to a couple of plots in Boston's oldest Catholic cemetery, however, the boss stated in his will that he wanted burial in the Riverside National Cemetery with California's fallen veterans. His children seemed interested only in his estate, despite their rejection of "crass materialism." As all documents had been filed in California, it was done at the offices of *The Riverside Times and Review* staff attorney, the law offices of Chutzpov, Goniv & Metzschmuck. You remember them. The matter was over in an hour and a half, with the poor, disaffected offspring mumbling about the "unfairness" of it all, the "rotten system," and "capitalist greed" on their way out of the law offices. But there wasn't diddly-squat they could do about it. The will was airtight, especially against airheads.

The funeral service was held a week later at the Riverside Mission Assistencia and presided over by Cardinal Patrick Pedaphony. His final mass before retirement had drawn five thousand persons, a surprising number since the boss had left the "big time" years earlier. It was apparent that during his sojourn on earth he had influenced more souls than expected. The people who knew him best and respected him for his good qualities, sat in the front rows: Margaret, Steve, Tara, and Karl from US Immigration, fellow publishers, "the troops of the trade," even a couple congressmen and one senator, but his children and ex-wife did not attend. His oldest and best friend, Leilo Torquemada, gave a brief but a colorful eulogy of their days on the docks and in the army which brought laughter and tears to the guests. The best eulogies always have this quality. He looked up above the frescoes toward the ceiling and winged saints beside the Throne.

"My old friend, if there is corned beef and cabbage in heaven, wait for me. I will cook the best you have ever had, I promise."

They all filed past. Steve paused for a moment, took a metal object from his pocket, and placed it inside the casket. No one could see what it was, and he would not say. When a Times' cub reporter asked him about it, he just said, "Personal, not newsworthy." A publisher's word is tantamount to law and Boss Robyn's obituary would be done with dignity and grace.

Finally, there was the usual uniformed three-gun salute for a former army officer. The color guard troops removed the flag and handed it to the closest next of kin that had the decency to show, a niece. Briefly, a white seagull flew over and landed on the casket but quickly flew off. Steve was the last to leave the cemetery after Tara tossed some flowers on the casket. Then the maintenance crew covered the grave. Steve said a short prayer in Armenian, turned tearfully away, and mumbled inaudibly, "We'll find them. We'll find them."

-30-

AFTERWORD

All good things come to an end. Fortunately, so do some bad things; like CIS systematic corruption we dare hope. We part company on bittersweet notes of pleasure and pain, hope and despair, loss and redemption. The characters and events of the story you have just read are pure fiction. Again, dear reader, it is up to you to decide. Dedicated to the memory of that colorful, cantankerous, curmudgeonly newspaper editor, Robert Wilcox Robyn, the author wishes him godspeed to the place where all the great newspaper magnates go, with the certain knowledge that the other lords and ladies of the press are waiting to usher him to his new rolltop there. They who died with a pen in their hands can now publish with confidence, assured that Boss Robyn will get out the morning edition of the *Valhalla Times*. Finally, may every good sex maniac, wherever he is, (or in this day and age of playmate-of-the-month school marms), wherever she is, continue to sell newspapers. No one else wants to anymore.

In Memory of the giants - actual and fictitious (many more are deserving - I don't know about all of them)

William Randolph Hearst
Joseph Pulitzer
Joseph R. Knowland
Catherine Graham
Eugene C. Pulliam
Norman Chandler
Lord Beaverbrook
Crotchety Old Colonel Robert McCormick
Axel Springer (for magazines)
Henry Luce (for magazines)
Self-proclaimed "Man of the Century" Hannibal Hamlin Hardy
Robert Wilcox "Boss" Robyn
"Madam" Speaker Sandra G. Lusepuzi (newspapers and other enterprises)

SOME OF THE CHARACTERS

Steven Ara Melkonian - middle-aged Armenian-American hack reporter, turned tort lawyer, returned to newspapers and still looking for his "breakout."

Robert Wilcox Robyn - pronounced "ROW-bin" old-time crusty, cantankerous, city editor determined to turn the *Riverside Roach*, his just-purchased "underground hippie rag" into *The Riverside Times and Review*, a respectable city daily.

Luis Leilo "Da Torque" Torqemada - Cuban émigré attorney and restaurateur. Personal "career counselor" to John B. Ouine, confidant, community organizer, activist, *bon vivant*, purveyor of blocks of Lakers game tickets and other things. Owner of Restaurante El Malecon (front) and "Party Dolls Gentlepersons Club" (back), aka "Da Torques," a high class Pomona nudie bar and favorite watering hole of mid to high-level straight male and lesbian female INS personnel. The elite - usually judges, district counselors, and bureaucrats with a GS-14 rating or above, have controlled access to the backrooms for special occasions and tension relief. Members only and club key required. Lower ranks need not apply.

Karl Kirel Keibalski - Former All-America fullback at Ohio State University, 225 pounds of raw Slavic fury. Played on the great legendary Coach Stoney Oates teams. Played 1970-1973 in the same backfield with two-time Heisman Trophy winner quarterback Harvey Grissom. The trophy might have gone to Keibalski, the only time two players on the same team were up for it. But just before the Michigan game, he turned in his gear and left college, no one was knew why. Goes north and plays in the Canadian league until a knee injury forces him out. Takes up criminal investigation and joins the Cleveland INS anti-alien smuggling task force unit for the Great Lakes area. Makes lateral move to LA Asylum as a mole to gain knowledge of alien smuggling rackets on the southern border. Have a field day conspiracy theorists!

John (sometimes Jean) Pierre Beauregard Ouine - pronounced "we-NAY" not "we-NEE", as he is fond of saying. Now the director of the Los Angeles Asylum Office this former INS investigator came up through the ranks from level one border patrolman. Also, proud of his southern heritage and claims to be a descendent of a Civil War Confederate general. This war has produced descendents most uncivil. On the take and wants the national director's job. Lotsa luck, fella!

Harriet McCornnell - political activist and former LA Asylum supervisor. Resigned to form her own mini-firm after falling out with Director Ouine over alleged alien maltreatment.

Lazarus Longstreet - National Director of the United States Asylum and Refugee office at headquarters in Washington DC and a most shadowy figure; also a descendent of a Civil War Confederate general, or so he claims.

Gaylord Uomo Newskum - Colorful, flamboyant Director of the San Francisco Asylum Office. His politics and administrative philosophy is just too "out there" even for the inveterate bourgeois liberal views of the Unholy Troika, Longstreet, Falabenko, and Van Rumpelsteen.

Sean Faggerty - ex AID official, unsuccessful immigration attorney, aspiring Asylum Director wannabe. Now Deputy Director of LA Asylum. Wants to move on to HQ and get Longstreet's job and a title that is just about etched in stone.

Isadore (Izzy) Finkelstone Falabenko - a pluperfect bureaucrat, recently promoted to first-line supervisor. Judiciously solicitous and desirous of…you guessed it Longstreet's job at headquarters.

Hortensia Luz Martinez de Falabenko –h is nymphomaniac wife and source of his recent coronary bypass surgery. Emotional, power-driven, and a bit ruthless. Hispanic, hot, and horny, she's just gotta have it all.

Laura Schmelbalz - pronounced "SHMEL-bahlz" not "SMEL-bawls", as she is fond of saying. Director who immediately preceded John B.Ouine as LA Asylum head. Promoted to INS District Director with perks that included the premier office suite that takes up the entire fourteenth floor of The Federal Building in LA. Demoted and reassigned as Deputy Director of the Miami office for running activities that included burning documents, losing files, and besmirching honest employees. Main peccadillo was her private B & B (Bar & Brothel) on the thirteenth floor of the LA Fed but beat the rap on that one as it was founded during the Hernando Da Silva tenure.

Maximilian Van Rumpelsteen - newly minted U. Cal Berkley (Boalt College of Law) immigration attorney. Class valediction as undergrad, finished first in law school class. Joined Oakland branch of the prestigious Gavin Bully Law Firm but lacked the family pedigree and contacts to make partner (neither to the manner nor to the manor born.). Switches to a lower-level immigration firm which he immediately dislikes and then reluctantly joins LA Asylum for the steady paycheck. Tries to hide his resentment but it occasionally surfaces in the ruthless manner in which he organizes his "lunch club" and makes his play for advancement.

Isaac M. Chaiklin - woeful first-line supervisor generally disliked by subordinates. Has PhD in Psychology from California State University at Pebble Beach. His poor interpersonal skills lead to nervous breakdown - he couldn't cure his own case. Recovers during Esalen sessions at Big Sur. Part-time Psych Prof at California State University at Rodeo Drive (night school). Once attended kumabya group therapy outing sessions with singer/ actress Magdalena. Likes to tell people she begged him to share a sleeping bag with her at a Big Sur retreat. No credibility here - he's gay and everyone knows it, but likes to puff about the celebrities and influential persons he knows.

Audry Hepburn Santorello - aka Clitoretta La Pasta – Italian-American babe lawyer turned Asylum officer after brief stint as Norwalk Superior Court deputy DA. Suddenly quit a promising career there; no one knows why. UCLA undergrad and Pepperdine Law College. Charter member of the Blue Max Lunch Club.

Mike Magnesia - crude, gross, and ill-mannered, no class, first-line supervisor. Farts when he's talking to subordinates because he can just like President L.B. Johnson used to crap while talking to his high-salary advisors because he could. Wanders daily into Audry Santorello's office to ask "relevant" questions pertaining to fine points of immigration law. Ex low-level AID clerk. Busted and sent home for "improper conduct" with local Somali girls during a middle school construction project.

Pabu Punjah Punjahbih Pootahngheehr - US customs official and part owner with his brother Jawaharlal Siddhartha Nirvana Pootahngheehr of the Namaste Pootahngheehr Hotel just north of the 91 Freeway on Anaheim's Lime Street, a popular no-tell motel, watering hole, bar and grill-beer joint for those without the means or status for Leilo's "Party Dolls." With room rates by the hour, it serves as a quick pick-up joint for Asylum officers and clerical people. Licensed fakir, swami, and kumbaya practitioner, Pabu sometimes double-hats as Isaac Chaiklin's "spirit guide."

Theodore Theophalus Penrod - A failed litigator and resident weirdo who came to Asylum from private law practice in San Pedro branch of Hutzpov, Goniv and Metzschmuck where the managing partner at his medium-sized firm fired him after he got caught sexually harassing two secretaries. Twice divorced, he chose both his spouses, two Russian ladies, from ads he located in the INS fraud unit's "escort catalogue" and now complains his salary doesn't cover alimony payments. What a winner.

Malcolm Muddleston - former unsuccessful immigration lawyer now nondescript "company man," had one JC Penny burlap suit to his name. Paying ninety-nine cents at a thrift shop he acquired it for his graduation and now wore it every day to compliment the perennial stubble on his face. Law school buddy of Faggerty and Barfield. Does what he's told, doesn't make waves; grants lots of cases in exchange for "outstanding efficiency reports" and bonuses.

Orenthal Donald Barfield - aka O-Don, Old Barfy, or "a Barf. Corrupt immigration lawyer protected by the ABA - Old Boy network, but senses the Department of Justice hounds are closing in on him and they are. Once a senior immigration partner in the general practice medium-sized firm of Hutzpov, Goniv and Metzschmuck, and former Asylum officer, he left under mysterious circumstances to "found" his own law office. Significant ties to Chinese gangsters known as snakeheads. Likes to bring his clients to interviews wearing $5,000 Armani suits and driving silver-toned James Dean Porsche because he can. Classmate of Sean Faggerty and Malcolm Muddleston at the La Jolla University Mahatma Gandhi College of Law and Meditation near San Diego (Non-ABA approved). Now target of state attorney general determined to see him disbarred.

Oswald Harvey Hinkel - the supervisor who fires Don Barfield for conflict of interest and later surveys his Rolling Hills law office running reconnaissance for the Asylum Director. An extremely self-contained character, little is known about his personal life.

Rita Redonda Rincon - part-time Asylum officer, full-time hot babe; name appropriate as just about every male officer has "cornered" her at one time or another. Proud achiever of three pregnancies, one acquired with the help of a husky marine guard at the US Embassy compound in Bangkok. Sunburst smile, seductive (Dolce & Gabbana) blouses, slacks, and curvy figure contributed to the last two of three mishaps.

Tara Hoa - "Hwah" not "Ho" Do not *ever* say "Ho." INS special investigator; born into a Vietnamese refugee family, she hails from Westminster, California. This Asian-American uberchick is qualified eighth degree black belt in three martial arts plus Israeli army Krav Magah. Expert pistol shot, knife thrower, and swords-woman. Stunning beauty with 170 IQ - do not spa with her. Karl Keibalski - this means you.

Margaret Chase Smith Hamlin - Sturdy Mainer, and rock-ribbed Republican lady, one of the last, maybe even the very last of a dying breed, the stoic granite New England mama; a little bit Abigail Adams, some Clare Boothe Luce, and a lot like her own namesake, Senator Margaret Chase Smith. Great-great-great granddaughter of Abraham Lincoln's first vice-president, Hannibal Hamlin, she is now newly appointed Director of the San Francisco office. Once an investigator always an investigator, or so the saying goes, her low-key balanced personality is sought as a counterweight to the psycho-neurotics who generally populate the Asylum subculture. Will maintain low profile while she leads an undercover investigation team.

www.ingramcontent.com/pod-product-compliance
Lightning Source LLC
Chambersburg PA
CBHW060004210326
41520CB00009B/822

* 9 780692 501603 *